LETTERS FROM THE FUTURE

LETTERS FROM

THE FUTURE

LINKING STUDENTS AND TEACHING
WITH THE DIVERSITY OF EVERYDAY LIFE

Edited by

Deborah A. Brunson, Brenda Jarmon,
and Linda L. Lampl

Foreword by Michelle Howard-Vital

STERLING, VIRGINIA

Published by Stylus Publishing, LLC
22883 Quicksilver Drive
Sterling, Virginia 20166-2102

Library of Congress Cataloging-in-Publication-Data
Letters from the future : linking students and teaching with
the diversity of everyday life / edited by Deborah A.
Brunson, Brenda Jarmon, and Linda L. Lampl ; foreword by
Michelle Howard-Vita.—1st ed.
    p.   cm.
Includes bibliographical references and index.
ISBN 1-57922-186-6 (cloth : alk. paper)—ISBN 1-57922-187-
4 (pbk. : alk. paper)
1. Multicultural education—United States. 2. Education,
Higher—Curricula—United States.
3. College students—United States—Correspondence.
I. Brunson, Deborah A. II. Jarmon, Brenda. III. Lampl,
Linda L., 1942–
LC1099.3.L48   2007
370.117—dc22
                                                    2006030835

ISBN: 1-57922-186-6 (cloth) / 13-digit ISBN: 978-1-57922-186-7
ISBN: 1-57922-187-4 (paper) / 13-digit ISBN: 978-1-57922-187-4

Printed in Canada

All first editions printed on acid free paper
that meets the American National Standards Institute
Z39-48 Standard.

Bulk Purchases

Quantity discounts are available for use in workshops
and for staff development.
Call 1-800-232-0223

First Edition, 2007

10   9   8   7   6   5   4   3   2   1

To my family who has known me, loved me, and supported me in all my efforts to grow and to become. I also offer special tribute to my parents, Robert (deceased) and Ola Draper.

—DEBORAH A. BRUNSON

I dedicate this, my first edited work, to my late grandparents (Fred and Ida Jarmon, Beatrice Palmer and Avery Johnson), my parents (Carlton and Lillian Jarmon), and my daughter and son (Lynette Hickerson and Terrance Jarmon). I am who I am because of your continued support and love. Know that I love each of you from the depths of my soul and I will be eternally grateful to God for the family he gave to me.

—BRENDA "BJ" JARMON

To the memory of Grace Branham Lampl and Carl Lampl, who together provided a lifelong learning lab on culture, and to the memory of Georgia Porter Curry, who had just begun to teach the world about diversity when Hodgkin's disease claimed her in 1977.

—LINDA L. LAMPL

CONTENTS

FOREWORD

Fundamentally, education is about change and transformation. So often teachers do not know the influence of the lives they have lived or the influence of their instruction on the lives of students who will help create our country's future. This might be particularly true regarding our knowledge of the value of diversity education or the outcomes of educating diverse students. These types of influences are sometimes not explained well by quantitative research, yet one can argue that they are significant factors that influence the development of a more diverse and equitable society.

Letters from the Future: Linking Students and Teaching with the Diversity of Everyday Life provides an opportunity to explore the influence of diversity education through narratives written by former college students to the teachers with whom they had diversity-related classes. As did their instructors, students took a different journey to the course and traveled divergent paths through these classrooms as they sought to expand their understandings of racial and cultural identities in the United States. Some came to study more about diversity in order to excavate society's political underpinnings; others came to fulfill a personal challenge to learn more about diversity and the racial and cultural identities of themselves and others. The narratives these students offer demonstrate how personal experiences contribute to identity construction. Students and teachers provide insight into the sensitive and obsessive areas of racial, cultural, and social identities. These insights are rarely exposed in most homes, schools, or workplaces. It is difficult to read these personal narratives without coming away with a sense of urgency for more discussions that go beyond conversations based solely upon stereotyped, preconceived notions about the identities of others.

By hearing from faculty who taught these diversity courses and how they were each shaped by the racial, cultural, and political climates of the times, we can better understand and decipher the complex pedagogies that influence teaching and learning in these and other classrooms. We can also extrapolate lessons from the particularized experiences of the contributors in this volume and place them within the broader, generalized experiences that have framed diversity education in the academy. Devorah Lieberman's chapter in the opening section provides this expansive perspective. Her essay aptly frames and articulates the current status of diversity education at colleges and universities, and thereby provides a solid contextual foundation for *Letters from the Future.*

Lieberman affirms that colleges and universities have both moral and practical reasons for addressing diversity more thoroughly. American institutions of higher education are becoming more diverse, yet some students, faculty, and staff continue to experience alienation on college campuses. She argues that institutions of higher education should address diversity in the curriculum, in the retention of faculty and students, in learning styles, and in the development of inclusive college campuses. Integrating diversity more fully in higher education will require a thoughtful process and evaluation of the institution's diversity efforts. *Letters from the Future* contributes to this integrative process and reflects the diversity initiatives that Lieberman articulates.

The contributors to this interdisciplinary volume bring a wealth of educational philosophy and pedagogy to the diversity dialogue. Disciplines represented include education, biology, social work, criminal justice, political science, English literature, communication, and sex education. Topics are expansive and provide thoughtful reflection upon teaching and learning diversity so that these lessons may better prepare our future generations. Examples of the breadth and depth of these chapters are reflected in McDonald's comparison of Afrocentric and Western literature, Sheridan's candid discussion of growing up under Jim Crow and how the experience influenced his academic career in political science, and Campbell's professional struggles to integrate a diversity-focused pedagogy within his standard, traditional communication course.

In chapter 5, "Literature, Self-Discovery, and Identity: Cultural Difference and Its Impact on Black Students' Language Engagement," Brown McDonald (with students Copeland and Gramenz) examines differences between Afrocentric literature and Western literature. Brown McDonald's analysis reveals that students of color are at a disadvantage within a dominant culture that does not mirror their experiences and concerns. Because of this dissonance, students of color are not motivated to be as engaged as other students. Further, more knowledge about the cultural backgrounds of diverse students could inform instruction design in higher education and result in more engaged (and achieving) students.

Sheridan's commentary, for example, takes us back to the painful Jim Crow history of America and portrays how the dismantling of Jim Crow policies and practices served as motivation for his academic and political pursuits. For Sheridan, racial tensions greatly influenced how he saw the world and how the world saw him. Because of the omission of the contributions of African Americans in most of his academic studies, Sheridan gravitated toward studying and teaching the role of African Americans in the American political system. After reading the students' accounts of their experiences years after taking his course, Sheridan admits surprise that the public school system did not do a better job of sharing and teaching the stories of a more diverse group of people. He concludes, "To love America one need not be ignorant of America's faults. . . . We are strengthened not weakened by knowledge of racial and diversity issues" (p. 84).

Another professor, Scott Campbell, approaches diversity from a midwestern background and relates his experiences teaching in a culturally diverse university. He affirms that his background did not put him on an equal "cultural footing." Thus, one of Campbell's goals was to make sure that students shared their diverse cultures and learned to understand and appreciate them. His personal challenge was to integrate within his pedagogy new methodology that would support this multicultural imperative. He found that providing safe spaces (e.g., small groups) would encourage more interaction among these diverse participants and invite his students to consider new ideas, perspectives, and pathways.

Based upon the students' narratives, it seems that diversity courses can challenge students to confront, deconstruct, and reconstruct their preconceived notions about the worth and value of persons from other races, cultures, and traditions. Moreover, the effects of the courses seemed to extend, for students, to their professional lives. Most students offered that the diversity course had formed a foundation for how they treat others in the workplace. Needless to say, the commentaries and narratives from future generations support the assumption that the ability to understand and respect the diversity of another is fundamental to understanding and developing personal identity. Only with respect and knowledge can future generations of Americans thrive in a culturally diverse environment. One student stated, "As we interacted with each other, we opened the door to alternative possibilities in our lives. . . . I felt this experience was more like a gathering place where we learn and evolve together" (pp. 121–122). Whether the reader is teaching or participating in a diversity class, these reflective commentaries and narratives underscore the influence and importance of providing a basis for individuals to understand and expand upon racial and cultural identities.

Michelle Howard-Vital
Interim Chancellor
Winston-Salem State University
Winston-Salem, North Carolina

ACKNOWLEDGMENTS

We first give thanks to God, the Creator, who is the author and finisher of our lives.

We stand on the blood, sweat, and tears of those who have gone on before us—our ancestors. Those who fought valiantly to bring justice and liberty for all—they too, like the contributors to this volume, came from diverse backgrounds, languages, geographic locations, cultures, ethnicities, genders, various social and economic statuses, and they fought hard so that we might enjoy the privileges that we have today. Truly, diversity is more than race.

We are eternally grateful to the faculty and student contributors to this book, for without them, Deborah Brunson's original idea that started out as a verbal concept would not have come to fruition. Our sincerest thanks go out to the marvelous contributors who are the steadfast anchors of this work.

We also acknowledge Stylus Publishing for giving us the opportunity to share the voices of our colleagues and our students particularly when our hallowed academic halls and walls are in need of culturally sensitive and culturally competent diversity strategies. Our prayer is that this book will be a catalyst to inspire others to create similar works and pave the way for society to embrace a mission that can facilitate a road map to action.

Last, but certainly not least, we thank our family members for their support, love, and encouragement in our various professional journeys. Family is our rock and God is our supplier.

PART ONE

FOUNDATIONS

DIVERSITY INITIATIVES, INSTITUTIONAL CHANGE, AND CURRICULAR REFORM IN HIGHER EDUCATION

Devorah A. Lieberman

Higher education is undergoing reform to an extent that has never before been considered, examined, or addressed. These reforms stem from internal and external pressures. Internal pressures are most often related to financial costs around maintaining a quality institution and delivering a quality education, increasing expectations from faculty and staff, rising enrollments, and raised student learning expectations. External pressures are most often related to changes and expectations around external funding, demographics, community needs, accrediting and political bodies, and business-related items (Lieberman & Guskin, 2003). Diversity and multicultural issues are dimensions that thread through most of these internal and external pressures. As institutions wrestle with these pressures and translate them into campuswide reform initiatives, it is critical to address the multiple facets of diversity that affect and are affected by the reform processes. Specifically, this chapter addresses ways to integrate issues of diversity into the institutional reform process in ways that answer the following six questions:

- Why is "diversity" an area of concern in higher education?
- How does higher education today address issues of diversity?

- What diversity initiatives, especially those related to faculty and instructional development, have the greatest impact and why?
- What are examples of diversity initiatives and curricular issues on various campuses?
- How *do* we and how *can* we assess diversity initiatives?
- What are lessons learned about institutional readiness, institutional change, and diversity initiatives?

Why Is "Diversity" an Area of Concern in Higher Education?

At no other time in U.S. history has higher education been as diverse as it is today. The growth and changes in American society and its commitment to higher education for all qualified students has meant a tremendous increase in the numbers of college and university students. To illustrate this, student enrollment in higher education increased from 156,756 in 1880 to 597,880 in 1920, to 3,639,847 in 1960, and 14,304,803 in 1994 (Snyder, 1997). As enrollment increased, so did student diversity. The following data illustrate this increase. As of 2001, higher education enrollment was 28% nonwhite, 55% female, and 43% over the age of 25. The increase in African American students, 40.2% between 1976 and 1994, was greater than that of Caucasian students at 14.8% (Nettles & Perna, 1997). Latino enrollment has increased by 39.6% since 1990. Carter and Wilson (1997) claim that the 4.6% increase in Latino enrollment in 1995 was the largest one-year gain among the four major ethnic groups. Asian American student enrollment has doubled since 1980, with the largest growth at four-year institutions (Carter & Wilson, 1997). In 1992, Asian American enrollment accounted for nearly 5% of the total enrollment at colleges and universities (U.S. Department of Education, http://nces.ed.gov/programs/digest/d99t186.asp). Finally, international student enrollment has also continued to increase.

Documenting the numbers of students from underrepresented groups who enroll in college is only a piece of the big picture. It is equally as important to document data about diverse students who earn college degrees (Harvey, 2002). "Nationwide, students at Division I institutions in 2000 posted a graduate rate of 56%, which was unchanged from the previous year and a 1% decline from 1995" (p. 21). Though African American and American Indians recorded small gains in graduation rates at Division I institutions from

1998–1999, the matriculation rates for both remained below the corresponding rates for Caucasian students. The six-year graduation rate for African Americans at Division I institutions increased from 37% in 1998 to 38% in 1999. The Latino Division I graduation rate decreased from 47% in 1999 to 46% in 2000. The one-year decrease was the largest among the four major ethnic minority groups. In 1999 Asian Americans had the highest graduation rate at Division I colleges and universities—66%, among the four ethnic minority groups. The rates also exceeded the corresponding rate for Caucasian students. With a Division I graduation rate of 38%, American Indians joined African Americans in posting the lowest graduation rates among the other ethnic minority groups in 2000.

The needs of the diverse students attending college must be anticipated. In anticipating these needs, it is necessary to put in place support systems in the academic environment that further a positive and supportive campus climate that enhances all classroom and cocurricular activities. While statistics demonstrate an increasing percentage of minority students who attend and graduate from college, there continue to be growing concerns about the college experience voiced by students within minority populations (Lieberman & Guskin, 2003). Examples of these concerns are

1. Students report feeling marginalized inside and outside the classroom.
2. Students report a lack of course work that addresses diversity across the curriculum or, where appropriate, within specific courses.
3. There is an exclusion of content or inaccurate historical representation within the curriculum content dealing with the social and cultural backgrounds of diverse students.
4. There is greater disparity in minority representation between undergraduate and graduate student populations.
5. The hiring practices of content specialists within the discipline do not take into consideration the diversity that candidates could bring to a department or reflect the demographics of students reenrolled in departmental offerings.
6. Junior faculty report ineffective retention methods as they proceed through the promotion and tenure process, given the special demands placed on them by students, the institution, and sometimes the community.

Institutions of higher education across the country recognize that it is necessary to address issues relating to increasing diversity among faculty, staff, and students. These demographic and social trends underscore the moral and practical reasons for institutions to address the characteristics that attract and retain students from underrepresented groups while concurrently creating an institutional environment that is welcoming, nurturing, comfortable, and educational for all.

How Does Higher Education Today Address Issues of Diversity?

Administrators within institutions across the country recognize the need for systemic change at every level to address the issues that arise when serving an increasingly diverse student, faculty, and staff population. It is also necessary to raise understanding about the assets that diverse faculty, students, and staff bring to an institution.

Diversity issues that are being addressed and documented by institutions of higher education today include but are not limited to campus climate; curriculum design and reform; diversity, pedagogy, and the scholarship of teaching and learning; recruitment and retention of a diverse faculty, staff, and student population; and faculty and staff development.

Campus Climate

Campus climate includes the overall environment of the college or university. The environment is a variable that has significant impact on student access, retention, and academic success. Efforts to address issues of climate on campus have emerged, in part, from the body of research that reports nearly universal experiences of difficulty with the prevailing institutional cultures among specific groups of students (Smith et al., 1997).

Institutions define a positive campus climate as one that works positively to welcome and to retain diverse faculty, staff, and students. The more welcoming and nurturing the campus climate, the more the institution is perceived as recognizing the assets that diverse students bring to the curricular and cocurricular activities, that diverse staff bring to their areas of employment, and that diverse faculty bring to the classroom context and their research colleagues. Further, a positive campus climate is perceived as one where minority students, faculty, and staff do not feel marginalized from the majority and where diversity is welcomed and encouraged.

Conversely, a negative campus climate adversely affects student, staff, and faculty recruitment, success, and retention. The literature on campus climate and its negative effects on minority student populations centers on nearly universal reports of feelings of alienation, hostility, and difficulties fitting in to prevailing institutional cultures (Smith 1989; Smith et. al, 1997). Beckham (2000) speaks of a consistent theme of alienation experienced by students of nontraditional backgrounds in their campus environments. He refers to this as symptomatic of a deep, underlying problem that has not been adequately addressed.

Curriculum Design and Reform

Bringing diversity issues into program and course curricula requires a thoughtful process that includes classroom management, student learning outcomes, and assessment. These efforts range from including multicultural materials in course content through academic program redesign. "Perhaps the most significant shift observable in [the] literature has been the judgment that changes in curriculum and pedagogy are needed not just to 'satisfy' certain groups of new students. Rather, these changes are needed to fulfill institutional and societal concerns about preparing all students for a pluralistic society and world" (Smith et al., 2000, p. 31).

Many new course curricula are designed with student learning outcomes that include successful participation in a multicultural society. Existing curricula are redesigned in ways that newly infuse these diversity outcomes through a process of reform. For example, Nowak-Fabrykowski and Price (2001) assisted faculty members who were interested in "restructuring their courses in order to reflect a multicultural approach to course content and pedagogy" (p. 24). This was an extension of a campuswide initiative to foster greater awareness and commitment to diversity among faculty, students, and staff in both curricular and cocurricular areas. James Banks (1996) focuses much of his scholarship on ways to bring multicultural education into traditional and nontraditional classrooms and course content.

Diversity, Pedagogy, and the Scholarship of Teaching and Learning

As the higher education student body becomes more diverse it is necessary to think more broadly both about pedagogical methods and about student learning styles. An increasing body of literature substantiates the importance of recognizing ethnic and cultural diversity among students as well as in the surrounding community while engaging each as a resource and an asset in the learning environment. The examples in the following section begin to clarify a few of the pedagogies cited in the literature that are recommended for enhancing the multicultural classroom and the community-based learning environment. These examples merely serve as a reminder that paradigmatic pedagogical shifts are needed when introducing alternative learning activities while also managing student interaction and the understanding of the materials. Each example should be adopted with care when redesigning a traditional course or designing a new course. While the literature is replete with the call for integrating diversity and course design, there is a paucity of research that systematically examines corresponding diversity, teaching, curriculum design, and student learning outcomes. With the advent and acceptance of the Scholarship of Teaching and Learning as well as the Scholarship of Application in higher education, professors have an opportunity to pursue research questions addressing curriculum design, teaching strategies, diversity, community-based learning, and student learning. These research efforts will result in dissemination of good practice at national levels (e.g., conferences and publications).

These expanded forms of scholarship support alternative and nontraditional forms of promotion and tenure policies and guidelines. They also provide applicable classroom examples that are theoretically based and are also grounded in rigorous, systematic research resulting in evidence-based contributions to an existing body of knowledge. Consequently, the quality of research will be advanced as well as the practice in the classroom. Portland State University in Oregon (www.pdx.edu) and Wagner College in New York (www.wagner.edu) offer financial support to faculty who conduct research that focuses on diversity issues in relation to teaching and learning. The financial support furthers the research and its presentation at national conferences. These forms of research that result in presentation and publication are positively recognized and evaluated in the promotion and tenure process. Some examples of pedagogical strategies follow.

Making classrooms inclusive

Classrooms that are intentionally inclusive focus on strategies that strive to create an environment in which students learn from one another, bring their personal experiences to enhance the course objectives, feel respect for and are respected by the professor and their colleagues, and contribute to classroom management and developmental learning. When the course content includes multicultural issues that may give rise to emotional issues among the students, the following strategies are suggested.

Providing informal interactions in class

Ortiz asserts that informal paper interaction and peer-led discussions in class are effective for all students, but especially for first-year students who prefer this as their primary vehicle for learning about multicultural issues (as cited in Smith et al., 1997).

Offering instructor-led discussions

Fourth-year students found that instructor-led discussions and activities were most effective for them and they supported and preferred instructors playing a large role in the learning process. Students with prior discrimination and racism experiences have much higher expectations for educational interventions, trainers, and instructors. These students found their peers were better sources of information than instructors or trainers.

Exposing students to diversity issues

Hasslen found that pairing white students with students of color reduces myths and fears of difference (as cited in Smith et. al., 1997). Benns-Suter (1993) found the use of simulation methods to be effective in stimulating thinking about multicultural issues. Grant and Secada (as cited in Smith et al., 1997) suggest that the most effective pedagogical strategies involve intense exposure to diversity issues. The more time spent learning the content, the more varied the presentation, and the more course work covering diversity issues, the more likely learning will be successful.

Reducing myths and stereotypes through panel discussions

Smith et al. (2000) found that the most effective way to reduce myths and stereotypes about gay and lesbian issues was to have panel discussions with time for questions and answers. Literature about students with learning disabilities and performance in the classroom maintains that when students with learning disabilities are given the same amount of time to perform tasks as students without learning disabilities, students with learning disabilities perform at a significantly lower standard. However, when each group is given more time to complete the task or exam, there was no significant difference in performance or accomplishment.

Using service learning to reduce stereotypes

Connecting students with diverse communities through community-based learning or service-learning opportunities also reduces myths and stereotypes about the differing cultures and ethnic groups (Voegele & Lieberman, 2005). As service learning and civic engagement pedagogies become ever more present, students will encounter more diverse community-based interactions than they otherwise would have. "Given the economic, racial and ethnic stratification of our neighborhoods and schools, college campuses frequently are the multivalent space bringing people from all kinds of backgrounds into potential relationship with one another" (McTighe Musil et al., 1999).

Inviting speakers to campus

Colleges and universities often bring well-known individuals to campus to address diversity, racism, or bigotry. This may take place in a public forum where students are encouraged or are offered extra credit to attend. This invited speaker may attend particular classes to address the topic. Though the institution and the participating faculty are often well intentioned, they may find that their impact on students has been anything but positive. The problem is not so much what the speaker says but the tension that precedes and follows the event (Stern, 1990). What occurs after the event may be portrayed in a way that makes some students feel marginalized or put in a position where they are not able to defend an attitude or an opinion about their race or their culture. "The greatest pain for the students who feel unfairly maligned may be that their fellow classmates cannot—or will not—understand why they feel so hurt. Lines are drawn and victimized students react angrily, in protest if they are strong enough numerically, in silence if they are too few" (p. 13).

Engaging students in the large classroom

Oullette (2002) addresses issues of diversity when engaging students in the large classroom. He recommends that when a diversity-related incident emerges in the large-class setting, the professor should "accommodate the unexpected through strategies of experiential learning theory and practice, which can make a large class appear smaller through brief writing responses to a focused question, dyad responses, sharing circles, caucus groups or fish-bowl exercises" (p. 104). He further points out that often in the large classroom Caucasian students are afraid of saying the wrong thing in diversity-related situations or discussions "leading to a classroom climate permeated by a kind of paralysis as white students become almost completely silent. Students of color may feel hyper visible and further alienated. By reframing student comments in historical or discipline-specific contexts, teachers can level the perceived risks of active participation" (p. 104).

Discussing socioeconomic class diversity

Cullinan (2002) includes socioeconomic class in teaching and learning about diversity and discrimination. Including issues that involve socioeconomic class broadens student understanding of intercultural issues, differences, and similarities. Cullinan suggests that the following goals guide the inclusion of socioeconomic issues in student learning:

- Explore ways in which class differences are identified in the United States;
- Discuss reasons for different views of socioeconomic class differences;
- Identify some of the ways students first learn about class differences;
- Identify ways in which discrimination based on socioeconomic class differences can damage relationships;
- Identify and explore individual development and customer service for both colleagues and students;
- Develop strategies for identifying and preventing discrimination based on socioeconomic class.

Recruitment and Retention of a Diverse Faculty, Staff, and Student Population

Two lessons are important to keep in mind in relation to recruiting and retaining faculty, staff, and students from underrepresented groups. First, institutions often focus on recruiting minority faculty, staff, and students without heeding the needed resources to support these individuals once they are in the institution. Second, recruitment and retention is something that everyone should participate in, not just a few. It takes human involvement and commitment to recruit and retain minority individuals, not only financial resources (Smith, Wolf, & Busenberg, 1996). Some of the primary actions higher education departments have taken to recruit candidates from underrepresented groups include, but are not limited to, the following:

- Crafting an inclusive job description, that describes a department culture that welcomes and encourages diverse composition and perspectives;
- Taking the initiative to network within the discipline to attract appropriate candidates;
- Contacting minority organizations within the discipline about the open position;
- Contacting relevant department chairs at Historically Black Colleges and Universities (HBCUs), at Hispanic-Serving Institutions, and at Tribal Colleges;
- Including community minority leaders on search committees;
- Connecting candidates with people on campus and in the community who are interested in diversity issues ("Recruit and Retain" in the *Academic Leader,* 2002, pp. 1–5).

Some institutions have a central body, other than the Office of Human Resources or the Office of Affirmative Action, that is available to assist departments in following through on any of the above points. Portland State University, for example, created the Diversity Hiring Resource Team (DHRT), which comprises an individual from the Office of Affirmative Action, an individual from the Office of Human Resources, a department chair, faculty who have successfully helped with recruiting their respective departments, and the vice provost and special assistant to the president. Portland State University increased its percentage of minority faculty from 6% to 13% between 1999 and 2003 since the inception of the DHRT. For more detail on the Diversity Hiring Resource Team, see http://oaa.po.pdx.edu/diversity. Wagner College is in the process of forming a Diversity Hiring Resource Team.

It is not uncommon for institutions to have an elaborate plan for recruiting faculty, staff, and students with little or no strategic plan around retention issues. Once faculty, staff, and students have agreed to become part of the institutional whole, it is important that retention issues are considered. Administrators should be aware of and sensitive to issues that may arise that are particular to the faculty, staff, or students. For minority faculty, these may include assisting with balancing their time to serve the institution, the classroom, and a research agenda. Or, this may include social issues that have an impact on feelings of inclusion, exclusion, or marginalization. For minority staff, this may include sensitivity to the work environment, assistance with learning particular tasks, or inclusion in the workplace environment. For minority students, this may include assistance with course work, or social issues that lead to feelings of inclusion, exclusion, or marginalization.

Diversity recruitment and retention are issues for everyone. When an institution is guided by this principle, it becomes self-evident why its members should participate in activities related to minority recruitment and retention. A clear example of this diversity principle contributing to institutional health and vitality relates to student recruitment. If an institution staffs a single position that is the "minority recruitment" position, it should logically follow that fellow recruiting officers should also be concerned with addressing issues of diversity when recruiting students. However, there is often the assumption that "There is a person hired to focus on diversity issues, so it is not central to my job." We should clearly communicate to anyone who recruits for the institution that attracting the most diverse student population is a top priority. It also becomes important to consistently inform everyone in academic departments or disciplines that obtaining a diverse faculty is likewise a priority, and that there is an institutional expectation that this priority will influence how these entities recruit and interview prospective candidates. Unfortunately, minority faculty often comment on how welcoming their colleagues were during the interview process, and then how insensitive they became once the minority faculty member joined the campus community. Some of this inconsistency may be alleviated if, during the recruitment process, minority candidates meet with other minority colleagues across the institution to discuss the challenges they may encounter and avenues of assistance they may receive. Newly hired minority faculty maintain that their most positive experiences revolve around interactions where other faculty reached out to them in ways that helped them to navigate the promotion and tenure system, the university system in general, and to become affiliated with a social network within the institution and the community.

It takes more than financial support to retain a diverse campus population successfully. It is not uncommon to hear administrators say that they could not retain minority faculty, staff, and students. Upon closer examination, minority faculty and students who leave an institution claim that they left not because they were not supported financially (e.g., funding for research), but rather they felt marginalized within the institution. As stated earlier, basic funding is critical to conduct outreach and to support faculty and students. But just as, if not more, important is the feeling that one is respected and included within the institutional environment.

Faculty and Staff Development

Few faculty or staff would be unwilling to support a diverse and welcoming campus climate or to educate students to be successful in a diverse society and a diverse professional environment. However, most would also admit that they have never developed the skills and content knowledge necessary to do this with ease and with success. Campuses are turning to faculty and staff development support for bringing this knowledge and these skills to the campus community.

Offices of faculty development are the places on campuses that most frequently further efforts to support diversity training inside and outside the curriculum. Often the Faculty Development Office partners with the Office of Multicultural Affairs to offer broader and deeper campus support. The types of support include but are not limited to the following:

- A diversity speakers series
- Workshops on embedding diversity issues in the curriculum
- Sessions on developing new courses that focus and/or include diversity issues
- Sessions on redesigning existing courses to include diversity issues
- Sessions on creating a classroom climate that is inclusive and student centered
- Sessions on how to facilitate difficult dialogues about diversity in the classroom
- Training on how to write a job description in order to attract the broadest and most diverse pool of candidates
- Strategies for interviewing job candidates so that they understand the diversity that exists on campus and in the community
- Recognizing and unlearning racism

Examples of each of these types of sessions or workshops can be accessed at http://www.pdx.edu/cae/diversity and http://www.universityofmaryland/diversity.

What Diversity Initiatives, Especially Those Related to Faculty and Instructional Development, Have the Greatest Impact and Why?

Bonilla and Palmerton (2001) make the following recommendations for faculty developers who are furthering diversity on their campuses:

- Get your community talking about race and gender. Listen. Its members have much to share.
- Although you will hear things that are truly discouraging, they need to be heard and given legitimacy.
- Assume people are doing the best they know how, and wherever possible catch them doing things right. Focus on trying to understand, not on judging.
- Use a multiracial, multiethnic, male-female faculty development research team whenever possible. The more lenses you bring the better you see.
- Use the "choir."
- Hitchhike on a current administrative concern.

Bonilla and Palmerton have found that when they present their diversity findings in a campuswide forum, it is fruitful to seek assistance from faculty who have demonstrated and support multicultural teaching. This strategy tends to temper skepticism from fellow faculty colleagues. This process avoids having faculty preach to the choir but actually opens the door for the skeptics to be more thoughtful as they hear information from their respected colleagues. Those in the "choir" feel empowered, and skeptics have another chance to listen with potential positive intention.

They found that coupling diversity and multicultural issues with other administratively based initiatives served to further the diversity initiative within the administration. For example, if "assessment of student learning" is a campuswide initiative, it may be useful to suggest ways that topics related to diversity could strengthen the assessment initiative. Jacobson, Borgford-Parnell, Frank, Peck, and Reddick (2002) found that faculty were more effective in their teaching when they developed a teaching portfolio that had special emphasis on diversity issues in the course curriculum and classroom management. They found that "inclusive practices portfolios" fostered greater faculty reflection and development.

In the 1990s, the Ford Foundation supported a selected group of 19 higher education institutions to develop diversity initiatives on their campuses. A central theme among most of the campuses was faculty and curriculum development. Based on the Ford-funded projects, "engaging a faculty member in new scholarship and pedagogy changed more than a single course; it potentially altered all the courses that faculty member might teach. Faculty members at campus after campus were universal in their praise of the intellectual awakening that seminar and workshop opportunities triggered" (McTighe Musil, Garcia, Moses, & Smith, 1995, p. 27).

The Ford Foundation research concluded that faculty development and diversity were critical, though no one model was better than the next. For example, some institutions addressed faculty development through a series of four day-long symposia, others designed a five-week summer seminar that met regularly, others offered a series of seminars throughout the quarter or semester, and others met throughout the year in small learning communities.

What Are Examples of Diversity Initiatives and Curricular Issues on Various Campuses?

The *Diversity Web*, a publication of the Association of American Colleges and Universities (AAC&U), is one of the most comprehensive resources that brings readers examples of how campuses across the country address issues of diversity (http://www.diversityweb.org/Digest/). Each publication connects theory to practice and cites specific diversity practices that occur on particular campuses. It focuses on five particular diversity and multicultural themes: diversity innovations; research and trends; research, evaluation, and impact; conferences and publications; and position openings.

There are many diversity initiatives that are currently underway on campuses across the country. The following list reviews the programs of some of these universities and colleges and their efforts to make significant changes regarding diversity issues that address the campus climate, the curriculum, and student learning.

Arizona State University
(http://www.asu.edu/provost/intergroup/)

Former ASU president Lattie Coor publicly proclaimed that cultural diversity would be central to the university's core mission and university goals. In particular, in 1997, ASU formed an Intergroup Relations Center (IRC) that focuses on positive relations among students, staff, faculty, and administrators. The IRC assumes that diversity is an asset for campus climate and sought to provide activities that promote this philosophy at all levels of the campus. Three important goals of the IRC are to create intergroup education and training for the campus and the community, establish a clearinghouse for information and intergroup relations at ASU, and provide support for research on the impact of programs and activities on intergroup relations as well as information that faculty can use to revise and develop course curricula.

University of California at Los Angeles
(http://diversity.ucla.edu/)

UCLA has worked in a variety of areas to address diversity issues through the Chancellor's Advisory Group on Diversity. This Web site, which was developed by the advisory group, provides a comprehensive review of campus initiatives to strengthen diversity at UCLA. The Faculty Diversity Web (http://faculty.diversity.ucla.edu/) provides a number of resources to assist in recruitment and retention of faculty of color, including a Faculty Search Toolkit and a link to databases of potential minority candidates across various disciplines. Additional issues addressed on the faculty site include gender equity; programs that promote a fair, positive, and open academic environment; and family-friendly initiatives.

University of Michigan, Ann Arbor
(http://www.umich.edu/~igrc/)

The Ann Arbor campus is well known for its Program on Intergroup Relations (IGR) a social justice education program. This initiative seeks to develop among students an understanding of and appreciation for intergroup relations. The IGR is a collaboration between the College of Literature,

Science, and Arts and the Division of Student Affairs. Students may complete multidisciplinary course work that incorporates experiential methods and implementation of dialogical communication models. Participants also have access to cocurricular experiences. IGR has expanded its work to include a community outreach program called "Summer Youth Dialogue" where U-M undergraduate students work with Detroit high school students of various ethnicities.

Rice University (http://rice.edu/diversity)

Rice has a multilevel approach to meeting its diversity mission (see descriptions below, taken from the university's Web site). Many of these programs are listed under its Diversity Showcase link (http://www.google.com/u/rice?num = 10&q = Diversity + Showcase) and include such initiatives as

- The Americas Project™: "This undertaking is designed to create a leadership forum where emerging economic, political, and cultural pacesetters throughout the Western Hemisphere can engage in dialogue on important topics of hemispheric consequences. The Americas Project brings together approximately fifteen fellows selected competitively from the various countries of the Western Hemisphere."
- Rice Nominator's Circle: "Initiated in 1998, the Rice University Nominator's Circle consists of K–12 teachers, counselors, administrators, and community leaders who assist Rice in identifying and reaching out to underrepresented students of color. Each year a new group visits Rice University for an orientation and workshop about the admissions and financial aid process."
- Pride at Rice whose purpose, stated on its Web page, includes:

  provide a healthy and safe place for Rice University students who are discovering their sexual orientation to find understanding and develop a network of support;
  educate the Rice community on gay, lesbian, bisexual, and transgender issues, cultures, and history through various programming efforts;
  provide a place for GLBT, questioning, and straight students and others to meet, gain information, and socialize;
  provide a forum for the friends of GLBT people to learn about the community and show their support.

- Mellon Mays Undergraduate Fellows Program at Rice: "In partnership with the Mellon Foundation, the Mellon Mays Undergraduate

Fellows Program at Rice is aimed at increasing the number of students from diverse backgrounds who choose to enroll in PhD programs in the humanities, anthropology, mathematics, mathematical sciences, statistics, physics, geology, ecology, and earth sciences."

University of Wisconsin State System (http://www.wisc.edu)

The state system developed a 10-year statewide plan titled "Design for Diversity" (http://www.ssc.wisc.edu/~whansen/reg_bgd3.html) to increase underrepresented groups on all system campuses. The plan, a very ambitious program, states:

> The problems associated with minority education and serving the needs of the economically disadvantaged cannot be short-term concerns. Similarly, this design for diversity should not be interpreted as a quick fix to a specific problem but rather as a series of long-term efforts designed to break the cycle of growing under-representation of minorities and economically disadvantaged people and to provide increased multicultural understanding and greater diversity throughout the system. Finally, this ambitious program cannot be successful without the cooperation and strong commitment from others—the elementary and secondary schools, state government, business and industry, community leadership, and young people and those who influence them. The UW System accepts and stands ready to fulfill its responsibilities and to work with others in this important area.

The plan's goal is to have a statewide system adopt a multicultural teaching and learning environment focused on preparing students to live and contribute to a multicultural society. This plan is specific in pursuing goals for significant increases in diverse student enrollment, diverse faculty and staff hiring, and relationships with other institutions to increase the "pipeline" of students of color going on to college.

Portland State University, Portland, Oregon (http://www.pdx.edu)

Portland State University created the Diversity Hiring Resource Team, a volunteer team of five faculty and staff who meet with departments that are advertising for a tenure-track position. The team assists the department in writing its advertisement so that the position description will be attractive to the most diverse candidate population. The team helps the department think of ways to reach out to diverse audiences through personal contacts, through disciplinary organizations, and through particular institutions. When the final candidates come to campus for their interviews, they meet with team members to facilitate responses to diversity questions that the interviewing departments may need assistance with.

University of Maryland, College Park (http://www.inform.umd.edu/EdRes/Topic/Diversity/)

The University of Maryland provides one of the most comprehensive diversity databases in the country. The database includes general diversity resources, curricular examples, institutional initiatives, and example syllabi.

University of Washington (http://depts.washington.edu/diversity)

This institution includes initiatives that most actively engage faculty and staff. Specifically, UW has a Center for Curriculum Transformation (http://depts.washington.edu/ctcenter/), a diversity program implemented through UW's Financial Management wing (http://www.washington.edu/admin/finmgmt/diversity/index.htm), and an "Inclusive Teaching" resource provided through the university's Center for Instructional Development and Research (http://depts.washington.edu/cidrweb/inclusive/). The Center for Curriculum Transformation was created in 1993 through external funding from the Ford Foundation with additional support from internal academic offices. Its mission, as stated on the Web site, notes that:

> The Center for Curriculum Transformation promotes and supports curriculum development aimed at teaching and learning to think critically about cultural diversity. This mission is supported by a Faculty and Senate Resolution on Cultural and Ethnic Diversity (3 March 1994). The Center assists both individual faculty members and academic departments in developing courses and curricula that include the study of race, gender, ethnicity, nation and nationhood, class, disability, sexuality and religion, and their intersections. The Center also disseminates research on curriculum transformation and pedagogical innovation through a web site and publications.

The Financial Management Diversity Initiative developed teams to support the diversity aspect of its overall quality improvement model, including mentoring and training, as well as programs, events, and publications that address work environment and diversity in the workplace.

"Inclusive Teaching" is an online resource that faculty can use to increase their understanding of the philosophy and pedagogy that supports the academic success of all students. Three major headings include "Perspectives on What Excludes Students"; "Strategies for Inclusive Teaching"; and "Resources for Inclusive Teaching."

Wagner College, Staten Island, New York (http://www.wagner.edu)

Wagner College has begun taking a strategic approach to addressing diversity among its campus community. First, as provost, I stated during my position interview that diversity would be an issue of deep concern during my tenure. During my first year, I met with key individuals and groups about diversity and campus climate. With a goal of enhancing campus climate to attract and retain a more diverse student body, faculty (tenure track and adjunct), and staff (administrative and nonadministrative), I issued a call for interested students, faculty, and staff to apply to form a Diversity Action Council (DAC) whose objective was to articulate a Diversity Blueprint for Wagner College. The DAC would serve as an advisory body to the provost and to other policy-recommending bodies on campus. The campus blueprint would take into account the hiring process, the curriculum, study abroad, classroom management, community interaction, cocurricular activities, and research support. In addition to encouraging faculty to integrate diversity and multicultural issues in their course curricula, the blueprint required students to complete a number of courses that have been assessed by a campuswide, faculty-elected committee as integrating "diversity" and "intercultural" content throughout their curricula.

Three specific activities occur annually on the Wagner campus, all initiated, facilitated, and evaluated by faculty. First, all freshmen, as part of their "learning communities," are required to attend a student-written, faculty-directed diversity play accompanied by a "talk back and reflection session." Second, a year-long speakers' series titled Academic and Cultural Enrichment (ACE) sponsors speakers, panels, and activities that generally revolve around a diversity theme. Faculty and staff suggest the speakers to a faculty-selected ACE coordinator. The series topics are communicated across the campus, and faculty require students to attend particular sessions that complement their course content and student learning outcomes. Third, Wagner hosts an annual Diversity Fair during which four ethnic groups from within the broader community come to Wagner to share ethnic and cultural information. The Staten Island community is invited to this event, which is also attended by Wagner faculty, students, staff, and administrators. The Diversity Fair was initially developed by a faculty member and has grown into a program that is widely celebrated throughout the campus and the community.

How *Do* We and How *Can* We Assess Diversity Initiatives?

There are many approaches to diversity assessment and evaluation. Though campuses continue to struggle with and believe in addressing issues of diversity, without assessing and evaluating the goals that we strive to achieve, higher education will not learn from what we do on our own and each others' campuses. Some common diversity assessment and evaluation areas are:

1. The percentage increase of students, faculty, and staff from underrepresented groups
2. The retention rate of students, faculty, and staff from underrepresented groups
3. Goal setting and measurement of student performance (by demographic group) in courses. For instance, the Center for Urban Education at the University of Southern California has designed, tested, and implemented the Diversity Scorecard, which identifies diversity areas a campus strives to improve: retention, access, institutional receptivity, and academic excellence. The scorecard allows each institution to identify its goals and then to measure its baseline, target, and equity issues by demographic group.
4. The James Irvine Foundation Diversity Evaluation Project (http://www.aacu.org/irvinediveval/overview.cfm) provides assessment and evaluation tools for campuses that have chosen to institute campuswide diversity initiatives.
5. Portland State University created a diversity rubric to measure a student's increase in empathy and cultural awareness from the beginning of the student's freshman year until the close of the freshman year. Since "Intercultural Awareness" is a goal of the university's gen-

eral education requirements, this rubric became the tool faculty used to read student work submitted at the beginning of the year and at the end of the year and assess any increase in empathy and intercultural sensitivity.

What Are Lessons Learned About Institutional Readiness, Institutional Change, and Diversity Initiatives?

One would be hard pressed to find an institution of higher education that did not have a statement of diversity or equal opportunity within its mission statement, its office of affirmative action, or its hiring practices. Posting these goals are the basic first steps toward institutional readiness for thinking broadly and deeply about diversity and multicultural issues. Institutional change does not advance past these general postings until faculty, staff, and students fully realize the academic and personal benefits that come from having a diverse student body, diverse faculty, and diverse staff. It is critical that the upper administration finds ways to articulate publicly its own personal beliefs in these issues. These messages can be conveyed through public addresses to the campus community, through promotion and tenure practices, through research support, and through hiring and promotion practices. Faculty, staff, and students must populate the committees that recommend policy about diversity within and across the curriculum. Basic persuasion theory posits that changing behavior changes attitudes. When those who are the most skeptical of diversity issues come to realize that internal and external pressures are changing the cultural and demographic makeup of higher education and that these changes enhance the student learning experience, the faculty research and classroom experience, and the campus climate, then will come the consistent and deeply felt changes that we continue to discuss.

References

Banks, J. (1996). *Multicultural education, transformative knowledge and action: Historical and contemporary perspectives*. Columbia University, NY: Teachers College Press.

Beckham, E. (2000). *Diversity, democracy, and higher education: A view from three nations*. Washington, DC: Association of American Colleges and Universities.

Benns-Suter, R. (1993). *The utilization of simulations in multicultural education.* Millersville, PA: Millersville University. (ERIC Document Reproduction Service No. ED 364613)

Bonilla, J. F., & Palmerton, P. R. (2001). A prophet in your own land? Using faculty and student focus groups to address issues of race, ethnicity and gender in the classroom. In D. Lieberman & C. Wehlburg, (Eds.). *To improve the academy: Resources for faculty, instructional and organizational development* (pp. 32–48). Bolton, MA: Anker.

Carter, D. J., & Wilson, B. (1997). *Minorities in higher education. Fifteenth annual status report 1996–1997.* Washington, DC: American Council on Education.

Cullinan, C. (2002, May/June). *Adding class to the mix: Preparations, methods and cautions for including socio-economic class in teaching and learning about diversity and discrimination.* Paper presented at the National Conference on Race and Ethnicity in Higher Education, New Orleans, Louisiana.

Harvey, W. B. (2002). *Minorities in higher education 2001–2002.* Washington, DC: American Council on Education.

Jacobson, W., Borgford-Parnell, J., Frank, K., Peck, M., & Reddick, L. (2002). Operational diversity: Saying what we mean, doing what we say. In D. Lieberman & C. Wehlburg, (Eds.). *To improve the academy: Resources for faculty, instructional, and organizational development* (pp. 128–149). Bolton, MA: Anker.

Lieberman, D., & Guskin, A. (2003). The essential role of faculty development in new higher education models. In C. Wehlburg & S. Chadwick-Blossey, (Eds.). *To improve the academy: Resources for faculty, instructional, and organizational development* (pp. 257–272). Bolton, MA: Anker.

McTighe Musil, C., Garcia, M., Hudgins, C., Nettles, M. T., Sedlacek, W. E., & Smith, D. (1999). *To form a more perfect union: Campus diversity initiatives.* Washington, DC: Association of American Colleges and Universities.

McTighe Musil, C., Garcia, M., Moses, Y., & Smith, D. (1995). *Diversity in higher education: A work in progress.* Washington, DC: Association of American Colleges and Universities.

Nettles, M. T., & Perna, L. (1997). *The African American education data book: Higher and adult education* (Vol. 1). Fairfax, VA: The College Fund/United Negro College Fund.

Nowak-Fabrykowski, K., & Price, A. (2001, winter). Culture, identity and curriculum. *Multicultural Education, 9*(2), 24–25.

Oullette, M. (2002). Teaching for inclusion. In C. A. Stanley & M. E Porter (Eds.), *Engaging large classes: Strategies and techniques for college faculty* (pp. 97–108). Bolton, MA: Anker.

Recruit and retain. (2002, May). *Academic Leader: The Newsletter for Academic Deans and Department Chairs, 19*(5) 1–5.

Smith, D. G (1989). *The challenge of diversity: Involvement or alienation in the academy*. Washington, DC: School of Education and Human Development, George Washington University.

Smith, D. G., Garcia, M., Hudgins, C. A., McTigh Musil, C., Nettles, M. T., & Sedlacek, W. E. (2000). *A diversity research agenda: Campus diversity initiatives*. Washington, DC: Association of American Colleges and Universities.

Smith, D. G, Gerbick, G. L., Figueroa, M. A., Watkins, G. H., Levitan, T., Moore, L. C., et al. (1997). *Diversity works: The emerging picture of how students benefit*. Washington, DC: Association of American Colleges and Universities.

Smith, D. G., Wolf, L. E., & Busenberg, B. E. (1996). *Achieving faculty diversity: Debunking the myths*. Washington, DC: Association of American Colleges and Universities.

Snyder, T. D. (1997). *State comparisons of education statistics: 1969–1970 to 1996–1997*. Washington, DC: National Center for Education Statistics.

Stern, K. S. (1990). *Bigotry on campus: A planned response*. New York: American Jewish Committee.

Voegele, J., & Lieberman, D. (2005). Failure with the best of intentions: When things go wrong. In C. Cress, P. Collier, V. Reitenauer, & Associates (Eds.), *Learning through serving: A student guidebook for service learning across the disciplines* (pp. 99–112). Sterling, VA: Stylus.

2

THE POWER OF NARRATIVES IN THE PROCESS OF TEACHING AND LEARNING ABOUT DIVERSITY

Brenda Jarmon, Deborah A. Brunson, and Linda L. Lampl

With Deborah "Debbie" Cardamone, Mary Cole, Sherick A. Hughes, Martin Jarmond, Audrey Mathews, James McFarland, and Daniel R. Vicker

M
any books and journal articles focus on teaching diversity and multiculturalism, but often the writer's viewpoint is geared toward addressing pedagogy and learning exclusively from the perspective of the teacher. Rarely does the reader hear from students about their learning experiences within the academic setting. It is even more infrequent that those who teach or do research in diversity hear from former students about how the classroom experience has intersected with their life encounters beyond the course. Thus, we felt it a significant contribution to the diversity arena to edit this volume where the voices of teachers and their students converge around diversity lessons that have been taught, learned, and experienced.

This book is an interdisciplinary edited volume that provides insights into the power of narratives related to the educational experiences that occur between teachers of diversity and their students. Through a letter addressed to their former teacher, we hear how these students have encountered diversity since leaving the classroom. Their narrative observations and reflections focus upon key lessons learned or ideas that were challenged in the teacher's classroom, and how these lessons are connected to or disconnected from their professional and/or personal lives. Further, framing these narratives through a letter to their former teacher provides a unique opportunity to hear the voices of these students beyond their classroom experiences. Because we believe in the "power of narratives" as a powerful conduit for effective diversity and multicultural pedagogy, we invited several of our colleagues who teach in the diversity arena to contact former students who could collaborate with them and us on this project. This chapter provides an overview of narrative as a pedagogical method and explores the potential influence of this method upon teaching and learning diversity. Letters from the former students of Brenda Jarmon, Deborah Brunson, and Linda L. Lampl have been integrated throughout this essay, to provide a frame of reference for scholarly observations about the narrative as an effective instructional technique.

Narrative as Pedagogy

The use of narratives and stories in the classroom has been the focus of increasing attention among educators in recent years (Baxter Magolda, 2001; Butler & Bently, 1996; Kenyon & Randall, 1997; Kerby, 1991; Rossiter, 1999; Taylor, Marienau, & Fiddler, 2000). This whole notion of narratives is fruitful ground for adult educators who know by instinct the value of stories in teaching and learning. The person experiencing the event often feels compelled to relate these life occurrences and actions, thus giving credence to the importance of narrative in the human experience. Rossiter (1999) has conceptualized the narrative perspective as an organizing construct for adult development by identifying five elements that frame the narrative-development process:

1. Narrative knowing is based on a constructivist, interpretive epistemology;
2. Narrative is a central structure in human meaning making; thus, the life course and individual identity are experienced as story;
3. Temporality and narrative are integrally related; time is constitutive of meaning;
4. Narrative is historical; thus, development can be understood retrospectively, as an interpretation of the life story; and
5. Individual and cultural narratives are interrelated (p. 59)

It is therefore not surprising that many educators—who as human beings also participate in this storytelling process—have come to acknowledge and appreciate the power of narratives in teaching and learning. Narrative, as it is conceptualized here becomes much more than "storytelling in the classroom." The pedagogical value of narrative rests in its ability to explain how one has *applied* what one has learned, or how one expects to make that application in everyday life. As teachers of diversity, this certainly rings true for us and is what prompted us to ask former students to articulate what they learned from our courses and how they have applied these learning outcomes in their professional/career endeavors. For example, the letters below from two of Deborah Brunson's students reflect the ability of our students to articulate their own experiences, drawing upon concepts and language encountered in the academic classroom. These selections also provide insights about how adult educators facilitate learning through narrative both during the classroom experience and beyond it. Rossiter (1999) proposes that two key goals of the educator who is sensitive to the narrative perspective are to facilitate learning and to facilitate narrative receptivity.

Mary Cole, *graduate student and job recruiter (Florida)*

Dear Dr. Brunson,

Just recently, I decided to pursue my graduate degree in mental health counseling. Someone asked me, "What do you think will be your biggest contribution as a mental health counselor?"

This made me think—this is the kind of question that forces us to pay attention to how we define ourselves and as a result, how we "label" other people. I asked myself: What is the greatest contribution I can make? But more important, does this relate to how I live my life today?

I graduated from college six years ago. My decision to go back into academia was easy—I genuinely missed learning about people, how we communicate and what connects us as human beings. This was a concept that became an integral part of my life during my education at the University of North Carolina Wilmington (UNCW). After deciding to major in communication studies, I had hoped to somehow capture the essence of being an empathic communicator. As this idea took shape over the years in school, I was able to develop a genuine awareness for other people from all walks of life.

While many professors encouraged me as an undergraduate student, I enrolled in several courses with you. Each time I found you to be a true inspiration. I had considered my background to be "fairly diverse" upon entering college, but it was in fact during the last few years of school that I truly learned the power of certain words like culture, identity, and gender. Our classes seemed to be filled with exciting material, and I had never before been exposed to such candid discussions. The same friends that I would laugh with outside of the classroom were also profound, insightful people inside the classroom with their own deep values and identities. It was difficult for me at first to speak. We immersed ourselves in sensitive topics that other people in my life had simply avoided because it was a challenge to their balance. Previously, these subjects had been oversimplified in many of my other classes, but your supportive class environment encouraged all of us. The more I began to speak in class, the more I realized there was a great need for simple awareness of what others were feeling. The more I tried, the easier it became. The wisdom I gained still exists in my life today.

These experiences ignited a spark in me. My classroom work and heavy group interactions led me to my current career as a recruiter. Every day I speak with people from all walks of life from all over the world. My job is not only to search for new careers for them, but also to understand them on a more fundamental level. My UNCW experience enables me to respect their different needs and to appreciate the incredible variety of their experiences. Every day I learn something new!

So many times in the therapy field, counselors forget that every client is different, that each one embraces a unique perspective within his or her own private world. Therapists are constantly challenged to remember that clients are truly alive in their own experiences based on what life has brought to them. At times, it can seem too emotional, too consuming, and even too exhausting to commit sensitivity to a client's reality. However, my contribution is simply to remember, believe, and apply this very concept! It is not easy and no one is perfect. However, it seems to me that the more I try, the easier it becomes . . . just like in your class! We are different from each other, yes. Nevertheless, we are all still human beings, searching to validate our identity through communication, awareness, and, above all understanding for one other.

Debbie Cardamone, *college instructor in communication studies (North Carolina)*

Dear Dr. Brunson,

I remember your Interracial Communication course in which we discussed ways to reduce prejudice in the world. I can still hear you saying,

*"Persuasion, education, and contact are three ways to reduce prejudice."
Prior to my undergraduate years at the University of North Carolina Wilmington, I had little or no contact with anyone who would be considered the "other" in my small hometown of upstate New York. My world was one of sameness: same race, same ethnicity, same religion, and same socioeconomic class. Until your course, I had not experienced contact with anyone different from myself. Today, contact is a means for me to meet others, reduce anxiety and uncertainty, discover common ground, and begin to persuade and educate those around me on the richness that diversity adds to our lives.*

As a graduate student of communication studies at the University of North Carolina at Greensboro working with undergraduates, I often reflected upon the strategies you used to build a spirit of community among our diverse student body. As a nontraditional student, I was aware of what it felt like to be the "other" on a campus dominated by students half my age. Along with creating a safe, supportive climate in our classroom where respect and tolerance were central, the engagement you fostered was transformational in bridging our differences. The contact you orchestrated among students of different races, religions, genders, and ages through round-table, panel, and small-group discussions was instrumental to our assimilation. We became a "melting pot" by choice.

In a graduate service-learning course, Communicating Common Ground: Diversity and Dialogue (part of Communicating Common Ground, a national initiative program), course creator Dr. Christopher Poulos requested each graduate student to serve as a facilitator. I selected the theme "Race in America: The African American Experience." Reflecting on the positive impact of your teaching methods regarding interracial and intercultural communication, I wanted "my" class, like yours, to make a difference. The most insightful information I gleaned in your course came from students speaking from their hearts, sharing their experiences and feelings about race and prejudice, without fear of judgment. I decided to approach my class in a spirit of openness by sharing my intention to inspire meaningful dialogue. I began by sharing a personal narrative of my experience as a recipient of religious prejudice. I wanted my students to understand that I was sensitive to their concerns. I recall you sharing with us that as a child you could not attend a "whites only" amusement park. I felt your pain, and my shame as a white person. By sharing your personal story, I sensed your sincerity and the importance of the issues at hand.

Drawing upon your teaching and example, we made contact in my class.
I heard stories of hurt and of anger. I heard stories of forgiveness and of hope.
I witnessed listening and empathy as students genuinely searched for common
ground among their differences. Thank you Dr. Brunson.

These powerful testimonies underscore the impact of the narrative perspective that Deborah Brunson modeled in her classroom—a perspective she used to share her own narrative story, which led to profound insight for students Mary and Debbie. It allowed them to connect new knowledge with lived experience and weave it into existing narratives of meaning. Gudmundsdottir (1995) notes that pedagogical content can be thought of as narrative text, and teaching as essentially the exercise of textual interpretation. Educators not only tell stories about the subject, they story the subject knowledge itself. In doing so, they aim to maintain some interpretive space in which the learner can interact with the subject. Rossiter (1999) underscores the notion that learning is integrally involved with the interpretative process, and that the teacher becomes a partner with the learner in facilitating change through narrative: "According to the narrative orientation, then, we can appreciate that transformative learning involves a restorying process on the part of the learner" (p. 68). This approach is an important departure from more traditional pedagogies and philosophies of teaching and learning.

The traditional teaching structure typically places instructors at the front of the class, disseminating their knowledge to students who later, with delight, restate the same knowledge in order to demonstrate their understanding. Considerable research has examined the efficacy of lecture-based instruction (Lowman, 1995), and it would not be prudent to dismiss the lecture as an unsound pedagogical practice. When carefully organized and used in moderation, lectures can present up-to-date content not in the text; help students organize complex material; motivate students to seek more information; and model problem solving, critical thinking, intellectual curiosity, and enthusiasm (McKeachie, 2002). At the same time, lectures alone are not adequate to facilitate deep understanding (Halpern & Hakel, 2003). Educators still need to encourage and promote reflective narratives within their instructional practices, with the expectation that such exercises will uncover important implications about education and its values. The most significant implication one would hope to articulate is that students' beliefs about themselves and about their academic disciplines have an impact on their learning

(Halpern & Hakel, 2003). For example, two letters from Linda L. Lampl's students (Daniel and Audrey) are evidence of this very important implication, as are the letters from Mary and Debbie.

Daniel R. Vicker, *Senior Management Trainer (Florida)*

My mother is from South Carolina and Dad is from Wisconsin. I attended first and second grade at a public elementary school located in my neighborhood. None of my classmates were of color. I attended 3rd through 6th grade at an integrated school that grouped students in multiage classes where we learned at our own pace in teams. I attended 7th through 12th grade in a more traditional school environment. A racial divide began for me suddenly in the 7th grade that continued through high school, as my circle of friends slowly became white.

This experience probably increased my interest in culture and led me to take intercultural/interracial communication. I was older than most of the students in that class, and I remember thinking of myself as somewhat of a mentor to the other students. I could act on this role because the class was a blend of experiential learning and Socratic dialogue, giving me the opportunity to speak my thoughts and influence the direction of the discussion. I remember one class discussion on institutional discrimination and its influence on the racial makeup of the employees of government agencies. At the time, I had just finished a master's degree in public administration and was working for the state legislature. I remember the instructor saying something like "Institutional racism affects the hiring practices of the people in government agencies, and this has created inequality." I remember thinking of affirmative action and other things I believed were true about the positive strides in racial equality that were being made in government that I had learned in public administration. I immediately blurted out, "There's no discrimination in hiring practices in government." The room of about 60 students suddenly became silent and then erupted in a scoffing type of undercurrent. The instructor looked at me in shock and said something like, "If you don't think there is then you need to open your eyes." The other students seemed to concur. I suddenly realized that I was probably wrong. It was a significant emotional event realizing that I was ignorant of this issue.

I remember playing two experiential games called BaFáBaFá and Star-Power, which I have used several times since that class. Both helped me see and feel the troubles with cross-cultural communication. I am able now to work on my attitudes, values, and beliefs around racial and intercultural relationships/communication almost every day from a position of power I gained from those games. I look at almost every encounter with some sensibility to myriad cultural differences.

I currently teach leadership to government workers, and I try to use my intercultural sensibilities to reach them and to teach them. After 14 years, I still feel I am a better person in all my relationships because of the lessons I gained from that class. Recently I have traveled to Egypt and to Kuwait to deliver leadership training and I can say without a doubt, my ability to connect with people of different cultures has been greatly enhanced.

Audrey Mathews, *attorney, human resources (Florida)*

Dear Professor Lampl,

As a black female, born and raised in Tallahassee, my exposure to diversity was limited to gender and race (specifically black and white). My formative years did little to open my eyes to people's differences. My family lived in a predominantly white neighborhood, where I was oftentimes the only black participating in extracurricular activities or in a classroom. Nonetheless, as I entered Florida State University (at the ripe age of 18) I believed that I was tolerant and very accepting of others. However, after registering for your class, I quickly learned that diversity was more than race and gender.

I recall during the first week of your class, you took pictures of all the students and requested everyone to complete a survey. I remember commenting on the survey that we needed something harder and more challenging than what the first week's introduction to multiculturalism provided. Reviewing the course syllabus and gathering my material for class, I felt this class would be a breeze. I was confident your class would be one of my "easier" courses to complete for the semester. I had no idea what lay ahead of me. Our classroom discussions were very candid and affirmative action (purpose, logic, and justifications for/against) was always a topic of interest for my classmates. Attending your class left me upset and frustrated, but also encouraged me to self assess my personal biases and understand the makeup behind someone who was not like me. Rarely did our classroom discussions run within the allotted time. More often than not, students continued our discussions gathered in front of Ruby Diamond Auditorium, or as we headed to our next class. Your class was one of the few classes where we did not *watch the clock.*

Following my undergraduate work at FSU, I graduated from Nova Southeastern University law school and followed a career path that led me to human resources. Previously, I prepared strategies and defenses for employers sued pursuant to Title VII allegations and conducted remedial training for employees on—yes, you guessed it—diversity. Years later, I still refer to useful resources and tools that were first introduced to me in your class; an article, a videotape, or simply a classmate's opinion to assist me facilitate training and/or presentations.

Presently, I work for one of the nation's largest providers of electricity-related services with annual revenues of more than $9 billion and employing over 12,000 personnel. I manage my company's Equal Opportunity Employment and Affirmative Action Programs. I am also responsible for the revitalization of the company's past diversity initiative efforts (training, community involvement, recruiting efforts, and communication to employees/customers) and moving forward, I am preparing the company for new and emerging employment trends.

Your class continues to be a huge influence in my life. Not a day goes by that diversity is not intersected in my life (social or professional). As I write this letter, I think how silly I must have seemed to remark that your class was easy. It is ironic, don't you think? Your class (over all the many courses I've completed) was the most influential to me, has the most practical use of application, and continues to challenge me daily. Thanks for making things difficult for me; it has kept me gainfully employed!

Certainly, these letters bear witness to the impact of the narrative metaphor as applied to adult development (e.g., Cohler, 1982; Hermans, 1997; Rossiter, 1999). This approach sees developmental change as experienced through the ongoing construction and reconstruction of one's life narrative. Once again, learners connect new knowledge with lived experience and weave it into existing narratives of meaning—a wonderful way to examine and teach diversity and multicultural education. Using this narrative orientation to teach diversity and multicultural education is grounded in an understanding of narrative as a primary structure of human meaning, and narrative as metaphor for the developing self. We believe that narratives can function as a powerful medium of learning, development, and transformation in the diversity arena. A prime example of the narrative metaphor as applied to adult development is James McFarland's letter:

James McFarland, clinical social worker (Florida)

> Dear Dr. Jarmon,
>
> Cultural Competence is alive and well in the field . . . it has to be, or you could find yourself as a social worker invariably on the "losing end." One of the things that we discussed a lot in your class was the idea of openness to other cultural beliefs and norms, no matter how different they may be.
>
> Poverty, I've come to learn, has its own culture, and so does wealth. The North has its culture, and the South has its own cultural rhythms and ways, too. Living and working as a therapist in rural South Florida you need to be flexible and remember where you are. Often you would focus on the importance of geographic location and language as important diversity tools. I wished I had paid more attention because you were right on the money — diversity is more than race! For example, where I work, if you can't muster the compassion and liquidity of thought required to deal effectively with people from all walks of life, you can easily find yourself up against tremendous odds.
>
> Case in point from my own personal experience was an incident just this past year in which I found myself in a circuit courtroom being stared down by a very menacing and powerful southern conservative judge, fielding a barrage of sarcastic questions from him. The judge had inadvertently happened upon one of my treatment plans for a client who was not only a ward of the state but a child that this judge had "taken a likin' to."
>
> This child was sexualized very early in her life and had a myriad of sexualized, very explicit behaviors, one of which was public masturbation for hours at a time. My treatment plan addressed this problem very clinically with a standard intervention of redirecting the behavior to more appropriate private settings together with a modicum of foster parent supervision to be certain that the child's behavior was not excessive, nor involved objects or materials that could injure the child.
>
> After reading the treatment plan aloud in court, the judge was livid, and subsequently issued a subpoena for me to come in to the court to "explain" why I was "teaching a little girl to masturbate at all, let alone with the parents watching!" Your words rang clear: Rule number one—know the

playing field (what is the culture, mind-set, norms of the area you work in),
and talk to the players in a language that does not assault their sensibilities.

When I crafted that treatment plan, I hadn't acknowledged a couple of
very important facts about where I was working, or who I was dealing
with—the "playing field" was a rural county in the middle of the Florida
Bible Belt, replete with a conservative judge who believed that people like
me were opening Pandora's box to all things immoral and improper. You
see, in southern cultures, women are to keep their "modesty," and to openly
talk of things such as sex and masturbation, let alone with a male, is tanta-
mount to heresy.

I spent an hour and a half in the courtroom explaining my treatment
plan, and the judge finally relented, stating, "I understand that this is the
treatment standard, but I don't have to like it. I want a woman counselor
to do therapy with this little girl too." Had I been a little more in tune to
the culture, I could've phrased that treatment plan in a way that would've
kept me out of the courtroom, and doing what needs to be done: helping my
kids.

Not all those who have written narratives tell positive stories—the majority do, but not all of them. Some have related quite unpleasant experiences such as James's; however, his learning curve was enhanced as he
recalled and applied social work and diversity concepts gleaned from Jarmon's lectures. It turned out that James had an intellectual reorientation that
resulted from learning something profoundly novel (e.g., the judge's attitude) that shifted James's attitude to a new area that he had never considered.
Interestingly, most of the narratives found throughout this volume have focused on personal learning (i.e., a change in self-perception) and cognitive
learning (i.e., changes in intellectual understanding). Both are effective
modes of learning for human diversity issues and multicultural education.
These infinite expressions of interpretive interplay among teachers, learners,
and content provide unlimited opportunities for uses of narratives and story
in adult teaching and learning. We cannot reduce narrative to a handy tool
kit of techniques; however, we can recognize the dimension of learning that
leads us beyond ourselves to the real world and we can conclude that narrative—in its many manifestations—functions as a powerful medium of learning, development, and transformation. Former students Sherick and Martin

offer two more stories that illustrate the developmental and transformational potentials in narrative:

Sherick Hughes, *assistant professor of education (Ohio)*

> *Dear Dr. Brunson,*
>
> *Upon entering the University of North Carolina Wilmington, I struggled with the typical human dilemma of leaving home as a young man: man versus man, man versus nature, and man versus himself. Like many other freshmen, I changed my major. I went from computer science to communication studies. I realize that we are who we think we are, and who we think other people think we are, but the degree to which I looked to others to find out who I was at that time was troubling. Dr. Brunson, you helped me begin the focus on redefining myself to make social choices I could live with and feel proud of through two classes that explored human diversity from the inside out—Interpersonal Communication and Interracial Communication.*
>
> *When I took Interracial Communication and Interpersonal Communication with you, Dr. Brunson, I was certainly somewhere between stages in Cross's Nigrescence Model of Racial Identity. The pedagogy of the courses involved diversity education through self-exploration of "perception, self-presentation, listening, relationship development, and resolving interpersonal conflict." I even kept my syllabi and most of my notes and the course packs for the courses. The courses provided much depth and breadth to my knowledge of one-on-one interactions. Three assignments in particular remain in my head, most likely because I use remnants of them even today, over seven years later: (1) personal style inventory, (2) sex and gender education with emphasis on perception checking, and (3) BaFáBaFá.*
>
> *Now, of course, I understand that two courses do not account for everything that changed in my life. I understand that lived experiences do not follow formulaic stages in any contrived way for most of us. In addition, I understand that we move in and out of "fixed research-prescribed" stages, are between stages, skip stages, remain in one stage an entire lifetime, and even regress to a stage after momentary progress when the goal is antioppression. I too constructed my identity in a dynamic way, but I must say that I did seem to hit every stage in Cross's model. I was trying to find my "self" at the predominantly white-experience-based UNCW—to find my way in life away from home as a burgeoning adult, scholar, social servant, activist for*

social distributive justice, and as a young black male scholar in the academy. I will say that it is highly unlikely that I would have changed in the same ways, or with the same speed without you, Dr. Brunson, and the classmates that structured my learning experiences.

Materials from those courses were useful in graduate school and they continue to be useful in my life today. I am now a tenure-track professor of education at the University of Toledo. I teach a course dealing with family, issues of race, ethnicity, gender, sex, sexual orientation, and developmental pathways. I have started a nonprofit agency, G3, Inc., which offers free diversity education and streamlines free resources to connect local universities with local school needs. And, I still consult with you to learn from your pedagogy of diversity and perseverance for justice.

Martin Jarmond, *assistant athletic director of development (Michigan)*

Until the time that I entered my freshmen year of college at predominantly white University of North Carolina Wilmington, my educational experiences and settings had been very racially diverse. For the first time, I could look around a classroom and not see one single person who looked like me. Unknown to me then, I would eventually develop an awareness and appreciation of the responsibilities of representing one's race.

One day in Dr. Brunson's diversity class, she asked our class a peculiar question: "How many of you have never *had a class with or had any significant interaction with an African American?" Almost half the class raised their hands, a response that totally shocked me. That night I called my mom to talk with her about my astonishing classroom experience. She talked to me about a sense of responsibility (to my race) that had never come to my conscience. She insisted that I be on my best behavior in class, take part in class discussion, and radiate a positive attitude . . . from the way I dressed to the way I spoke. "Some of those classmates might develop a stereotype of all blacks from what they observe from you, fair or unfair, so make sure that it's a positive one." Those classroom experiences, coupled with my mother's words of wisdom, gave me diversity training and awareness that has been fundamental to my educational, professional, and social development. It taught me the value of understanding our differences, helping me to have more effective and meaningful communication, and ultimately more "success" in such interactions.*

I entered graduate school at Ohio University, again as the only black in my program. By and large, graduate school was a positive and enriching experience. There were a few instances, however, and one crisis where I had to "draw upon" what I had learned. The worst experience occurred late one night when someone placed a sign on my parking space that read "NIGGER PARKING ONLY." This was the first time that I had encountered such negative, outright racism. It was so comforting (and cherished to this day) how my white classmates rallied around me. Their overwhelming support helped me turn a negative experience into a positive affirmation of my value to my classmates.

Moving on from graduate school to the real world, I again find myself in the position as the only minority in the office. I am the assistant athletic director of development in the athletic department at Michigan State University. Here I am faced with a much more diverse work environment besides race because of being a 24-year-old surrounded by much older coworkers. My job responsibilities revolve around developing and implementing strategies to solicit donations from MSU alumni and supporters, usually older, white individuals.

Much of my current career success can be traced to awareness and competencies learned in Dr. Brunson's diversity course. Working in the field of development, my job is all about stewardship, nurturing relationships, and gaining insight into what is important to a donor. I still reflect on my unique position to be stereotyped . . . so my "other" job is to make sure I leave a positive one. Diversity class was the catalyst for the lessons learned from my mother and experiences that followed my time at UNC Wilmington.

As editors, we hope that these students' letters and the ones that follow in *Letters from the Future* will demonstrate narrative as a powerful pedagogy—a pedagogy that can potentially produce fundamental change in individuals' worldviews. Rossiter (1999) explained this potential for change: "It is through narrative that people renegotiate meaning as they deal with what is out of the ordinary. In this renegotiation, one's story is enlarged so as to include unanticipated events, inexplicable happenings, or contradictory perspectives. Furthermore, the cultural and familial narratives in which our lives are embedded come to our awareness at times of change and conflict" (Bruner, as cited in Rossiter, p. 68). Note that we interchangeably use narratives, letters, and stories to examine the fact that our students' letters deal with human experiences, and that we tend to perceive the letters as authentic and credible sources of knowledge based on what students have learned in our classroom, which has so profoundly affected their view about diversity and multiculturalism. Our student letters have provided us with their "landscape of action" and their "landscape of consciousness" (Bruner, 1986) whereby we can share students' learning experiences and offer our readers more in-depth meaning to the importance of enhancing our diversity repertoire. In doing so, we create the opportunity to conduct more research in this area, to add to the diversity and multiculturalism database, and to promote a growing paradigm of new thought about the importance of narrative to diversity teaching and learning.

Teaching diversity has an obvious connection to the real world. A "power of narratives" perspective contributes to the classroom—real world connection, and to the continuing development of pedagogical and interpretive methods that engages the academic community in a progressive orientation toward diversity teaching. It is important for us as teachers to understand the primary structure of human meaning and how narratives as metaphors for developing self are a great way, we believe, to teach our students and to understand that we, too, have our own narrative metaphors to tell as well. Thus, our student letters indicate that when we shared our narratives, their learning processes were strengthened, thus substantiating our resolve that both student and teacher can more effectively engage in unlimited interplay among themselves with diversity content—an effective way to enhance teaching and learning in the diversity community. Yes, narratives are indeed a powerful dimension of learning, development, and transformation.

Sonia Nieto (2002) says it profoundly as she discusses language, culture, and teaching with input from participants: "if a community is created in which all voices are respected it seems to me that itself is a noble first step—a deeper sense of bonding and caring can develop despite the real differences that exist" (p. 247). It really is about respect and tolerance and gaining credible feedback that substantiates what we have felt about our diversity courses. Our student letters, as well as the many letters you will read throughout this text reflect Nieto's concept of community. It is our earnest hope that we will create a "community of narratives" that will inform, transform, and give new meaning to the importance of teaching and learning about diversity.

The importance of this topic is repeated throughout our book. Certainly, the chapter that precedes our essay, authored by Devorah Lieberman who has become one of the most prolific writers about diversity and higher education, bears witness to the significance of this topic. Her discussion about the necessity of thinking more broadly both about pedagogical methods and about student learning styles further substantiates the importance of using various pedagogical strategies to support teaching and learning about diversity. *Letters from the Future* was developed to invite opportunities for its readers to expand their understanding of diversity teaching and learning across the academy. With that in mind, we have assembled teachers from a variety of disciplines to contribute their voices: Muriel Lederman (biology), Earl Sheridan (political science), Patricia Brown McDonald (English), Scott W. Campbell (speech communication), Randy K. Dillon (speech communication), Karen Bullock (social work), Billy R. Close (criminal justice), Leila E. Villaverde (education), and Steve Chandler (sex education). As editors, we hope that this diverse offering across disciplines and pedagogics will promote more exchange of ideas about diversity, and about hearing from our students so that we may learn from them.

References

Baxter Magolda, M. B. (2001). *Making their own way: Narratives for transforming higher education to promote self-development.* Sterling, VA: Stylus.

Bruner, J. (1986). *Actual minds, possible worlds.* Cambridge, MA: Harvard University Press.

Butler, S., & Bently, R. (1996). *Lifewriting: Learning through personal narrative.* Scarborough, Ontario, Canada: Pippin Publishing.

Cohler, B. (1982). Personal narrative and the life course. In P. B. Bales & O. G. Brim Jr. (Eds.), *Life-span development and behavior* (Vol. 4, pp. 205–241). New York: Academic Press.

Gudmundsdottir, S. (1995). The narrative nature of pedagogical content knowledge. In H. McEwan & K. Egan (Eds.), *Narrative in teaching, learning, and research* (pp. 24–38). New York: Teachers College Press.

Halpern, D. F., & Hakel, M. D. (2003). Applying the science of learning to the university and beyond: Teaching for long-term retention and transfer. *Change, 35*(4), 36–41.

Hermans, H. J. M. (1997). Self-narrative in the life course: A contextual approach. In M. Bamberg (Ed.), *Narrative development: Six approaches* (pp. 223–264). Mahwah, NJ: Erlbaum.

Kenyon G. M., & Randall, W. L. (1997). *Restorying our lives: Personal growth through autobiographical reflection.* Westport, CT: Praeger.

Kerby, A. P. (1991). *Narrative and the self.* Bloomington: Indiana University Press.

Lowman, J. (1995). *Mastering the techniques of teaching* (2nd ed.). San Francisco: Jossey-Bass.

McKeachie, W. J. (2002). *Teaching tips: Strategies, research, and theory for college and university teachers* (11th ed.). Boston, MA: Houghton Mifflin.

Nieto, Sonia. (2002). *Language, culture, and teaching: Critical perspectives for a new century.* Mahwah, NJ: Erlbaum.

Rossiter, M. (1992). NEWACE social action theatre: Education for change. *Continuing Higher Education Review, 56*(3), 168–172.

Rossiter, M. (1999). A narrative approach to development: Implications for adult education. *Adult Education Quarterly, 50*(1), 56–71.

Taylor, K., Marienau, C., & Fiddler, M. (2000). *Developing adult learners: Strategies for teachers and learners.* San Francisco: Jossey-Bass.

PART TWO

TEACHERS AND STUDENTS: LESSONS TAUGHT, LESSONS LEARNED

3

BIOLOGICAL DIVERSITY

Muriel Lederman

With Jill Sible, dayna e. wilhelm, and Laurie Spotswood

This chapter relates the pedagogical journey of a working molecular biologist who became engrossed with feminist analyses of science and realized that these critiques should be part and parcel of science. To implement this perspective, Lederman developed a molecular cell biology course that integrated the social studies of science with scientific content, to make explicit how epistemology and praxis are constructed and exclusionary. The awareness may increase the diversity of practitioners, as students come to understand the reasons for their "otherness." The responses to this course of another instructor (Jill Sible), a graduate teaching assistant (dayna e. wilhelm), and a student (Laurie Spotswood) are shared.

T he term "biological diversity" can mean the broad range of species within an ecosystem or the different forms of genes, called alleles, within a population of organisms. I would like to put new twists on this term by relating it both to the position of women in science and the nature of science itself. I write as a woman who was trained as a biologist, spent many years at the bench, obtained a tenure-track position at the age of 50, and was a moderately productive molecular biologist until retirement. Late in my career, I became immersed in feminist science studies, in parallel with coming to understand the dynamics of diversity (or lack thereof) in the academy. My pursuing these issues led me to realize that how we teach sci-

This project was supported by National Science Foundation Grant HRD-0332843 and approved by Virginia Tech's Institutional Review Board.

ence most often reinscribes the social conditions and disciplinary conventions that make science inimical to women and other groups. I eventually developed a strategy that I think might overcome this barrier.

Here, I will describe how I came to a pedagogy that might make the choice of a life in science more appealing to those who are currently underrepresented in the discipline. My plan would be to teach the science curriculum while incorporating the insights provided by the history, philosophy, and sociology of science and by feminist science studies. This approach promotes new conceptualizations of diversity in biology; biology as a discipline becomes more diverse when seen through sociocultural approaches. Concomitantly, teaching in this fashion may promote the diversity, defined in the traditional sense, of scientific practitioners, by encouraging members of underrepresented groups to persist in science once they become aware of how science's epistemology and practices are socially constructed to their exclusion, and how change can be effected. I will also share how the pedagogy was implemented and some preliminary assessment results.

Why So Few Women in Science?

As I write, the tidal wave of response to the comments made by Larry Summers, the former president of Harvard University, seems to be receding. It was he who suggested that women might be inherently incapable of engaging at the highest levels of science, mathematics, and engineering. What do we know about their ability? Fewer women than men attain the highest scores on measures of math ability such as the SAT. Women's brains are smaller than men's. Women and men use different portions of their brains for certain tasks. The problem with differences is that they are automatically ranked—one state must be better than the other. And it matters who gets to do the ranking, since those in power tend to validate their own characteristics. When these items of information (one would hardly call them data) are used as the basis for claiming a biologically/genetically based difference between the sexes, a correlation is being converted into causality. It is ironic that those who accept this reasoning would never permit it in a scientific paper.

Summers's biggest faux pas may have been to state openly what is most often unspoken and naturalized, in other words, "Of course, we all know that women don't do well in science." This perception may be at the bedrock of the failure of women and girls being offered the same opportunities to have lives in science as are boys and men—they are subtly discouraged from becoming engaged with these disciplines during their early lives and schooling. Nevertheless, public policy encourages women and some minorities to join the scientific workforce, but not for reasons of social justice. Instead, their participation would be a means to gain economic advantage and increase competitiveness for the nation as a whole. Advancing diversity as a route to riches sends the message that we will recruit and train more workers from among those not previously encouraged or thought able only because there are not enough recruits from the groups traditionally represented for us to prevail and be profitable in the global economic sphere.

It is instructive to understand the origins of the current practices of science as a prelude to attempting structural change that would make the playing field equal for all. Science, as an entity, sets itself up as the only means to explain natural phenomena. Scientists do not acknowledge that the methods and practice of science are fabricated—literally—having been developed in the 17th century in Europe. The origin of modern science is grounded in the Cartesian dualism that separates mind from body, giving supremacy to the cerebral over the corporeal. Superimposed on the deprecation of the body per se is the especial denigration of the female body; if Man were to gain control over nature through science, the power of the female as the source of life had to be overthrown. Evelyn Keller (1992) says that, at the Enlightenment,

> a metaphoric convergence between women, life and nature . . . bound these terms together in a new way, and in doing so, contributed to changes in all their meanings . . . the newness lay in the conjunction between women, life and nature as the locus (or refuge) of secrets that did not belong to God. It is in this move . . . that the language of secrets acquired its most radically new implication: not respect for the status of things as they are and must be, but first permission, then, a challenge, and finally, a moral imperative for change (p. 59).

The debasement of woman/nature opened nature's secrets to the investigations of the new science and the exploitations of industry (Merchant, 1980).

The reconfiguration that Keller credits with creating modern science also effectively removed woman from the enterprise. Dichotomies were set up so that the desirable attributes of science were defined as male and their opposites were made to be female, for example; male/mind, female/body; male/rational, female/emotional; male/logical, female/intuitive. In other words, science became a male or androcentric endeavor, not only in practice but also in epistemology. In contrast, the female was declared to be " 'other,' " and precisely "the 'otherness' of nature is now what allows it to be known" (Bordo, 1999, p. 69).

This micro history of Enlightenment epistemology from a feminist perspective shows that the science of that period was essentially created by a social contract. The natural philosophers invented and agreed to the rules of their game. The new principles had, as their defining features, the mechanization of nature (evidenced by the use of mechanical metaphors), the mechanization of knowledge making (especially through the use of mathematics), the separation between humans and the objects they investigate (defining nature as "other" was necessary for this schism), and the use of knowledge in the service of socially defined goals (Shapin, 1996). These principles have come down to us through the centuries, and they, too, like the naturalization of the inability of women to do science, are unspoken. Scientists are trained to follow these rules as the way to do "good science," without examining how these rules came about. They do not question the methods and practices they engage in, the rules or the conclusions they draw from them or how their results are put to use.

To break through the barriers of male-dominated science, to increase its diversity, requires the realization that it may be the nature of science itself that is inimical to women and other minorities. Lemke (2001) claims that science has been shaped "historically by the over-representation and under-representation in its ranks of different social categories of people: men and women, Europeans and non-Europeans, wealthier and poorer classes, young and old" (p. 299). In the past, the homogeneity of practitioners (men, Europeans, wealthy, the young) may have resulted in a science that reflects the gender and racial ideologies of western societies (Brickhouse, 2001); thus, it is perhaps not surprising that its norms are alienating to those who were excluded from its development.

Virtually all scientists are unaware of these norms, and this naïveté spills over into science education. Because most collegiate science educators are practicing scientists, they have so internalized the culture of science that when they teach the methods and results of scientific inquiry, they simultaneously and unconsciously transmit and validate this culture as normal, natural, and not to be questioned. Seymour and Hewitt (1997) found that women students feel psychologically alienated from the realities of science and engineering pedagogies. Since they "lack prior experience of the educational norms and attitudes they encounter on entry to science, mathematics, and engineering majors, women do not know what to make of them, or how to respond appropriately. The system . . . does not relate to the [different] way in which they were taught to learn, nor to the models of adult womanhood which their socialization encouraged them to emulate" (p. 260). We may change science education to make students aware of the cultures of science, as they have been explicated by feminist science scholars working from a variety of standpoints, as well as by historians, philosophers, and sociologists of science as a route to increasing scientific diversity, in both senses of the term.[1] If we make these cultures explicit and if they carry equal weight with scientific facts in science education, if we make clear otherwise invisible scientific norms, attitudes, institutions, and practices, we may be taking the necessary first steps for women and members of underrepresented groups to persist in an environment in which they are, to a large extent, "other."

A Personal Transformation with Respect to Science

It was a long and winding road that led me to the pedagogy described above. A life-changing commitment to feminism and a personal and intellectual transformation preceded my effort to change science education. As a college student, I was entranced with the possibility of understanding the workings of the cell through the activities of the molecules contained within. In 1965, I was a graduate student in the zoology department at Columbia University. My dissertation project was directly at the cutting edge of the first wave of molecular biology, the attempt to understand gene action rather than the contemporary project of altering gene action. I was to use biochemical techniques in vitro, in a test tube, using components of broken cells and off-the-shelf chemicals, to confirm the observation of Jacob and Monod (1961) on how the production of the enzyme b-galactosidase is regulated in bacteria.

---

1. The following works are resources for the feminist and social studies of science: Barnes, Bloor, & Henry, 1996; Fehr, 2004; Figueroa & Harding, 2003; Fleck, 1935; Hacking, 1983; Haraway, 1991, 1997; Harding, 1986, 1991, 1993, 1998, 2004; Hubbard, 1990; Keller, 1985, 1992; Kuhn, 1962; Latour, 1993; Latour & Woolgar, 1986; Lederman & Bartsch, 2001; Longino, 1990; Mayberry, Subramaniam, & Weasel, 2001; Narayan & Harding, 2002; Shapin, 1996; Wyer, Barbercheck, Giesman, Ozturk, & Wayne, 2001.

Eventually, I was able to show that the enzyme was synthesized in the in vitro system and that when I added another protein called "repressor," the synthesis of b-galactosidase was inhibited (Lederman & Zubay, 1968). This result was extremely exciting since it corroborated Jacob and Monod's in vivo analysis in the most definitive way, through in vitro experiments.

I continued to do in vitro protein synthesis in various guises for another decade, but eventually, I came to question its validity as a surrogate for what was occurring in the living cell. What criteria made me decide that I had the "optimal" conditions for protein synthesis? How did I know when I had achieved a "true" reflection of what occurs in nature? I concluded that I had no way of knowing how the in vitro system related to what occurred in vivo. I still remember the almost physical shock when I realized that major accomplishments in my scientific career were not as definitive as I thought.

This insight came to me during a meeting of faculty members at Virginia Tech with interests in the history and philosophy of science, a precursor to the current Department of Science and Technology in Society. It was at about this time that I was introduced to feminist science studies, which I immediately realized gave me both permission and context to deal with my loss of faith in the science that I had previously treasured. The only way to learn something well is to teach it—I became an autodidact in feminist science studies by developing and teaching a course for the women's studies program called Gender and Science. Being affiliated with the women's studies program was wonderful—a group of smart, savvy women, who, over time, opened my eyes to more feminist theory than I ever thought I could comprehend. I had the acquiescence of the biology department—if only because the course could fulfill the newly introduced university requirement for a writing-intensive course in the major field—although it would not count toward the 42 hours of "real biology" required for the major.

Feminist science studies confirmed that my disillusion with science was not idiosyncratic—my epiphany about my research was part and parcel of a much larger critique of science. Feminist science studies showed me that this critique was not only acceptable, but also intellectually exciting, perhaps even more challenging than doing science. My doubts about traditional science turned out to fit perfectly with constructivism, which holds that the rules of science are defined and adhered to by practitioners. Science does not discover that natural world but rather invents it—as my colleague Barbara Reeves, a historian of science says, "If history is a story we tell about the past, science is a story we tell about Nature" (personal communication, 1994). My research is an example of how practitioners decided that postulated biological mechanisms must be confirmed in vitro. The unexamined premise of this mantra is that in vitro experiments accurately represent what occurs in vivo.

Indeed, much of molecular biology may be manufactured. Evelyn Fox Keller (1992) says, based on the work of Nancy Cartwright and Mary Hesse, that:

> the understanding of the remarkable convergences between theory and experiment that scientists have produced requires attention . . . to the particular and highly local manipulation of theory and experimental procedure that is required to produce these convergences. . . . Scientific laws may be "true," but what they are true of is a distillation of highly contrived and exceedingly particular circumstances, as much artifact as nature. (p. 30)

I once heard a graduate student exclaim, "I made it work!" He was so happy he obtained the desired results without understanding that the design of the experiment and the result were a circular, self-fulfilling prophecy.

Following this reasoning to its logical conclusion, I ended up questioning fundamentally our knowledge of the natural world, perhaps reaching the point of considering that this knowledge is irretrievably flawed. It may be that the center will not hold, that there's no there, there. Donna Haraway, one of the most original thinkers in feminist science studies, has reached a similar understanding: "It seems to me that the practices of the sciences—the sciences as cultural production—force one to accept two simultaneous, incompatible truths. One is the historical contingency of what counts as nature for us; the thoroughgoing artificiality of a scientific object of knowledge, that makes it inescapably and radically contingent. You peel away all the layers of the onion and there's nothing in the center" (Penley & Ross, 1991, p. 2). A student in the transformed molecular cell biology course described in the next section stated, "In a small sense, science can be viewed to some as a lie."

I, for myself, could be this skeptical about science and still remain comfortably a faculty member in a biology department. However, in the long term, I felt uneasy presenting the processes by which we know the natural world and the information obtained through these processes as definitive and conclusive to students. Therefore, I needed to meld all my doubts about science with the critiques and analyses of other scholars in order to teach biology in a way that was intellectually rewarding and placated my conscience.

A Personal Transformation with Respect to Science Pedagogy

My reaching the point of finding it necessary to challenge traditional science teaching was another convoluted journey; one path of that began when I was appointed coordinator of the Biological Sciences Initiative at Virginia Tech in 1996. Funded from the Provost's Office, this cross-college endeavor's goal was to support opportunities for life sciences students, faculty, and departments that were not otherwise available to students, faculty, and departments. One of the first decisions was to hire two instructional designers to help faculty understand their teaching style and its consequences, and to provide the resources to implement a university goal: incorporate computer-based learning into instruction. Through these enormously talented individuals, Patricia Bevan and Zeke Erskine, I began to learn about educational theory and how instruction might interact with these theories so that students do not perceive their science classes as just memory mazes.

With their help, I redesigned my senior/graduate-level course in virology, which has an emphasis on the molecular mechanisms of viral replication rather than on viral infectious diseases. The goals of the course were, to quote from the materials given initially to students, "to understand the kinds of experiments that virologists used to obtain this information and what particular information is obtained from a particular sort of experiment, and to design and interpret experiments that answer questions in virology, including how to approach a problem and what constitutes an appropriate answer." The first goal was addressed during a "class meeting," rather than a lecture, when the instructor modeled how virologists approached and solved problems. These meetings were interactive, with lively give and take as opposed to a lecture. The second goal was met in a discussion section during which students were divided into groups to solve an authentic problem and were required to provide their conclusions both orally and in written form. However, I quickly realized that the course revision perhaps helped students understand their science better, in the sense of grasping processes rather than just memorizing facts, an admirable goal within a science department. At the same time, it made me aware that alterations widely promoted as better teaching strategies, such as problem-based learning, were self-serving and not revolutionary (Lederman, 2001; see also Mayberry, 1999). Thus my revision had not advanced my aims relevant to a broader vision of science.

I came to the conclusion that the contemporary frameworks for how students learn, which classroom protocols are based around, do not mesh well with what I had come to believe about science. For example, there could be a parallel between students constructing information for themselves, as in the educational theory of constructivism, and the other sense of constructivism, the social construction of science, which holds that practitioners have constructed an interpretation of those aspects of nature under investigation. However, it seems to me very unlikely that science instructors will come to believe that students have any level of agency in structuring their own learning (inventing a story for themselves), when they themselves do not understand that what students learn is itself a story that has been invented about nature. As another example, Lave and Wenger's apprenticeship paradigm (1991), under which we learn by doing, translates within science education to a recommendation that all college students have a research experience. However, immersing students in the rules of the laboratory reinscribes the features of science that have been promulgated by those who develop and maintain its characteristics to the exclusion of those whom they consider "other."

At about the same time, I was a founding member of a feminist pedagogies faculty study group, convened under the auspices of the Center for Excellence in Undergraduate Teaching. Two of the initial members were quite sophisticated in feminist theory and gave a solid introduction to educational theory from this perspective. Although they did not return, the group continued for another six years, changing its focus to consider feminist pedagogies specifically for the sciences. We engaged constantly, on a theoretical level, with the question, what differentiates feminist pedagogies from "just good teaching?" and concluded that the hallmark of feminist pedagogy is a commitment to social justice. This pedagogy is based in the realization that

> both science and science education reflect the inequities of the societies in which they are embedded both with respect to equality of opportunity and also with respect to how these fields are themselves constructed. The theories and practices of both traditional science and science education reproduce these inequalities in ways that are, on the whole, hidden from researchers, educators, and students. Feminist analyses of science aim to make this construction obvious and to use the insights gained in this process to create an instructional philosophy, feminist pedagogy, which overcomes these

disparities. . . . Science educators, with their access both to bodies of scientific knowledge and to students training to become scientists, are in a unique position to effect this change. (Augustine et al., 2002, pp. 17–19)

As these strands in my understanding of pedagogies came together, the result was the belief that the route to social justice and increasing diversity in science, from both perspectives given in the introduction to this chapter, was to integrate the social critiques of science (history, philosophy, sociology, feminist studies) into science teaching. Their absence, to quote Sandra Harding, "indicates to students that no one thinks these studies important to learning to do science or for making reasoned decisions about scientific issues in public life. This is unfortunate, since . . . philosophical, sociological and historical assumptions form part of scientific understanding about nature" (1994, p. 329). The deeper and more difficult task is to have the social studies of science accepted as what Kuhn (1962) would call "normal science," that the study of the processes by which scientific knowledge is obtained and the consequences of the use of that knowledge are just as important as the knowledge about the natural processes themselves.

Pedagogical Transformation

Under a grant from the National Science Foundation, a novel pedagogy for the sophomore-level Cell and Molecular Biology course (BIOL 2104) required of all biology majors at Virginia Tech—a Research I, land-grant institution—was implemented by myself in spring semester 2003 and by Jill Sible in spring semester 2004. dayna wilhelm was Dr. Sible's graduate teaching assistant, and Rebecca Scheckler of the University of Cincinnati is continuing to assess the outcomes of the course.

One way to conceptualize the transformed course is through the term "tools":

- What are the experimental tools that cell and molecular biologists use? What are their strengths and limitations?
- What are the epistemic tools that cell and molecular biologists use? In these disciplines, what is the proper way to ask a question, what are the proper techniques and instruments to answer a question, and how should the results be interpreted?

- The social studies of science will be used as a "tool" to scrutinize the scientific tools. This might include investigating the reasons for primacy of in vitro experimentation, the focus on deciphering mechanism, the relationship of mechanisms elucidated in vitro to the context of a cell or organism, and the relationship between pictures of cells, diagrams of processes, and a living cell.

For the new course, students were asked to adopt a critical stance in order to see the assumptions, concepts, and practices of science in a new way. Linkage to science studies reinforced scientific content, and science studies made explicit how the culture of science influences its theories and practice.

The scientific content of this version of Cell and Molecular Biology includes mechanisms and regulation of DNA replication, transcription, and translation; protein structure, function, and trafficking; signal transduction; the cell cycle; and so on. In addition to the required text (Cooper, *The Cell: A Molecular Approach*, 2000), there were additional readings in the social studies of science, excerpted from, for example, H. F. Judson's *The Eighth Day of Creation* (1996), Lily Kay's *Who Wrote the Book of Life?* (2000), Robert Olby's *The Path to the Double Helix* (1974), and Robert Proctor's *Cancer Wars* (1995). In contrast to the typical section of BIOL 2104, which has over 100 students, the (restricted) registration was 35 in 2003 and 47 in 2004. Even though the course was advertised as being different from usual, all students said they enrolled simply because this section fit their schedules rather than because of interest in the new content. The exams were not simply multiple choice, but instead were in the fill-in-the-blank and short essay format.

We developed a set of questions whose answers required that students use the social studies of science as a tool to scrutinize particular and general instances of scientific practice; their written responses contributed to their final grade. For example, on the first day of class, students were asked, "What does an experiment in molecular cell biology involve? Please touch on the biological materials used, the instruments used, the sorts of questions asked, and what makes the results obtained acceptable to other scientists." What was shocking about the responses was that the students had virtually no understanding of what constitutes an experimental science and expressed uncertainty about their ability to answer the question. They were asked the same question at the end of the semester, in order to evaluate change in knowledge of molecular cell biology. This example, edited for spelling and grammar, shows a change to a sophisticated understanding of the science:

- *Before:* An experiment in molecular cell biology involves biological materials, special instruments and acceptable uses of experiment(al) techniques.
- *After:* An experiment in molecular cell biology involves a clearly defined question that a scientist wants to solve to enlighten the world, at least that's what I thought coming into this class. However, after taking Biology 2104, I believe an experiment does not have to be hypothesis driven, rather it can be data driven or may even be a simple desire to make things more efficient. Some examples of data-driven experiments are microarrays where massive amounts of data are collected then a question is derived from comparison of the data, and the human genome project where the entire human DNA was sequenced with no clear question being asked in that instance as well.

The next set of excerpts shows the most extreme example of change in a student's worldview that we observed:

- *Before:* Experiments in molecular cell biology involve techniques and treatments at a variety of levels . . . the subject matter covers all forms of organic life and the questions asked could cover topics from the very specific to the somewhat broad. . . . The results will be acceptable if the methods are clear, concise, and well-documented.
- *After:* An experiment in cell and molecular biology is really an experiment not only in the *biological science* of the cell, but also in the *political science* of the research area. Through this semester I have had an eye opening to the politics behind the research and how this drives every part of the scientific experiment itself. A scientist is not only at the mercy of his own background and knowledge, or even equipment, but truly at the mercy of his *peers* and, more important, the political correctness of his *perceived* research motivation.

As well, at the end of the class in spring 2003, more students stated that following the scientific method was necessary for an investigator's results to be accepted than had made this claim at the beginning. During the semester,

I never explicated the scientific method, nor did I endorse it. I wonder if students conflated the totality of the paradigms of research in cell and molecular biology, which I *did* make explicit, with the scientific method, making sense of these paradigms by applying a term they were familiar with.

Another question we asked was: "Hans-Jorg Rheinberger (1998) has suggested that our representations of the natural world, e.g., in pictures and diagrams that describe the results of our experiments, are compared with each other, rather than with Nature. Do you think he is correct? What is the consequence of this for science?" In 2003, most agreed with the statement and, as well, made the related point that it was necessary to study the cell, not in isolation, but within the context of an organism. Students have come *on their own* to conclusions developed by philosophers and sociologists of science. Three students thought that representations have value since they depict previous results and scientists can build on already known information, avoiding starting at square one every time research is carried out. This claim is strikingly reminiscent of Thomas Kuhn's statement about the development of normal science: "Being able to take no common body of belief for granted, each writer on physical optics felt forced to build his field anew from its foundations (1962, p. 13). A graduating senior said, "Because these data were published, and other scientists were able to complete the experiments, the results were believed to be fact." This echoes Bruno Latour, "a fact is what is collectively stabilized from the midst of controversies when the activity of later papers does not consist only of criticism or deformation, but also of confirmation" (1990, p. 42). In other words, a fact becomes a fact when other people cite it in a progressively more "abstract" manner, making it a certainty without referring to the experiments the claim is based on.

The goal of this project is not to have students blindly learn facts and accept "science as it is." If it were, an assessment instrument based in male subjects could be used (Perry, 1970), since it would echo science as developed by males. Rather, we hope to help women understand the rise of "science as it is," the character of its epistemology, and what their place in it might be—a perspective that is somewhat outside of science. Accordingly, the assessment is grounded in an epistemology that arises from subjects who themselves are outside of science. It is built on the progressive stages described in *Women's Ways of Knowing* by Belenky, Clinchy, Tarule, and Goldberger (1986)—from silence, the inability to articulate a stance for oneself, to constructed knowledge, in which the learner formulates a position using objective and subjective measures. If we find that exposure to the social studies of science helps women move through these increasingly sophisticated epistemological stages, then we are promoting the eventual success of women, even within "science as it is." The most advanced stage of Belenky's classification describes well creativity in science—realizing that knowledge is provisional and subject to change as a result of a variety of influences, having the perception of oneself as capable of creating knowledge, and having the self-confidence to actually change understandings of nature or the ways we understand nature.

This self-confidence can be described as self-efficacy, the belief that one can accomplish a particular task or behavior (Bandura, 1977). Here are two examples of student statements that indicate increases in self-efficacy, both in learning and in career choice: "We have exercises that help us broaden our understanding of what our own opinions are and what we really know. There have been questions about experiments and research that I would normally panic at, but I sat down and wrote what I knew and found out it was more than I thought." "It has honestly inspired me to go into biology as a career instead of my original plan of physical therapy. I am doing well in this class and I feel it is more real to life than a multiple choice test class. I have a broader and much better understanding and much more appreciation of the field. Since I am doing well I have more confidence and this class has definitely sparked an interest." Another student answered the question, "Did the course affect you in any other way, either in school or outside of school?" that was posed in a follow-up survey sent in 2004 to all the students in the 2003 course by saying, "Yes. I ended up signing up for a neuroscience grad school program almost directly because of the confidence that I gained in my ability to think as a scientist during this class. Also, scientific experimentation seemed more exciting to me after taking this course. If I ever end up teaching, I will try to model my own style after this style of teaching."

Student Letters

Jill Sible, the other instructor, might echo at least part of this last assertion:

Jill Sible, *associate professor of biology (Virginia)*

> *Dear Muriel,*
>   *Thank you for the opportunity to reflect on my experiences teaching BIOL 2104, Cell and Molecular Biology, for gender equity. Although my*

formal role in the project is that of "teacher," I feel more appropriately categorized as "student." My participation in this project has been one of the greatest (and most rewarding) learning experiences of my academic career. When you asked me to teach this special section of Cell and Molecular Biology, I must confess I agreed for two reasons, the first considerably less admirable than the second. First, you said the section size would be small, 35–40 students as opposed to the 100–150 students that I had become accustomed to teaching for this class. The second reason I agreed was because it was you who asked. I did not fully appreciate the importance or impact of teaching undergraduate science courses from a feminist pedagogical perspective, but I respected you as a scholar and hoped to gain a better understanding of the theory by putting it into practice. I also felt indebted to you for all of the tremendous mentoring you had given me during my pretenure years as I tried to balance my research and teaching careers and having babies.

The course was a radical experience for me from day one. I had taught this course six times before and earned high marks from student evaluations (including a 4.0 out of 4.0 the previous semester), so I figured it was just a matter of adapting the course to incorporate the social studies of science. As I sat down to modify the syllabus, I realized that teaching from a feminist perspective would require completely transforming, not just what I taught, but fundamentally how I taught. Listed among the course objectives on my syllabus was the following: "to learn to think as scientists." With the best of intentions, I had consistently put that objective into my syllabus every time I taught Cell and Molecular Biology. It was only after working with you that I realized that by encouraging students to "think as scientists," I was perpetuating the status quo. Implicit in that phrase was the concept that there was a right way for a scientist to think and that to become a scientist, one must think in that same way. I had no idea what a dangerous, exclusive norm I was promoting with that objective.

The transformative experience continued in the classroom. I had always prided myself on the interactive nature of my classes. I asked a lot of questions, the class responded, and the class asked a lot of questions as well. What I came to realize during this experience was that "the class" who participated was a small minority, perhaps 5% to 10% of the group. In fact, it was the students who already knew that material who were the most engaged in discussions of the material. Why?

Fortunately, the answer came from those quiet students who were will-

ing to talk with me one-on-one outside of class. They said that they were intimidated by the vocal students, who seemed to know it all, and they did not want to speak for fear of being wrong. After I heard that, I then began to pay attention to the way in which I encouraged class discussion. I would ask questions such as, "Who has heard of the polymerase chain reaction? Who knows what Watson and Crick did to win the Nobel Prize?" No wonder those students were reluctant to participate! I was not inviting them to participate. I was inviting only those students who were familiar with a topic before I had even discussed it in class. I was excluding those students for whom this course was most important.

When I realized that my approach to generating class discussion was discriminatory, I worked to change that approach. Instead of asking who knew about a certain subject I would say, "That's my best attempt to explain DNA replication. What is confusing? What is unclear?" I was now introducing the topic first, and then inviting discussion from those who did not understand, because those were the students I really wanted to engage. After we had discussed a topic, I also asked more questions to elicit students' opinions and I stressed that every opinion was valid. These changes led to a steady increase in student participation throughout the rest of the semester.

I implemented many other changes to the course as a result of this project—reflective writing assignments, drawing assignments, group projects—and I will keep many of these changes in the course, even when I go back to my standard class of 100–150 students. However, the change that matters most does not appear in the syllabus and is even hard for me to define. I possess a new self-awareness and self-criticism as a teacher. Almost subconsciously, I question my every act as a teacher with a renewed perspective.

And so I thank you, Muriel, for providing me the opportunity to be your student, and in doing so, giving me an entirely new perspective on teaching. For me, it is no longer a choice whether to include the social studies of science and apply feminist pedagogy to my teaching. I feel compelled by a moral obligation to do so. I know this approach will not be readily understood or adopted by many of our peers, but working for change, no matter how incremental, is worth the effort.

A complementary perspective on the course can be seen from the point of view of *dayna e. wilhelm*, Sible's teaching assistant during spring semester 2004.

dayna e. wilhelm, graduate student, secondary science education (Virginia)

Dear Dr. Lederman,

    This project was first brought to my attention when I was an undergraduate teaching assistant for Cell and Molecular Biology under Dr. Jill Sible in fall 2003. Dr. Sible offered me the position as the graduate teaching assistant for this experimental section of Cell and Molecular Biology this spring semester. In effect I feel as if I have taken this course three times, because in addition to the classes that I have participated in teaching I also took this course for my undergraduate degree. When I had accepted the position I found myself not only the student learning science, but also learning different methods of teaching.

    Having had the experience of watching how this class was organized before, I was intrigued by the idea of adding a contextual social science spin on the class. Some people have asked me if there is a problem with the amount of material that is taught because of all the added social discussions. However, I have found that more students retain a higher degree of the information from the class due to these discussions. In addition, the students are able to conceptually understand the material, associating theory with application, not just memorization for examinations.

    The applications and discussions encourage the students to think at a higher level and begin to create experiments and form opinions based on current controversial topics. For example, one discussion covered stem cells. Being that this is still a hot political controversy, we felt it especially important for us to discuss not only the definition of stem cells and biological origin, but also to discuss the implications of research to the real world. Other topics that were included in class were the Human Genome Project, cancer, challenging of "the Central Dogma" (DNA → RNA → Protein), and representations of science in textbooks. Students are able to apply these concepts by designing their own experiments dealing with cell biology. I have had multiple students compliment this class because of this very fact. The applications and discussions involving the concepts and the social concepts surrounding science, instead of only listening to a professor preach science to them, has given them contextual information to help them remember and fully comprehend the information. Another piece of feedback that I have received from the students was that they enjoyed being able to ask questions and give their input into the class.

I found that the biggest challenge during this project was getting the students to form their own opinions. For example, when discussing private versus public research, one student asked what the right answer was. I said there was no right or wrong answer, but their personal opinions should be supported by information they had learned in class. This student raised his hand again and asked me, "Well, what is my opinion?" This was the moment it became obvious to me that there must be a change in the way science is taught. Although the cell and molecular class was very small (only 47 students), these concepts may also be applied to a larger class. Though it will take more effort on behalf of the professor to implement these ideas to a larger class, the level of education from the class will be greater and some of the workload could be alleviated by teaching assistants to help grade writing assignments and lead discussions.

Science is a very social profession. There are collaborations and interactions in the field of scientific research that usually get overlooked in the classroom. The general stereotype of a scientist is a pale, mad scientist who is trying to make Frankenstein or some other evil concoction. This can make the field of science very unwelcome for many people. The reality of science and how science is done must be presented to students to encourage them to pursue positions in research biology.

The new course design implemented in Cell and Molecular Biology will hopefully act as a model to open students' minds and remove the stereotypes of biology. Hopefully through new methods of educating and encouraging future biologists with programs like this, the goal of increasing diversity in the field will be met.

Following are the thoughts of Laurie Spotswood, who was a student in the class during spring 2003. The before and after responses to the question, "What does an experiment in molecular cell biology involve?" cited as an example of changes in worldview, were written by Laurie, and some of that writing is reiterated here.

Laurie Spotswood, *clinical microbiologist (Virginia)*

When I signed up for a semester of Cell and Molecular Biology, I simply chose the section that best fit into my schedule. I never intended to take this type of biology class but I couldn't be happier that I did.

I, a white female, grew up in rural southwest Virginia, not exactly the melting pot of the East Coast. My experience with the issues of diversity and women's studies had been limited before attending Virginia Tech. I must preface the remainder of my letter by saying that I was not the typical college student. I entered the university directly after high school as a premed optioned undergrad. After two years of college I met my future husband, and after less than two years of marriage we had our first child. I decided to put off my last semester of school until my son was bit older, and I delayed my graduation. The day that my son started kindergarten, I started classes to complete my degree. It was after this return to college life that I signed up for this section of biology.

My memories of what led me to pursue a career in the sciences are few and fairly faded. I have always enjoyed science. I was the "Why?" girl who was always questioning and analyzing; no answer was ever enough. So science was the perfect fit. However, until this course I had no exposure to studies in the philosophical areas of science and research: how research is conducted, how the scientific assembly line works. I was disappointed to learn that the "boys' club" of prestige and notoriety that comes along with the title of "scientist" often dictates the direction of scientific research and the way in which we continue to ask the questions.

The accepted scientific models of today are like the bible of experimentation. These are firm beliefs that other scientific experiments are built around. The biggest reason for this idea of a scientific norm comes from scientific pride. The last century has been a snowballing of sorts in the advancement of scientific technology. I believe that the general public sees these technological advancements and forms expectations about the types of knowledge that should come from the scientific community. They expect scientists to have a firm grasp in and understanding of natural phenomena, and they expect the scientific community to be in agreement.

There is some expectation that our scientific knowledge matches our sophisticated, highly advanced technological society. And the scientists have too much pride to admit otherwise. How can they now admit that they may have been wrong for the past 50, 75, or even 100 years? Their pride won't let them. It's against all "boys' club" rules. And if not pride, perhaps fear of the loss of confidence and prestige that goes along with the stereotype placed on scientists. And so they conform their research to fit the accepted norm that they inherited from the previous generation of scientists. To go against or—

heaven forbid—disprove the accepted norm, would not only be controversial,
but might also seem to be an insult to previous "great men" of science. And
so the club remains true and guards these pillars of modern science with great
assiduousness, like a great secret to be held above all things and protected
with the attentiveness one would give to an unstable foundation.

Through the semester I had an eye opening to the politics behind re-
search and how this drives every part of the scientific experiment. A scientist
is not only at the mercy of his or her own background and knowledge or even
equipment, but truly at the mercy of scientific peers and, more important,
the social or political correctness of the perceived research motivation. I
would never have imagined that these factors would play such an integral
role in scientific research. In order for experimentation and results to be ac-
cepted by the scientific community, it must be proven and reproven against
a host of comparable contemporaries in that field of experimentation. In
other words, a charter member in the old boys' club of science needs to ap-
prove. This would lead us to question what happens to those more forward
or more independent thinkers in science who have a unique or new approach
to an old area of research. Unfortunately the answer you'd suspect is most
commonly the norm.

This kind of epiphany is not exactly encouraging to the budding young
female scientist in me. The luster that I had expected by joining the scientific
research community has given way to a realistic view of the muddy trudge
through the bureaucracy that is modern science. Yes, I still want to work in
scientific research. I just no longer have a rose-colored vision of what it will
entail. Women in science have an uphill battle. We were not the stereotypical
charter members of this club, and we have our work cut out for us. But by
taking this class, I have learned that I have an advantage over that stereo-
type. I feel no sense of traditional duty to pay homage to my predecessors. I
am not too prideful to ask the questions in a different way. If women are
going to get scrutinized anyway, why not pave a new path along the way?

This class was not the stereotypical science course, and yet I learned more
about the business of science from this one class than I have in any other.
And I am grateful that I have a new sense of the responsibility I have as a
woman in science—to myself and to the future scientific community.

Reflective Notes

What can we learn from the reflections of those involved with the course?
We must pay attention to the fact that both Sible and I had initially at-

tempted to teach our students to "think like a scientist," but moved away from that position in our transformed pedagogy. Nevertheless, students seemed to value being able to think in that manner, as shown by the statement from the neuroscience graduate student. Perhaps our making students aware of the social embeddedness of science had helped them create a holistic view of knowledge so that the social context reinforces the basic science information, and the information itself is enhanced and more readily internalized when seen in a social framework. To reiterate dayna wilhelm's sense of student learning, "The applications and discussions involving the concepts and the social concepts surrounding science, instead of only listening to a professor preach science to them, has given them contextual information to help them remember and fully comprehend the information."

Another thread that runs through the transformation is that students were given a voice in the course. Including a short essay component in exams literally allows students to express themselves in their own words. In contrast, the typical multiple-choice test requires that students select one version of the instructor's voice. Most important, both iterations of the course were interactive—students were active participants in a multilogue so that their voices were literally present. This is in contrast to the typical biology classroom where the instructor, as the fount of all wisdom, lectures to those assembled. The conventional setting turns students into passive recipients of what is deemed to be most important at the moment. It deprives students of the chance to speak science and to speak about science.

Without having the chance to talk (and write) science students do not develop several dimensions of professionalism. They don't acquire facility with the socially constructed rhetoric of the field, and lacking this ability, they are not recognized as scientists by their peers. Second, they feel alienated from the material; they have no feeling or opinion about science or the uses science is put to. Finally, there is no forum for them to express their opinions about science, even though scientific literacy, the ability to contribute to discussions about the uses of science, is a national goal (Barad, 2000). This sets a dangerous precedent, allowing scientists to appropriate the power to make scientific decisions that affect society without input from society.

Laurie Spotswood's words demonstrate precisely the kind of epiphany hoped for by the structure of the course, paralleling the commonly heard statement from women that they never "got" history until they took a women's history course. As well, she shows that this kind of deeper understanding of science can result not only in self-efficacy but in a certain sassy assurance that might change science for those who are now marginalized or excluded.

In our courses, we have taken the first steps toward democratizing science, considering both its practitioners and its epistemology. We seem to have been successful in our goals of increasing self-efficacy, sophistication about the nature of science, and in promoting women's entry into and persistence in scientific careers. Given these outcomes, Larry Summers's claims seem even more marginal.

To the Future

We can only hope that this pedagogy can spread and be adapted on a wide scale. Actually, it has continued and expanded at Virginia Tech. Here is a postscript dated March 2005 from dayna wilhelm:

> *Dear Dr, Lederman,*
>
> *I am in the process of co-lecturing a course of cell and molecular biology (spring 2005) and have incorporated the same principles of the NSF-funded experimental course. The class is much larger, with 110 students. I have benefited from having a co-lecturer who was open-minded enough to allow me to have input on the design of the course in ways that others would not normally have accepted. Throughout the semester we have incorporated a number of homework writing assignments that were very similar, if not the same, to the assignments given in the experimental section. Topics such as cancer, the Human Genome Project, challenging the central dogma, and challenging representations of processes and structures in textbooks have all been touched upon in this course. The grading of the assignments can be overwhelming at times because there are so many of the students' opinions to read. However, I feel that it is very important that the students express themselves and their opinions on science as a whole as well as on the scientific topics.*

Perhaps the faculty member dayna is teaching with will continue to offer Cell and Molecular Biology using at least a version of the transformed curriculum.

Another curriculum that integrates the sciences with other disciplines was recently implemented at Virginia Tech. It was conceived initially by three members of the feminist pedagogies group who sought to broaden the idea of the social embeddedness of science by creating interdisciplinary courses that would fulfill the university core curriculum requirements. Barbara Bekken, the only one of the three still at Virginia Tech, with support from influential units and the Provost's Office, collaborated with faculty and graduate students from multiple departments to offer the first semester of a four-semester sequence whose theme is "Living in the 21st Century." Its focus is "earth sustainability, examining critical resources that humans would want to sustain (e.g., water, energy, food) through a discipline-based (history, natural sciences, behavioral sciences, fine and applied arts) discussion of how humans interact with a particular resource" (Bekken, 2005, p. 3). This interdisciplinary spiral fulfills five of the seven areas of the core curriculum; quantitative reasoning was not included, while area one—writing and discourse—was linked by having students enroll in preexisting sections with nature themes.

The assessment strategy for this course is similar to the one we used for Cell and Molecular Biology; at the end of the course, Bekken asked her students to evaluate their semester's writings, as we had asked our students to describe experimentation in cell and molecular biology for a second time. Bekken's students also developed a sense of the true locus of science, "I thought that since this was an environmentally focused class, only environmental things should be sustained, but I was wrong" (Bekken, 2005, p. 12).

This pedagogy might be adapted to other educational levels; to continue from dayna's March 2005 postscript:

> *Being the teaching assistant for this course has made dramatic changes in my life. Seeing firsthand the problems occurring in the education of science has awakened a passion for teaching in me. I have since chosen to further my education in the field of science education. I am continuing research on other projects pertaining to science education including the assessment of scientist—teacher—student partnerships in K–12 education. I hope that through my experience in this project I will be able to improve the education system for science not only at the college level, but also perhaps at the K–12 level.*

This project has touched many instructors and graduate and undergraduate students in life-changing ways. We can only hope for the success of other projects designed to diversify science so that our daughters and their friends have the chance to lead fulfilling lives in science if they so choose. Even if they do not so choose, these projects will have impact by increasing social justice for all.

References

Augustine, D., Bekken, B., Eriksson, S., Harris, H., Lederman, M., Lehr, J., et al. (2002, spring). What is a feminist pedagogy for the sciences? *Newsletter of the Center for Excellence in Undergraduate Teaching*, Virginia Tech.

Bandura, A. (1977). Self-efficacy: Toward a unifying theory of behavioral change. *Psychological Review, 84*, 191–215.

Barad, K. (2000). Reconceiving scientific literacy as agential realism. In R. Reid & S. Traweek (Eds.), *Doing science + culture* (pp. 221–258). New York: Routledge.

Barnes, B., Bloor, D., & Henry, J. (1996). *Scientific knowledge: A sociological analysis.* Chicago: University of Chicago Press.

Bekken, B. M. (2005, April). *Making self-authorship a goal of core curricula: The Earth Sustainability Pilot Project.* Paper presented at the annual meeting of the American Educational Researchers Association, Montreal, Canada.

Belenky, M. F., Clinchy, B., Tarule, J., & Goldberger, M. (1986). *Women's ways of knowing: The development of voice, self, and mind.* New York: Basic Books.

Bordo, S. (1999). Selections from *The Flight to Objectivity*. In S. Bordo (Ed.), *Feminist interpretations of René Descartes* (pp. 48–69). University Park: Pennsylvania State University Press.

Brickhouse, N. (2001). Embodying science: A feminist perspective on learning. *Journal of Research in Science Teaching, 38*(2), 282–295.

Cooper, G. (2000). *The cell: A molecular approach* (2nd. ed.). Washington, DC: American Society for Microbiology Press.

Fehr, C. (2004). Feminism and science: Mechanism without reduction. *National Women's Studies Association Journal, 16*(1), 136–156.

Figueroa, R., & Harding, S. (2003). *Science and other cultures: Issues in philosophies of science and technology.* New York: Routledge.

Fleck, L. (1935). *The genesis of a scientific fact.* Chicago: University of Chicago Press.

Hacking, I. (1983). *Representing and intervening: Introductory topics in the philosophy of natural science.* Cambridge, UK: Cambridge University Press.

Haraway, D. (1991). *Simians, cyborgs, and women: The re-invention of nature.* New York: Routledge.

Haraway, D. (1997). *Modest witness @ second_millenium. FemaleMan_meets_ Onco Mouse.* New York and London: Routledge.

Harding, S. (1986). *The science question in feminism.* Ithaca, NY: Cornell University Press.

Harding, S. (1991). *Whose science, whose knowledge: Thinking from women's lives.* Ithaca, NY: Cornell University Press.

Harding, S. (1993). *The racial economy of science: Toward a democratic future.* Bloomington: Indiana University Press.

Harding, S. (1994). Is science multicultural? Challenges, resources, opportunities, uncertainties. *Configurations, 10,* 310–330.

Harding, S. (1998). *Is science multicultural? Postcolonialisms, feminisms, epistemologies.* Bloomington: Indiana University Press.

Harding, S. (2004). *The feminist standpoint theory reader.* New York: Routledge.

Hubbard, R. F. (1990). *The politics of women's biology.* New Brunswick: Rutgers University Press.

Jacob. F., & Monod, J. (1961). Genetic regulatory mechanisms in the synthesis of proteins. *Journal of Molecular Biology, 3,* 318–356.

Judson, H. F. (1996). *The eighth day of creation: Makers of the revolution in biology.* Plainview, NY: Cold Spring Harbor Laboratory Press.

Kay, L. E. (2000). *Who wrote the book of life? A history of the genetic code.* Stanford, CA: Stanford University Press.

Keller, E. F. (1985). *Reflections on gender and science.* New Haven, CT: Yale University Press.

Keller, E. F. (1992). *Secrets of life, secrets of death.* New York: Routledge

Kuhn, T. R. (1962). *The structure of scientific revolutions.* Chicago: University of Chicago Press.

Latour, B. (1990). *Science in action: How to follow scientists and engineers through society.* Cambridge, MA: Harvard University Press.

Latour, B. (1993). *We have never been modern* (C. Porter, Trans.). Cambridge, MA: Harvard University Press.

Latour, B., & Woolgar, S. (1986). *Laboratory life: The construction of a scientific fact.* Princeton, NJ: Princeton University Press.

Lave, J. & Wenger, E. (1991). *Situated learning: Legitimate peripheral participation.* Cambridge, UK: Cambridge University Press.

Lederman, M. (2001). Mutating "virology": How far to feminist? *Feminist Teacher, 13,* 193–201.

Lederman, M., & Bartsch, I. (2001). *The gender and science reader.* New York: Routledge.

Lederman, M., & Zubay, G. (1968). DNA directed peptide synthesis. V. The cell-free synthesis of a peptide with ß-galactosidase activity. *Biochemical and Biophysical Research Communications, 32,* 710–714.

Lemke, J. L. (2001). Articulating communities: Sociocultural perspectives on science education. *Journal of Research in Science Teaching, 38*(3), 296–316.

Longino, H. (1990). *Science as social knowledge: Values and objectivity in scientific inquiry.* Princeton, NJ: Princeton University Press.

Mayberry, M. (1999). Reproductive and resistant pedagogies: The comparative roles of collaborative learning and feminist pedagogies. In M. Mayberry & E. C. Rose (Eds.), *Meeting the challenge: Innovative feminist pedagogies in action* (pp. 1–22). New York: Routledge.

Mayberry, M., Subramaniam, B., & Weasel, L. H. (2001). *Feminist science studies.* New York: Routledge

Merchant, C. (1980). *The death of nature: Women, ecology and the scientific revolution.* San Francisco: Harper & Row.

Narayan, U., & Harding, S. (2002). *Decentering the center: Philosophy for a multicultural, postcolonial, and feminist world.* Bloomington: Indiana University Press.

Olby, R. (1974). *The path to the double helix.* London: Macmillan.

Penley, C., & Ross, A. (1991). Cyborgs at large: Interview with Donna Haraway. In C. Penley & A. Ross (Eds.), *Technoculture* (pp. 1–20). Minneapolis: University of Minnesota Press.

Perry, W. G. (1970). *Forms of intellectual and ethical development in the college years.* New York: Holt, Rinehart & Winston.

Proctor, R. N. (1995). *Cancer wars: How politics shapes what we know and don't know about cancer.* New York: Basic Books.

Rheinberger, H-J. (1998). Experimental systems, graphemic spaces. In T. Lenoir & H. U. Gumbrecht (Eds.), *Inscribing science: Scientific texts and the materiality of communication* (pp. 285–303). Stanford, CA: Stanford University Press.

Seymour, E., & Hewitt, N. M. (1997). *Talking about leaving.* Boulder CO: Westview Press.

Shapin, S. (1996). *The scientific revolution.* Chicago: University of Chicago Press.

Wyer, M., Barbercheck, M., Giesman, D., Ozturk, H. O., & Wayne, M. (2001). *Women, science, and technology.* New York: Routledge.

4

CURRICULUM AND RACE

Earl Sheridan

With Frances Boyes, Tracie Davis, and James Fogleman

This chapter examines the impact of a course, Blacks in American Politics, on three southern-born white students. The author contends that students come to universities knowing relatively little about black political history or the historical role of racism on the American political system because these aspects are given little attention by many school systems or teachers. The course is designed to increase their knowledge in these areas and by doing so broaden their understanding of racial issues. Letters by the students indicate that the course did have this effect.

Early Beginnings: Realizations of Racism

Diversity and diversity issues have always been a part of my life. I am an African American male born in the South, in Wilmington, North Carolina, in 1953. I have lived in the South all of my life. So, I grew up during the era of Jim Crow and during the time in which that system was forced to collapse. Growing up during that period had a significant impact on why I decided to become a political scientist. It was a very political age, an age in which the meanings of many of America's most cherished political ideals were examined and reexamined. It was a time when who occupied the White House or a congressional seat had an impact on what restaurant I could eat in, or if I could go to see a Disney movie at the Manor Theatre downtown, or if I had to sit in a separate waiting room at my pedia trician's office. For me, politics was a way to demonstrably change things for the better, so I was quite interested in it. Moreover, the area of political science I chose to concentrate in was political theory, which deals with such timeless concepts as equality, freedom, and justice, concepts that are at the core of diversity issues, and concepts that were very much in debate in the 1950s and 60s.

I remember the pain of being excluded from certain arenas because I was black. As a boy I became interested in chess. I remember reading in our local newspaper about a chess club that had formed at the local YMCA. When I called to inquire about joining the club I was told that the YMCA was segregated. I never forgot the pain of such occurrences. But I also remember the courage of my older relatives and friends who took part in the sit-ins at that time. One of my proudest moments as a child was to be able to take part in a civil rights demonstration in which we marched to the city hall and sang freedom songs.

I witnessed the turbulent collapse of Jim Crow. As a high school student our schools were finally integrated. But the way that this was done, abruptly closing the all-black high school and sending us to two white high schools, led to violence and turmoil in the schools and the community. There were almost daily brawls and bomb threats in the schools and finally that turmoil spread into the community in the form of a riot in which two people were killed.

After graduation I attended Appalachian State University in the mountains of western North Carolina, a university with a very small black enrollment. Though my experience at Appalachian was mostly pleasant, even there the tentacles of racism would occasionally reach out and touch me. I would get a periodic tap to remind me that I was a black man in white America. On one such occasion I was in a dorm room with a number of friends, all of whom were white. Though I was a freshman at the time, I had been hanging out with this group of guys for months and allowed myself to feel completely comfortable with them. And they felt comfortable with me, perhaps too comfortable. One evening, one of the guys started telling us about his weekend and this club he had gone to. Without hesitation he said, "And all these niggers came in there." I was speechless, as if someone had sucked all the air out of me. Then a feeling of deep hurt welled up inside of me. Most of the other fellows seemed shocked too and embarrassed, but they did not seem to know what to say. Without saying a word I simply walked out of the room. As I walked down the hall I heard them reprimanding the one who had made the remark. "Well, that's what we call them," I heard him say. I did not know whether they were reprimanding him for harboring such racist feelings or for exposing them around me.

Even in graduate school I would occasionally overhear racist remarks. So throughout my childhood and early adult years the specter of racism was never very far away. That is one reason why diversity issues have always been important to me. This was reflected in my studies. As an undergraduate, I majored in political science and minored in history. And I pursued graduate degrees in political science with a concentration in political theory. As mentioned earlier, I like the broad philosophical examinations of such topics as justice and equality in political theory courses. I also liked the historical sweep of the courses. Though most of my teachers were white, I did learn a good bit about race and the historic role of black people in American society in my political science and history courses. These studies heightened my interest in diversity issues. As a graduate student I got a chance to teach a course in black politics. Black Politics was not my major area, and probably I was given the course simply because I was an African American graduate student. But I jumped at the chance to teach it and I began to blend more and more my interest in political philosophy and black politics.

As I finished graduate school and started my academic career back in my home town at the University of North Carolina Wilmington, my interest in race and politics was also heightened by the political climate in the country at the time. The triumph of political conservatism in the 1980s, with its attack on race-related issues like affirmative action, welfare, and busing, sharpened my interest in race and politics.

Race and Politics: Teaching for the Future

When I came to UNCW I began to teach Blacks in American Politics on a yearly basis. My views on race and education mirror that of W. E. B. DuBois in his earlier years. I believe that many white students harbor racist views out of ignorance. All that they really know of blacks are the stereotypical portrayals they see in the media or perhaps an impression from a chance encounter they may have had. They know little of the historical racism that existed in America because American schools do a poor job of covering this aspect of American history. Colleges and universities seem to place more emphasis on multicultural education than the nation's public and private schools. According to Urban and Wagoner:

The constituency for multiculturalism is clearly larger in colleges and universities—whose populations are more diverse—than it is in the schools and other parts of American society. Thus, educators and intellectuals who seek to introduce one or another aspect of multiculturalism into the schools often find a school system or a larger community that is uncomprehending of the problem and/or indifferent to the proposed solution (2000, p. 370).

Moreover, even if multiculturalism is a part of the curriculum teachers may not give it the same coverage as other topics. From what I can tell, many teachers gloss over issues of race and racism. When I talk about segregation, or the civil rights era, or talk about anyone other than Martin Luther King Jr. in my classes, students, sometimes both white and black, are shocked by what they learn of the era. They have never been taught the depth of racism in America. We are so proud of our country here, and the ideals of freedom and democracy we feel it exemplifies, we want to cover up the warts. We want to ignore its transgressions. As James W. Loewen showed in his wonderful book, *Lies My Teacher Told Me* (1995), even many history textbooks have ignored race and diversity in telling America's story. So, students do not know of our racist legacy. They just think that one day America started to give preferential treatment to African Americans.

Furthermore, despite the increased commitment of universities to teaching diversity and multiculturalism, it is argued that a discussion of racism and its historic role in American society has diminished. Tony Platt (2002), for example, argues that there has been a shift toward softening multicultural education, focusing more on the contributions of minorities to American society rather than on the effects of systematic racism. Platt calls this the "strengths" approach to diversity education. He laments, "In many multicultural textbooks, the 'strengths' approach tends to trump critiques of racism" (p. 44). And when racism is presented, it is presented as a declining legacy of the past. If this is the multicultural education that students are receiving, no wonder they continue to be ignorant of the role of racism in American political history, and I would add naive of its continuing influence on some issues. So, in my class I do not shy away from racism, which is not necessarily popular. I find that students are uncomfortable talking about racism and at the same time seem to view it as a relic of the past. However, it is my contention that you cannot really talk about diversity and American politics without confronting racism.

The great black educator and leader W. E. B. DuBois felt in his early career that education could be used to combat racism; if you tore down the walls of ignorance racism could be defeated. Cornel West explains DuBois' view this way:

> For Dubois [sic], education was the key. Ignorance was the major obstacle—black ignorance and white ignorance. If the black masses were educated—in order to acquire skills and culture—black America would thrive. If white elites and masses were enlightened, they would not hate and fear black folk. Hence America—black and white—could be true to its democratic ideals. . . . The world was thinking wrong about race, because it did not know. The ultimate evil was stupidity. The cure for it was knowledge based on scientific investigation. (1996, pp. 60–61)

This is very similar to the Socratic notion that "virtue is knowledge," that people do evil out of ignorance. If they truly know what is truly good they will do it. Thus the acquisition of knowledge can improve the virtue of a society (Sabine & Thorson, 1973, p. 45). In his later years DuBois grew disillusioned with this idea. He began to feel that racism was too tough an opponent and that education alone would not eradicate it. I agree. Racism *is* too tough an opponent. Education alone will not eradicate it. It is naive to believe that it is *only* ignorance that makes people racist. Many knowledgeable people use their knowledge to perpetuate racism. However, I do believe quite strongly that education can be *a* weapon against racism. It can help defeat racism. Many people do harbor racist beliefs out of ignorance. And if those people are open to learning and to new ways of thinking, their racist beliefs can be changed. That's what I try to do in my classes, to get students to look at America's political history in a holistic way that includes race.

I touch on race and diversity issues in virtually all the courses that I teach. I believe that diversity should be worked into our regular curriculum. However, the course that I teach, which is specifically dedicated to diversity issues, is Blacks in American Politics. The letters you will read are from students who took this class. Although the class is a political science class, I teach it in a historical manner. I am convinced that you cannot understand the present and current debates on diversity unless you understand history. Thus we discuss the role of blacks in the American political system from the founding of our nation to the present. I also point out to the class that blacks did not play a marginal role in the development of the American political system, but that blacks and issues of race have been central to the American political system. Though there are now very good political science texts on African American politics, like *African Americans and the American Political System* by Lucius Barker, Mack Jones, and Katherine Tate, and *American Politics and the African American Quest for Universal Freedom* by Hanes Walton and Robert C. Smith, I use texts with a more historical approach, such as *Running for Freedom: Civil Rights and Black Politics in America Since 1941* by Steven Lawson and *Black Leadership in America* by John White. In addition, I use lectures and discussions of readings from African American leaders from W. E. B. DuBois, Booker T. Washington, Marcus Garvey, and A. Phillip Randolph to Martin Luther King Jr., Malcolm X, Louis Farrakhan, and Lani Guinier. I also use segments from the PBS series *Eyes on the Prize*. This gives the class the chance to see and hear some of the people who took part in the civil rights movement, the famous and the not so famous. Seeing the newsreel footage and hearing interviews with people who participated often has a visceral effect on the students. I also sprinkle in my own experiences where pertinent. In the following letters three students from that class tell how that class affected them and their understanding of diversity issues.

Student Letters

Frances Boyes, graduate student (Massachusetts).

> *Dear Dr. Sheridan,*
>
> *I did not grow up with the legacy of the civil rights movement in my household; my parents never talked of their experiences with the African American community or their involvement in or impression of the civil rights movement of the sixties. I grew up in the rural South, in a white, middle-class family with a midwestern mother and southern father, both of whom are well educated. Most of my adolescence was spent in a small county on the Chesapeake Bay that had a fairly equal population of blacks and whites. My group of friends through grade school was a mix of white and black kids from various family situations. In my mind there was no difference between people because of the color of their skin.*
>
> *My family moved to Wilmington, North Carolina, when it was time to start high school, and my social situation changed. For the first time I saw*

kids segregate themselves into groups that were largely based on race. People whom I normally would have gravitated toward suddenly intimidated me. I did not socialize with many black kids outside the classroom. I was still able to have a diverse group of friends with many types of cultural and family backgrounds, but I was usually surrounded by a majority of white faces.

In high school there may not have been much social interaction between people of different races, but there was a large population of minorities present and in the classroom. This was not so in college. Many of my classes at University of North Carolina Wilmington had only a sea of white faces. The only exception during my five years in college was the course about the history of African American political involvement taught by Dr. Sheridan. I had always been interested in the civil rights movement and did not know much about the events that shaped it or the figures that moved it, and I felt it worthwhile to further explore this period of our history. It was an added bonus that the course was being taught by Dr. Sheridan, a professor I have great respect for and whose teaching style had proven to fit my learning style. There were about seven or eight African American students enrolled in the course of about 20 or so students, and this was by far the largest group that I had shared a class with. Even though I was there to learn about the political issues that the African American community had faced through our nation's history, I was still very intimidated. I certainly did not want anything I said to be offensive to anyone, and until I better understood the issues within the black community, I felt that it might have been best to maintain a low profile. After a few classes I realized that I was right to feel ignorant of the issues that were important to the black community in the past as well as the present. I had a lot to learn from Dr. Sheridan and the course. I realized that I had never known that throughout the history of our country there were many differing opinions and positions coming from within the black community itself concerning the best way to assert and gain their rights. I was naive enough to think throughout my life that all black people were unified behind a single idea and that they all fought for the same reasons and with the same strategy. I was so very wrong. I was exposed to the ideas of Booker T. Washington, W. E. B. DuBois, Malcolm X, A. Philip Randolph, and Marcus Garvey. Prior to this I never knew about any of the influential black thinkers except Martin Luther King Jr. I was certainly a better student and now a better person for having gained this more in-depth knowledge about the African American community and its political involvement.

Since taking the course and leaving school, I do not believe that much about how I see the world has changed. When my job requires me to hire people, I sometimes find that I ask myself if the color of the applicant has played any part in my decision. I know that the answer is no, but I do have that brief moment where I question my fairness as well as my perception of people. I then move on, confident that I am respecting every person's right to be given the same consideration. I still see the color of one's skin; I think it would be ridiculous to say that I did not. I do not, however, take for granted my supposed knowledge of other people and begin to make certain assumptions about them or their communities. The course on African American political history taught me that my assumptions about the black community were wrong, and they are probably wrong about other nonwhite communities as well. I sincerely believe that a large step toward trying to be the responsible and involved person I hope to become was exposing myself to new and diverse experiences and new knowledge. The most rewarding aspect of this part of my education is that it fits into my everyday life and I try to use the experience every day. The course was only an introduction to a part of our world that I had not previously known and was a foundation for decisions that I have made regarding my future goals and my chosen career.

Tracie Davis, *Town Manager (North Carolina)*

Dr. Sheridan,

As a nontraditional, divorced, single mother, undergraduate student, determining which classes to take to fulfill my political science major was always a challenging decision for me to make. After I determined the mandatory courses I needed to stay on track for my unforeseen graduation date, only then was I able to seek out classes that I found to be both personally interesting and applicable as they related to the real world and future job possibilities. When I discovered that you were offering a class titled Blacks in American Politics, my personal interest was piqued; however, I was not sure how the class would correlate with enhancing my future professional possibilities. Nevertheless, my personal awareness on the subject of race removed all questions I had on choosing to enroll in Blacks in American Politics.

The primary reason I was so intrigued with this class was that my white sister had just given birth to a beautiful baby girl, whose father was black. It would be an understatement to say that my southern parents and extended family took the news of our new interracial family very poorly. What I did not understand was the fact that my two sisters and I disagreed adamantly with my family's unbendable prejudice mentality that we were exposed to our entire childhood lives. Your class offered me a deeper understanding of the root of racial tensions.

One's first response to the question of the difference in my parent's value systems and that of their children may be integration in the public schools. Indeed, intermingling different races forced blacks and whites to get to know one another. Sadly, in my opinion, our knowledge of one another's diversity is a direct result of the lens that our parents and educators choose to filter their desired information. It seems to me that the sum is lesser than the whole, insofar as the value of black education in public schools.

After leaving public school in 1988, the depth of my education related to African Americans was limited to slavery, Rosa Parks, and Martin Luther King Jr. Period. *No wonder I could not understand the depth of hatred and discrimination I had witnessed toward people of different races that extended well beyond the bounds of my family. The scope of my public education did not encompass African American leaders such as Booker T. Washington and his support for the doctrine of "separate but equal" established by the Supreme Court decision in the case of* Plessy v. Ferguson. *Likewise, essays such as* The Souls of Black Folks *by* W. E. B. DuBois *were never required readings during my tenure in public school. In retrospect, after taking your class, it seems to me that efforts such as Black History Month is well deserved; however, it is at best, a token attempt to incorporate the history of blacks in our public education. To truly offer a better understanding of black history the subject matter should be incorporated unequivocally into the curriculum year-round from elementary through high school.*

I remember in 1999, when I would tell other students I was taking Blacks in American Politics *several people responded to me with the same question, "How many blacks are in that class?" Indeed, this statement speaks for itself. I would always give the same answer. "Three, including the professor, and I suggest that you consider taking this class. You will be impressed with Dr. Sheridan's ability to objectively, almost romantically, present the course material and engage a classroom of mostly white students on the factual and theoretical philosophy of some of our most revered founding fathers, great white political thinkers, and black leaders you never knew existed." Almost every time I left your class, I found myself very angry and ashamed of my own race for allowing such malicious treatment of other human beings. Several of your students shared this sentiment. Often we would meet after class for coffee and continue to discuss the day's lecture.*

Your thought-provoking dialogue resonated with us all. More important, you gave your students the freedom to come to their own decisions concerning the material presented in the class because you would not interject your personal opinions into the subject matter. You taught each topic in an unbiased manner. You offered opposing theories to each paradigm you presented to the class, therefore, creating an environment that naturally fostered classroom debates. Your incorporation of media such as the film Eyes on the Prize *provided imagery of the civil rights movement that mere words could never express. Those films increased my understanding of the great tension of those times and the struggles others had to bear for equality. To this day, I recommend those films to friends as must-see movies. The lessons I learned from your class about diversity continue to influence both my personal and professional life.*

As I previously stated, when I decided to take your class I was not sure how the class would fold into my professional career. I have worked in the field of management in the private sector and currently in the public sector. As a manager, some of the more complex issues I deal with are related to human resource and personnel matters. Unfortunately, I cannot disclose with you the details of some of my most challenging personnel dilemmas. Nevertheless, I want you to know the issue of diversity has caused my moral compass to spin. More than once, I have had to refer to Title VII of the 1964 Civil Rights Act to support my decisions and at times undermine my own job security. Your class provided me with a clear awareness of diversity and the sacrifice others have made in the name of equality. More important, this awareness has prevented me from making decisions that go against the inherent rights of equality for individuals and assisted me in dealing with difficult decisions related to diversity with great confidence.

Finally, the birth of my sister's interracial daughter changed my southern family for the better. I never hear the N word spoken anymore and racial jokes are no longer a part of family reunion entertainment. My niece is loved and cherished deeply by our entire family because of the person she is and will become. I also realized that my family held a different value system than I did because their experiences with diversity were greatly different from my own. Value systems are difficult to change and such change takes time; how-

ever, it is achievable. I believe that there is a light of many colors, shapes, and forms at the end of each challenging tunnel of life. Maybe the unknown fact that does indeed give us all hope despite the diversity challenges placed in front of many of us as children and young adults is the fact that not all children hold on to the prejudice of our past.

James Fogleman, *administrative coordinator, Department of Public Utilities (Virginia)*

I was born in 1963, in Wilmington, North Carolina. Wilmington has had a long and divided history with respect to race relations, and certainly, I was a product of my environment. Born a white male, my cultural norm was to be conciliatory toward black people, but there were absolute and clear boundaries. For surface and social purposes, it was OK to have black friends, but that was limited to case-by-case exceptions and was rarely deeper than cordial friendship. Much deeper and more intimately, we kids loved it when the adults let us overhear "nigger" jokes. We thought the whites who stood up against the blacks at the high school race riots in the 1970s were heroes, and if anyone had an uncle, cousin, or any other family member who was affiliated with the Ku Klux Klan that person was revered almost in a holy manner. If a white female was seen with a black male, she was shunned, ostracized, and if we could have gotten away with it, we desired her stoning within our hearts. I recall when the federal government decided to make a national holiday in honor of Dr. Martin Luther King Jr. the joke was that "we should have killed more of them." I was a racist.

In 1981, I joined the Army and I saw my social norms were out of sync with much of society, especially within the culture of the Army. One by one, I had to come to terms with understanding how hurtful and wrong many of my core understandings were. I finally accepted a peace within myself that racism was a thing of the past and limited to exceptional situations, no longer holding validity as a norm.

In 1993, I transferred to University of North Carolina Wilmington as a junior from Cape Fear Community College. By this time, diversity and racism were the farthest thing from my mind. However, I remembered I was back in Wilmington and to me, Wilmington had made significant growth insofar as race relations were concerned. I accepted the changes I'd seen to substantiate my belief that racism was nothing more than isolated cases, handled quickly and thoroughly by appropriate authorities.

By the time I took an American political thought course directly under Dr. Sheridan, I had established a good, comfortable rapport with Dr. Sheridan. One day, a race-related issue was in the news and a natural course of discussion transpired between Dr. Sheridan and me. I shared my belief with him that I thought racism and discrimination were isolated occurrences and I suspected overly inflated. I'll never forget his response to me that he wished I could spend one day in his shoes. This comment actually cracked open a door I thought I had shut and secured. I pondered this question with an open mind and realized that I've never received any factual and reliable information on the history and impact of racism and discrimination except what was spoken by word of mouth, or on television.

I decided to sign up for Blacks in American Politics during my senior year. When the course started, I remember two very distinct things: first, I was surprised how sparse the room was; only a handful of students had signed up for the course. Second, I was the only white student in the class, so not only was I ashamed there was not a greater interest in the subject, but for the first time in my life, I truly felt like a minority. I was afraid, at first. I feared everyone in the class knew my past. I feared this might be a course intended to cause a revolution to "kill whitey" . . . and I just happened to be in the room! I thought about dropping the course. As I pondered an excuse and what I would take in its place, I remembered what Dr. Sheridan had said to me on that one particular day. I then remembered why I signed up for the class—to learn what I had not been taught.

I decided to do my best to remove the cognitive filters I had put in place regarding blacks, racism, and discrimination, and actually "learn." The course did not attempt to pass judgement, but present facts stemming from post–Civil War social, political, and ideological perspectives; through the distorted influences of the media and filtered history teachings; to passive and active resistance; and to the schools of thought that have developed along the way. Two key influential individuals who had a profound impact on my understanding were W. E. B. DuBois, and the Reverend Vernon Johns. These men broke through my complacency and created an awareness in me that has not let me lower my own awareness of how discrimination and institutional racism remain underwritten evils that are still a threat to our society today.

I currently supervise 17 people, mostly classified within the "minority" context. My respect and regard for these individuals is absolute. I also accept the responsibility to ensure they work in an environment free of racial, sexual, and religious discrimination. I embrace our diversity and capitalize on our talent. The effect has been an atmosphere of positive interaction, productivity, and rare occurrences of disharmony. Would I have developed this level of understanding without risking my own understanding and interpretation of diversity and the effects of discrimination? Absolutely not. I would have been just another individual, likely with my head in the sand believing that discrimination and racism were isolated instances. Do I believe there is a need for clarification of factual history that has not been filtered down to the state of near meaninglessness? Absolutely. Now, more than ever before.

Responses and Reflections: A Lens to Focus Understanding

The three students who wrote the preceding letters had a key commonality—they are all southern whites. However, the fact that Frances lived for a time in the Chesapeake Bay area with its tremendous diversity and had racially diverse playmates did seem to have a more broadening effect on her racial views. What strikes me after reading the letters is how little the students knew of African American history and politics before taking this class. All three students indicated that their knowledge of African American leaders and history beyond Martin Luther King Jr. or slavery was sparse before taking the course. As mentioned earlier, I believe American schools at the elementary and high school level do a poor job of teaching diversity. The one thing that all three students agreed on about the course was that it broadened their knowledge of African Americans. They learned about the diversity of black thought, that black people are not monolithic but have historically expressed a variety of ideas on how best to achieve liberation in America.

For James and Tracie who professed that their upbringings on race had been somewhat unenlightened, the course, along with other life experiences, did have an impact on making them look at diversity issues with fresh eyes. As they have embarked on careers in the public sector their experience in the course has played a positive role in how they approach diverse populations.

Also striking was the educational effect of *being* in a racially diverse classroom. James talked about how it felt to be a minority in the class. And Frances talked about how different it was to be in a racially diverse class rather than the majority of her classes where there was a "sea of white faces." The experience of being around African American students and hearing them talk about racial issues in a classroom setting was certainly a vital part of this educational experience.

Finally, by examining the historical role of racism on black political life and by avoiding the "strengths" approach, I believe the students were made aware of the continuing role racism plays in American life. Indeed, in his letter James talked about the continuing existence of "discrimination and institutional racism." However, examining the role of systematic racism in American society does not negate a discussion of the "strengths" of black people, for it illustrates how strong African Americans had to be in order to persevere in a racist environment.

To love America one need not be ignorant of America's faults. We love our families and friends despite their shortcomings. It should be the same with our country. Elementary and high school teachers should not ignore or gloss over America's faults or the contributions of its diverse populations. We are strengthened, not weakened, by a knowledge of racial and diversity issues. Education is not a panacea when it comes to tolerance of diversity, but it can be a mighty potent elixir.

References

Barker, L. J., Jones, M. H., & Tate, K. (1999). *African Americans and the American political system*. Upper Saddle River, NJ: Prentice Hall.

Lawson, S. (1997). *Running for freedom: Civil rights and black politics in America since 1941*. New York: McGraw-Hill.

Loewen, J. W. (1995). *Lies my teacher told me*. New York: The New Press.

Platt, T. (2002). Desegregating multiculturalism: Problems in the theory and pedagogy of diversity education. *Social Justice, 99*(4), 41–46.

Sabine, H., & Thorson, T. L. (1973). *A history of political theory* (4th ed.). Hinsdale, IL: Dryden Press.

Urban, W., & Wagoner, J. (2000). *American education: A history*. (2nd ed.). Boston: McGraw-Hill.

Walton, H., & Smith, R. C. (2000). *American politics and the African American quest for universal freedom*. New York: Longman.

West, C. (1996). Black strivings in a twilight civilization. In H. L. Gates Jr. & C. West (Eds.), *The future of the race* (pp. 53–112). New York: Knopf.

White, J. (1990). *Black leadership in America, from Booker T. Washington to Jesse Jackson*. New York: Longman.

5

LITERATURE, SELF-DISCOVERY, AND IDENTITY

Cultural Difference and Its Impact on Black Students' Language Engagement

Patricia Brown McDonald

With Aquilla Copeland and Michael Gramenz

By examining differences between Afrocentric literature and European or Western literature, expressed as orature and literature, respectively, it becomes evident that the dominance of the latter's pedagogy has handicapped black students' language development. In the United States, black and other minority students are at a disadvantage for language development because they function within a wider, dominant culture that does not mirror their experiences and concerns. Because of this estrangement, black students are not motivated language participants; instead, they remain minimally engaged.

I grew up in the tiny 4,244-square-mile island of Jamaica and migrated to the United States at age 27. Almost 20 years later, I can safely say it was that small nation comprising 2.5 million people that has proved to be the most fertile academic ground on which I have ever stood. It was in the Jamaican classroom, both formal and informal, that my love of language and literature was kindled, and the reason for its kindling is simple: I read about myself from authors who were born and grew up in the Caribbean. It was not only the stories themselves, however, that developed my appreciation for language usage, it was the tone and style of the authors that placed me squarely in the heart of the work that also fostered my love. It was the words and stories of Afrocentric authors such as Michael Anthony, George Lamming, Samuel Selvon, Derek Walcott, and Chinua Achebe that caught my literary fancy and spurred my academic soul. It was their pen that delved deep within me leaving an indelible impression of the power of words. Without those authors, without those stories, without those words, I would never have formed a lasting relationship with language.

I hope I'm not giving the impression that as a Caribbean student I was only exposed to Caribbean writers. On the contrary, our classrooms were also imbued with Shakespeare, Chaucer, and Milton, among others, but it was Caribbean stories that danced into my heart making a lifelong impression, which consequently led me to become an English professor. Had it not been for those Afrocentric authors, I don't know what career path I would have taken, but I'm sure it would not have been a literary one. Without being exposed to language and literature that engaged my senses, written by my people, I would never have loved the subject. As my own passion of language development and literature was nurtured through contact with my own stories, so, too, I believe the passion of most students for the discipline can be nurtured, but there must be a hook! Students must first identify with the work itself before they can develop a healthy and lasting relationship with it, especially if they are to eventually understand and appreciate the wider offering of other literatures as well. If students feel connected to their learning, they will strive to do their best. What we read and who teaches us what we read is especially important in the literary field because it helps us re-create and make sense of our own experiences.

A former African American student, Aquilla Copeland, who took a composition class with me, was hooked after being briefly introduced one semester to an African American and a Caribbean author. After leaving my class, she constantly came back to me for more reading material that spoke to her sensibility, and in Aquilla's case, what spoke to a young, African American woman was Afrocentric literature. For her own edification, she wanted more. Aquilla has since embarked on a journey of her own to write her story:

> I was completely astonished to discover the truth. . . . I hardly know anything about my ancestry, and when I read books like *Krik? Krak!* and *Daughters of the Dust*, when authors vividly voyage through the inner and outer nature in the lives of the ancestors, I feel left out. . . . But, it kinda

gives me something to believe in—the fact that I, too, have a history. You see, now it's more than just about telling a story, I'm on a mission. I've never recognized the void, the space, inside me before.

Student Letters

Aquilla Copeland, senior undergraduate psychology major (Florida)

Dear Professor McDonald,

The semester that I spent with you in the spring of 2004 is definitely an experience that will have an impact on me for the rest of my life. Your unwavering dedication to teaching is seen in your willingness not only to teach students during the semester, but also your continual concern for former students, such as myself, who have also come to value you as a friend. Your teaching approach is analogous to the duty of a diligent gardener. With each and every encounter, you planted a seed in me that encouraged me to think individually and critically about literature. Even now that I'm attending a different college, you're ever present to aid me in cultivating my sprouting ideas.

I clearly recall your class. You assigned weekly reading assignments concerning a range of subjects, either from the textual reading assignments or from current events. The topics were, above all, stimulating because they involved controversial decisions, many of which directly affected college students. On such assignments I also remember how you gave students the option of orally presenting the paper to the class. This was a unique experience because it gave me an opportunity to hear the perspectives of other students, therefore challenging my own beliefs. On one such writing assignment, white students presented their perspectives on sensitive issues regarding black people. Overt verbalization of such sensitive topics has traditionally been limited either exclusively to blacks, or to whites who are experts on the subject matter. Although the white students were presenting their perspectives in a coherent and noncondescending fashion, the atmosphere initially felt awkwardly weird. You know, as if they were violating some implicit code of conduct. By the time the students had finished, however, as Zora Neale Hurston's Phoebe says, "I felt like I had grown ten feet." I had never been exposed to a classroom setting that freely permitted freedom of speech to that extent. Professor McDonald, your passion for literature and self-expression was transferred to me, giving me the desire to take on new challenges that I would not have otherwise been inclined toward.

My Awakening

It started at around 8:30 p.m. on Thursday night during Bible study. The pastor was standing in the pulpit before a small congregation of people, speaking in a low, monotonous voice that competed with the squealing sound of an old ceiling fan that hung above his head. My mind wondered. I glanced across the empty pews at my elderly grandmother who had a glazed look about her face, as if she were trapped in some hypnotic trance. On this particular night, she appeared to be surrounded by a soft, luminescent glow. As she sat there, nodding in agreement with the pastor, she looked so virtuous, so angelic, and yet so ancient. How had she got to that place in her life? At some time before, her wrinkled face must have been smoothed over by the hands of Youth. I watched as she continued nodding, rocking, and almost lulling herself to sleep; she always seemed to catch herself just before her head could collapse into her chest. It was difficult to imagine, but she must have once been a beautiful, vibrant young woman, full of hopes and dreams for her future.

She continued nodding.

Sitting there in church, I compared my grandmother to the courageous women who had overcome great adversity, especially the fictional ones that you had recently shared with me in the works of Hurston and Danticat. At that very moment, I realized that it was my duty to compose a novel of my own that would tell the story of my grandmother. When a person dies, the memories of them vanish somewhere with the corpse. Literature is the one way of keeping a person alive, a way of making that person immortal; everyone who ever reads a story about someone carries away a piece of the person.

Because my grandmother was a black orphan who grew up in a time when any legal documentation for poor blacks seemed useless, she knows almost nothing regarding her family history. All I know of my ancestry is my grandmother and the history of the native Africans who came across the Atlantic Ocean on slave ships. My objective for the novel, although unconscious at the time of conception, is to re-create a semifictitious history, not only for my grandmother to be remembered by, but also to give our family a historical foundation, which we've completely lacked up till this point. Rather than just telling a story, this novel gives me something to believe in the fact that I too have a history.

*Professor, you not only instilled in me a love and appreciation for novel-
ists but also a love and appreciation for my own writings. English was never
my major, but I realize that when it comes to self-expression through literature, ingenuity in not limited to professional novelists. Regardless of the topic,
we each have a unique story to tell. These stories must be told, or else we
suffer the loss of a great portion of our personal histories. It is not only our
duty, but also our privilege, as pilgrims on this journey to tell our stories and
write them down, thus immortalizing the ones we love. If we don't tell our
stories, they'll remain untold. Professor McDonald, thanks for being a wonderful instructor, source of inspiration, and above all, a diligent gardener.*

Orature: Written Oral Literature

Like myself, Aquilla had also read the literary greats, the so-called canons of
Western literature, but none had penetrated her psyche as did the Afrocentric
authorship of Edwidge Danticat (Haitian) Zora Neale Hurston, (African
American), and Jamaica Kinkaid (Antiguan). For Aquilla, these storytellers
exposed her to herself and opened up doors to a self-discovery she never
previously imagined. But, what constitutes Afrocentric literature that so differentiates it from the traditional European works that have become the literary staple for all students? What is it that Afrocentric writers possess that can
reach into the hearts and souls of black students and awaken their self-
awareness and stir their imaginations?

Black students share a predominantly oral culture that is integrally
linked to their African ancestry. While communication in all cultures is essentially rooted in orality, it is the contemporary nature of the oral tradition
in black cultures that makes the distinction relevant. A look at the chrono-
logical development of the written word in the early periods illustrates the
absence of written material from the African continent (with the exception
of the Sumerian cuneiform and Egyptian hieroglyphics). Africa's "literature"
was developing in other ways. For example, griots, oral historians, dating
from well over a thousand years, were the "history books" of their people.

What we have today, therefore, is the development of a written oral literature, or orature. Orature embodies the indigenous oral culture of Africa.
White students or "European" students, on the other hand, share a predominantly literary contemporary culture. Emmanuel Obiechina (1975) underscores the difference between the two traditions when he says the following:

> Differences in cultural transmission between the two traditions [that is, literacy and orality] produced different modes of preserving continuity between past and present. The oral tradition relies largely on human memory for the preservation and transmission of the cultural repertoire, and so develops elaborate mechanisms for helping the human memory. These include a high degree of ritualization of belief, action and concepts, of symbolization as a means of concretizing experience, and of routinization of everyday actions. (p. 33)

The difference between the two traditions is worth noting because the education system in the United States largely ignores oral language in favor of a written one. This dismissive view of oral language is historical—it is a view that is readily embraced by traditional educators because historically orality has been dismissed as irrelevant discourse. Susan Bassnett (1993) comments that the Western tradition disregarded one of the features most integral to the expression of African literature—oral culture: "Oral culture," she says, "was generally regarded as being of lower status so the existence of a tradition of epics, for example, was considered insignificant" (p. 18). Therefore, she continues, "belief in the superiority of their own [European] culture was a part of the politics of imperialism. . . . [and so] the rhetoric which dismissed African or Asian peoples as 'primitive' or 'childlike' also dismissed their art forms in various ways" (p. 18). Bassnett also states that Nigerian author "Wole Soyinka and a whole range of African critics have exposed the pervasive influence of Hegel, who argued that African culture was 'weak' in contrast to what he claimed were higher, more developed cultures, and who effectively denied Africa a history" (p. 6). Hegel contended the following:

> [Africa is] the land of childhood, which lying beyond the day of self-conscious history, is enveloped in the mantle of Night. . . . For it is no historical part of the World; it has no movement or development to exhibit. . . . What we properly understand by Africa, is the Unhistorical, Undeveloped Spirit, still involved in the conditions of mere nature, and which had to be presented here as on the threshold of the World's history. (as cited in Moses, 1995, p. 107)

Another acclaimed Nigerian author, Chinua Achebe, makes a similar comment regarding notions of European superiority as it relates to Africa. He points to Albert Schweitzer who he says symbolized "the immortal dictum in the heyday of colonialism": "The African is indeed my brother, but my junior brother" (1989, p. 68). Achebe continues:

> The latter-day colonialist critic, equally given to big-brother arrogance, sees the African writer as a somewhat unfinished European who with patient guidance will grow up one day and write like every other European, but meanwhile must be humble, must learn all he can and while at it give due credit to his teachers in the form of direct praise, or even better since praise sometimes goes bad and becomes embarrassing, manifest self-contempt. (p. 69)

Although oral literature has been acknowledged in more recent years, it is still stigmatized because of what Isidore Opekwho (1992) says is the seeming "simplicity of the lives of the folk from whom the materials were gathered—[who] because of their level of education and sophistication . . . were considered incapable of producing anything that may be considered literature in the same sense that one would see Shakespeare" (p. 4). It is the imbalance in emphasis on traditions, the preference for the written word over the spoken word that puts many black students at a disadvantage for language engagement, hence language development in the classroom. For example, in *Teaching English in Middle and Secondary Schools,* Rhoda Maxwell and Mary Meiser (1997) remind us that oral language "has most often been relegated to the speech courses or fragmented into isolated units" (p. 96). They also point out that in preparing English teachers for the classroom, oral language is often ignored while "secondary English textbooks reinforce the notion of the primacy of written expression, which generally appears in two varieties: literature and composition/grammar" (p. 96).

Additionally, Dorothy Strickland and Lesley Morrow (1998) in "Oral Language Development: Children as Storytellers," state that when oral language is applied in the classroom, its use is limited and is generally reserved for the kindergarten and early elementary years. Interestingly, Strickland and Morrow's view of oral language use is that of an unnatural development that needs structure. They say "storytelling is initially difficult for young children. They can be helped in their first attempts by your modeling the behavior for them. You may wish to tell a story several times before encouraging children to tell it" (p. 260). Strickland and Morrow's view of language development through storytelling, however, is in direct contrast to that of Jamaican-born educator and writer Glasceta Honeyghan (2000) who acknowledges the pri-

macy of oral language in the development of the black child. When Honeyghan reminisces on her own childhood days in Jamaica, she remembers being
told stories "under a dull moon glowing in the country night darkness"
(p. 406). The children, she says, were mesmerized by the telling of stories and
could be heard the next day retelling the same stories as part of their play.

Honeyghan tells of the symbiotic relationship that existed between her
growing up in a small Caribbean island and her subsequent appreciation for
the oral tradition and love of the sound of words. She says language came to
her in rhythms, and the score of the rhythms was indicative of the life of the
village. For example, she says there was the rhythm of death, the rhythm at
home, the rhythm in church, and the rhythm in school. Honeyghan recol-
lects these "rhythms" of the village as having an indelible mark on her appreciation of the power of oral language in language development. She also
traces the development of her own literary appreciation through what she
calls the "rhythms of the village." She recalls growing up as intricately related
to the daily activities of the village that had instilled within the children the
indigenous oral heritage of Africa—the elders who told stories to the young
under the moonlit nights, the games children played, church, funerals, wed-
dings, and much more.

Honeyghan regards all of these activities as the everyday sounds that affected her love for language and subsequent appreciation of literature. She
reiterates time and again that "many of those practices in that small village
worked toward effective literacy learning and have implications for literacy
instruction today" (p. 411). She continues, saying, "Those stories told to me
as a child taught morals, traditions, and traditional values. I now see a link
to a broader historical tradition—an integral part of African culture—linked
to the history of slavery and the survival of the human psyche" (p. 411).

Differences Between African and European Novels

What also needs to be taken into account in terms of black children and
language development are the sometimes very subtle and not so subtle differences between European novels and African novels. Such differences include
the relationship between the author and the work, the role of the protagonist
in society, the abundant use of proverbs and the supernatural in the narrative, the necessary fusion of history and fiction in storytelling, and the dis-
tinctive voice of the narrator/author speaking out directly to the reader.

Achebe (1989) summarizes that "one of the most critical consequences of the transition from oral traditions to written forms of literature is the emergence of individual authorship" (p. 47), a notion foreign to the African creative. He also says that quite apart from that fact is the more intangible effects of such transition: "The story by the fireside does not belong to the storyteller once he has let it out of his mouth. But the story composed by his spiritual descendant, the writer in his study, 'belongs' to its composer" (p. 7). He explains:

> This shift is facilitated by the simple fact that, whereas a story that is told has no physical form or solidity, a book has; it is a commodity and can be handled and moved about. But I want to suggest that the physical form of a book cannot by itself adequately account for the emergent notion of proprietorship. At best it facilitates the will to ownership which is already present. This will is rooted in the praxis of individualism in its social and economic dimensions. (pp 47–48)

Karen Winkler (1994) adds that "ironically, the African view of art is gaining currency among Western intellectuals, who have increasingly begun to argue that literature can never be politically neutral" (p. A9).

David Cook (1977), professor of English at the University of Ilorin in Nigeria, also exposes another important area of divergence between African and European literatures when he says the former produces a conceptualization of narrative borne out in the community-centered thinking of most African nations as opposed to "the hero in Western fiction [who] is characteristically an individualist" (p. 5). He says, "the situation may at first glance appear to be very similar; but the apparent similarity makes the actual difference all the clearer, since the protagonist in a typical nineteenth- or twentieth-century British, French, or American novel has as a rule quite a different relationship to his society" (p. 5). Chinua Achebe (1979) affirms that "African cultures are distinguishable from their European counterparts by their greater recognition of community. The European has come to view society as an adversary against whom the individual has to do battle in order to achieve his freedom, integrity, and self-realization" (p. 12), but "The African views his society (family, extended family, clan, etc.) as a fish might view its element, water at once limits and sustains its existence" (p. 13).

This notion of the separation between the individual and society is addressed in what Earl Miner (1990) distinguishes in his poetics of the affective-expressive, an Eastern poetics, as implicit and explicit poetics (p. 7). Implicit poetics, he says, belongs to cultures that identify literature as a separate branch of study; explicit poetics, on the other hand, occurs when literature is not seen as a separate branch, but rather is wholly incorporated into the web of human life (p. 7). A comparison by Innes (1990) of Achebe's and Joyce Cary's work underscores this implicit/explicit, individual/community relationship. Innes says although Achebe and Cary shared similar concerns of individual and society, their writings were vastly different (pp. 166–167). He explains:

> Where the two authors differ strongly is on the weight that should be given individual fulfilment. Cary's overriding interest is in the individual's need to overcome the barriers to self-fulfilment and self-expression, and here he shares with a majority of contemporary European male novelists a valuation of the individual as against his society and its demands. Hence Cary's novels are most memorable not for the worlds and cultures they portray, but for their central characters, as the titles of the novels imply. And those characters are celebrated not as types of their societies, but as eccentrics. (p. 166)

Chinua Achebe (1989) himself has had to respond to criticism that "berated African writers for concentrating too much on society and not sufficiently on individual characters thus failing to create 'true' aesthetic proportions" (p. 103). Achebe responds to such critics saying, "I wondered when this truth became so self-evident that (unlike the other self-evident truth) this one should apply to black as well as white. It is all this cock suredness which I find so annoying" (p. 103). In *Anthills of the Savannah* (1988), Achebe reiterates the idea of connectivity when the protagonist, Ikem, says "we all are connected. You cannot tell the story of any of us without implicating the others" (p. 60). This element of community and connectedness is important not only in highlighting the "siametic" relationship between individual and community but in demonstrating an important departure from European literatures.

A more glaring distinction between traditional Western literature and African literatures is the smattering, or absence, of the tenets of orature. It is a distinction underscored by Obiechina (1975) who says, "The most noticeable difference by native West Africans and those by non-natives using the West African setting, is the important position which the representation of oral tradition is given by the first, and its almost complete absence in the second" (pp. 25–26). Obiechina also compares the Europeanized Africa of Joyce Cary's *Mister Johnson* with Achebe's *Things Fall Apart* to clarify this point:

> If, for example, we compare Joyce Cary's Nigerian villagers and Chinua Achebe's villagers, we notice that Cary's peasants speak in straightforward English prose—with the exception of Mister Johnson, who speaks and writes "babu" English. Cary's Nigerian peasants speak like Cary himself, whereas Achebe's Nigerian villagers weave into the fabric of their everyday conversations, allusions from folk-tales, legends and myths, and back their opinions and attitudes with appropriately chosen proverbs, traditional maxims and cryptic anecdotes. In other words, whereas the nationality of Cary's peasants cannot be guessed at from the way they speak, Achebe's villagers' speech shows them unmistakable people who are closer to an oral than a literary tradition. (pp. 25–26)

In researching African oral literatures, Ruth Finnegan (1970) also speaks of the intricate nature of orality by addressing the tone and musical quality found in African expression. She notes that oral literature not only deals with the written word on the page, but also the impulse of rhythm that accompanies the words. Finnegan shows how word, meaning, and song are inseparable entities in conveying meaning in African literature:

> Tone is sometimes used as a structural element in literary expression and can be exploited by the oral artist in ways somewhat analogous to the use of rhyme or rhythm in written European poetry. Many instances of this can be cited from African poetry, proverbs, and above all drum literature. This stylistic aspect is almost completely unrepresented in written versions of studies of oral literature, and yet is clearly one which can be manipulated in a subtle and effective way in the actual process of delivery. The exploitation of musical resources can also play an important part, varying of course according to the artistic conventions of the particular genre in question. Most stories and proverbs tend to be delivered as spoken prose . . . an appreciation therefore of these sung forms . . . depends on at least some awareness of the musical material on which the artist draws, and we cannot hope to fully understand their impact or subtlety if we consider only the bare words on a printed page. (p. 4)

Finnegan also comments that "there are certain definite characteristics of this form of art which arise from its oral nature" (p. 1), and these characteristic forms "need to be understood before we can appreciate its status" (p. 1). Obiechina (1975) stresses that in terms of textual analyses, "reliance on the written word makes the novel very different from the prose literature produced in a traditional oral culture." He says, "the prose form par excellence of West African traditional society, language is often greatly reinforced by physical gestures, facial expression, voice inflexions and other arts of the performer" (p. 155).

Proverbs are also integral to African expression. It is a mode of ritualizing and routinizing common themes and concerns that is borne out in literary expression. Achebe (1959) explains the intimate relationship between proverbs and African expression when the narratorial voice in *Things Fall Apart* says, "Having spoken plainly so far, Okoye said the next half a dozen sentences in proverbs. Among the Ibo, the art of conversation is regarded very highly, and proverbs are the palm-wine with which words are eaten" (p. 7). Ryszard Pachocinski (1996) reiterates the importance of proverbs when he says, "they serve as the guardian and the carrier of the ethnic group's philosophy and genesis. The philosophy of life is built on the observations of nature; so is the concept of God" (p. 1). Obiechina adds that proverbs "are a natural part of speech of all traditional societies" (1975, p. 155); they "are said to be the kernel which contain the wisdom of the traditional people" (p. 156). He continues:

> These proverbs derive from a detailed observation of the behavior of human beings, animals, plants and natural phenomena, from folklore, beliefs, values, attitudes, perceptions, emotions and the entire system of thought and feeling which Durkheim called "les représentations collectives" of a society. They derive their effectiveness and force from the collective imagination which apprehends the underlying connection between a literal fact and its allusive amplification and which vivifies an experience by placing it beside another which bears the stamp of approval. The use of proverbs is one more way in which the individual expresses the primacy of society—even in the matter of language. (p. 156)

Rather than seeing proverbs as a natural form of African discourse, however, this type of writing runs at odds with Western ideals of narrative. It is a charge Obiechina says "needs special attention if only to answer the criticism of impercipient readers that the ubiquity of proverbs is an idiosyncrasy rather than a natural way or representing the linguistic reality of the world of rural novels" (1975, p. 155). The frequent discounting of proverbs in literature by the West is paramount to the West's understanding, or lack thereof, of African literature.

Obiechina also highlights another area of orature that is largely misconstrued and distorted when the "principles" of Western poetics arc applied wholesale to African literature—the supernatural. He says, "The supernatural is also an element that has a stronger hold on the oral tradition than on the literate tradition. Belief in magic, witchcraft and the gods tends to be in inverse proportion to scientific progress and control of the environment" (p. 33). He makes the following comment:

> Language whose function in the conventional European novel would be "largely referential" becomes in the traditional West African context largely allusive, symbolic, transformative. It creates a cosmos out of chaos through magical symbolism. . . . It has been called surrealism by European commentators but owes more to a sophisticated exploitation of the traditional belief in the omnipotence of the spoken word. The spirit of surrealism is foreign to the traditional experience. The surrealist image emerges out of the subconscious dreams of the private individual, but the traditional image derives from a collectively shared experience. (p. 175)

While the West makes solid distinctions between what is factual and what is fictional, Miner's (1990) lyric-based Eastern poetics of the affective-expressive congeals them in a manner more congenial to African philosophy. Such blending of two seemingly oppositional forces can coalesce harmoniously in the affective-expressive because in that poetics lyric shares a special relationship with history. This is so, Miner points out, because, "the lyric-based poetics of east Asia also included histories of certain kinds" (p. 83), and Murasaki Shikibu's *Tale of Genji* or *Genji Monogatari* is the first narrative work "giving us the closest thing we possess to a narrative-based originative poetics. In it Miner states that "*Genji Monogatari* contains discussions about art as perfectly natural episodes in the narrative" (p. 136). *The Tale of Genji*, presents a blending of factual and fictional material. Miner also importantly points out that far from being the norm, Western poetics, occupies a unique position in the study of literature: "western literature with its many familiar suppositions is a minority of one, the odd one out. It has no claim to be normative" (p. 8). The idiosyncratic nature of Western poetics must also be pointed out—it is the only poetics rooted in drama. As Miner says, "Far from being the inevitable, the view of literature dominant in the west is in a minority of one. The mainstream is instead a version defined out of lyric, with or without other kinds of writing" (p. 31).

It should also be noted that narratorial presence along with the involvement of the reader is another feature of orature where the narrator acts as storyteller. The narrator is also omniscient, speaking to us primarily in the third person. This oral function serves to keep the reader very close to the story, completely immersed in it by the narrator, and in this case, by the author as well. This idea of the inseparable convergence of history, or fact and fiction, is an important affective-expressive feature found in African writing—it is where much of the meaning of the fiction resides.

Although the concept of *monogatari* may be new to the Western world, it is found in an African tradition dating from as far as the 17th century among the Luba people of South Zaire. The concept of the *luba* attests to history as unfixed, subject to completion by personal observances and experiences. The *lukasa*, or *luba*, is "an instrument used for storing the coded history of the Luba kings, who flourished from the 17th to the early 20th century, and is described as "a small rectangular wooden panel produced by the *Luba* people of southeastern Zaire. Its surface is studded with the constellations of colored beads and iron pins [and] its slightly nipped-in sides are incised with meticulous hatching. A carved human head emerges from its top" (Cotter, 1996, p. 19). In the context of this study, the significance of the luba especially stems from its unique, functional way of recording the Luba past where the distinction between history and memory are "blurred." While the "creation myth remains a constant, the saga of kingship embedded in the *lukasa* will change with each new 'reader.'" (Cotter, 1996, p. 19). Importantly, "because memory boards are most often interpreted by court-trained historians, the history these readers offer will be an official history, with the past endlessly reshaped by the needs of the present" (Cotter, 1996, p. 19).

In the reading of the luba board, therefore, significant parallels are easily discernible between Miner's *monogatari* and the traditional African concept of "history." As Miner says: "there is no cause for surprise that we can derive something approaching a picture of historical actuality from fictional literature, providing of course we as readers know how to sort what is fiction. A fictional work is not entirely fictional. If it were, we could not comprehend it" (1990, p. 30). History, in this fluid sense, becomes a collective experience of fact, memory, and personal interpretation.

In an interview, Achebe refers to the American reviewer who "wondered condescendingly whether he was supposed to judge my *Arrow of God* 'as fiction, or as ethnic reporting of ancient customs'" (1979, p. 13). Achebe makes the following retort:

> What he did not know and was not prepared or open enough to learn was the simple fact that in *Arrow of God* Community is human character writ large, and my "ethnic reporting of ancient customs" a necessary portrayal of the nature and action of a personage of titanic proportions whose language is the symbolism of ritual and festival, and whose lifetime is not three score and ten years but the endless succession of the seasons. (pp. 13–14)

Apart from the natural beauty of oral language, such a mode of communication has far-reaching implications for classroom instruction. As Honeyghan (2000) points out, children can only benefit from being exposed to different ways of expressing themselves. She also says research has identified that storytelling fosters growth in language, and that there is a direct connection between storytelling and reading development. Glasceta Honeyghan's recollection of her childhood in a small Caribbean island is a powerful reminder of the "naturalness" of oral language. By allowing us into her world, she shows how much of our innate creativity is stifled when language becomes imbedded in a "foreign" format. If we listen to rap and hip-hop music, for example, the music of the marginalized African American population that began in rebellion to the strictures of white America, we again see the indigenous nature of black rhythm, which, at times, is pure lyrical genius.

Having myself grown up in a lyrical culture, I also have that sense of appreciation for the natural spontaneity of the rhythm of language, and I, too, have recollections of the impact of orality on my development: From math to childish retorts, all were intertwined in the fabric of rhythm. Multiplication tables had an easily remembered rhythm, "eleven times" being the favorite. Childish retorts would also musically roll off our tongues; for example, a very popular rebuke that I myself readily hurled back to any offender went like this: *Me a rubba/You a glue/Anting yuh sey/Bounce offa me/And stick to you.* The close relationship between the local language (Patwa) and academic English gave me a certain reverence for the gentle nuances of meaning conveyed in language.

The facets of black/African literature, or oral literature, make its content and delivery very different from white or European literature, which is primarily written. The differences between both forms of expression are very important because they can have a direct and marked impact on black student involvement, and consequently their language and literacy development. However, the consciousness of black students is not reflected in both content and mode of instruction within the American school system. Oral language, an important vehicle of black literacy development, is largely ignored, not represented, or poorly represented in a system that is insensitive to the needs of black students. Drawing upon the heritage of black students to bear on our present education system is imperative if, as educators, we are going to promote more than lip service in ensuring that all our students get a quality education.

Teaching Philosophy

Keeping in mind how heavily my background influenced my own language appreciation, I consistently try to make teaching relevant to the student's world. I try to translate what I learn of their individual and collective experience when I design and/or teach any course. Consequently, my teaching philosophy, both in and out of the classroom, is that there is never one way of arriving at any destination, regardless of the vehicle used.

I consider my teaching style to be that of facilitator. After laying down the groundwork from which to operate, I prefer that students learn to find answers themselves rather than have me give them answers; it would be presumptuous of me to think that I even have "answers." My primary goal is to develop in students the capacity for independent thought and action, the ability to express those thoughts and actions, and to take responsibility for them. In making my classroom student-centered, my success as a facilitator depends on students seeing me as approachable and nonthreatening. Keeping this requirement in mind, I encourage students to interact with me as much as possible during classroom sessions; I see dialoguing as an important part of student development. I also make myself available to students outside of the classroom. My students contact me through a variety of channels: posted office hours, telephone, E-mail, (most frequently used), and fax (most infrequently used). Students also feel comfortable "hailing" me anywhere they see me on the college campus.

I also think it extremely important that students feel comfortable to express their thoughts and ideas freely, so I try to foster a nonthreatening environment where they can tell their own stories; everyone stands to benefit from this type of exchange. I also strive to expose students to the wider possibilities of learning that exist outside the class. I do this to show students that learning is not confined to the four walls of the classroom; by definition, I do not restrict the word "classroom" to narrowly describe a room where instruction is delivered. To me, the classroom is any environment where learning and growth take place. If students can take what they have learned in the classroom and apply it to their daily lives, only then will true learning have taken place.

Additionally, I try to give students as much a chance at success as possible by integrating several teaching methods that take into account different learning styles. For example, student work may constitute a mix of lecture, individual and collaborative work, and discussion. In my classes, I emphasize independent thought and active research. Oftentimes, students are asked to choose a story to analyze from a selection of works, and when we analyze any literary work, students are asked to examine it from various perspectives: personal, critical, historical, social, and political. Students are also asked to explore the work from the point of view of the author. My approach to literary analysis is a holistic one; it embraces and puts into practice almost all of critical literary thought, with the exception of formalism, which discusses the work sans all else: biographical, historical, cultural, reader response, gender, deconstruction, and structuralism. For me, they all form parts of the whole.

Transitions

Because I grew up in Jamaica, I was able to fully participate in the dominant African culture of the country. I did not have to eke out opportunities to participate; I was totally immersed in it. I was in the majority, and daily events and entertainment reflected that majority culture. Being in the minority here in the United States, the situation for African Americans is not the same. As a minority culture, this group remains on the periphery. In terms of education, when African studies is incorporated into the curriculum, especially at the K through 12 levels, it is usually for anthropological examination and is taught in social studies classes. If students are assigned Afrocentric literature, it is only taught at the benevolence of the teacher and is still only marginally included. February, Black History Month, may be the only time of year when some educators feel obliged to teach anything relating to "Africanness," and so it is quite easy for a child to experience his or her entire school career without having to take any lesson or course addressing black studies.

My own son, Corlan, for example, who is in middle school and entering the eighth grade this fall, has not had any mandatory reading assignments that include black authors. The novels his teachers have assigned include titles such as *Gathering Blue* (Lois Lowry), *Alice in Wonderland* (Lewis Carroll), *The Golden Compass* (Phillip Pullman), *Frankenstein* (Mary Shelley), and *Brave New World* (Aldous Huxley). None remotely reflect anything Afrocentric. One day I asked him how he felt about reading these novels, and he mumbled, "They're OK but boring." Because I see that Corlan's exposure to literature is so heavily weighted against black authors, I decided to introduce him to a more inclusive reading list. Since reading Walter Dean Myers, he has been hooked. When I pick him up from school, my son's head is buried in one of Myers's books, which is not required reading. It is ironic that Corlan's exposure to black studies is so limited because we live in a very diverse geographical location in the United States—South Florida, and he has always attended public schools with sizable black student populations.

This year, I was especially pleased to read in the *Sun-Sentinel* in Fort Lauderdale that the Philadelphia School District is beginning to offer mandatory African and African American studies for all high school students (Dale, 2005). In taking this very necessary, long overdue, and, yes, controversial step, the Philadelphia School District will be the first in the nation to ensure that all its children are given the opportunity to learn about black America. How myopic and tunnel-visioned can we be not to see that everybody stands to benefit from learning about each other? For generations, black students have had to learn about white America; what can be so wrong to have white students learn about black America? Again, I go back to my microcosm of a classroom where I am painfully aware of the cultural inequities that exist and try my best to create some kind of equilibrium. My students journey to different worlds through literature where I try to get them to step over the race and culture line and to see the fictional characters as individuals like themselves. As Atticus Finch in *To Kill a Mockingbird* says, "You never really understand a person until you consider things from his point of view . . . 'til you climb inside of his skin and walk around in it" (Mulligan, 2005).

Michael Gramenz, a student who took Contemporary Literature with me felt as absorbed as Aquilla when he read a novel by a Haitian writer, Edwidge Danticat. Michael is a student who, as he states below, is able to accept diversity because that has been the hallmark of his upbringing. He was able to identify with characters whose demographics were quite unlike his own because he got beyond the race/culture divide.

Student Letter

Michael Gramenz, undergraduate in elementary exceptional education and a junior retail manager

> *I have always felt privileged growing up in South Florida with all of its diversity.*
>
> *Although I am a white male and grew up in a middle- to upper-middle-class neighborhood, I have always been exposed to other ethnicities. I grew up highly integrated into a Cuban family, and as a young child, my two best friends were black. School, from elementary through college, has always exposed me to all different kinds of people. I've known people from just about every walk of life growing up in West Palm Beach and am proud to live in an area as diverse as I do.*
>
> *Speaking of college, one class in particular, has prompted me to become involved in this project. It was my Contemporary Literature class with Professor McDonald, herself a black professor at the college. To digress briefly, I remember as a child my mother reading to me every night before bed because she wanted to make me love reading as I got older. This did not work, however. I hated reading and avoided it at all costs, resorting to things like renting movies to write book reports in high school. In this literature class, we began to read a novel and my first reaction was, "There's no movie version for me to rent." I decided that I'd just have to read it because I valued the grade I would receive for the class. To my surprise, I became completely engaged in* The Dew Breaker. *While reading, I felt as if I were in the stories*

themselves and cared about the characters as if I knew them. It opened my eyes to so much about Haiti that I never knew before because I was not yet born when the majority of those awful events took place. And so, after all these years, it happened for the first time—I not only loved the book, I wanted to read more. The experience I had while taking this class with Professor McDonald even prompted me to take another literature class, one which I don't even need to graduate. I developed a deep respect for my professor who reached me intellectually, as my teacher and as a person. through the experience of taking her class.

As far as where I am now in my life, I am majoring in elementary exceptional education and am finally leaving Palm Beach Community College after six long years of changing my major three times and dropping too many classes. I work in a retail store where I've been for three years, and it too has exposed me to many different people. I work with white, black, Hispanic, Middle Eastern, male, female and gay individuals, ages 19 through 50, and we all get along well. I think it's great that people come into our store and they see so much culture represented because I know in many of the higher-end stores such as ours, the staff is usually composed of mostly white women in their 30s to 40s. Outside work as well I am fortunate to have friends who are white, black, Hispanic, Middle Eastern, male and female, gay and straight, middle-aged and my age, who all show me something different from who they are and the things and places they enjoy. Although I may not always enjoy everything equally, they have all become a part of me that I will never forget. My life, as any life should be, has been a learning experience and through all of my educational and personal life, I value all of the lessons I've learned and all the people of every color, religion, ethnicity, age, gender, and sexual orientation that have been a part of my experiences.

Conclusion

It is no secret that in America minority students are largely regarded as low-level learners. We are constantly bombarded with stories in the media reiterating such findings. What we need to understand, however, is that minority students operate in an educational system that caters to the majority culture and expects minorities to function within that cultural framework. We must also keep in mind that students, by necessity, process information in a way that reflects their culture; this way of processing information becomes problematic for minorities because their cultural norms differ from the dominant white culture in ways that are not always obvious. For example, oral language development, an intricate part of black language development, is largely ignored and the literatures to which students are exposed largely reflect a "foreign" or European aesthete. This problem is further compounded when whatever culturally diverse material minority students are exposed to is usually taught by white teachers whose natural bias is in favor of their own European ancestry.

What is obvious, however, is the fact that we frequently see reports announcing the wide academic gap existing between minority students and their white counterparts. For example, an article by Mary Ellen Flannery in *The Palm Beach Post* titled "Most Area Black Students Stumble on State Tests," points out that black students are performing the worst on state tests that measure mastery of such subjects as regular reading (1998,). Another of the *Post*'s articles, "Unqualified Freshmen on the Rise at FAU, Study Finds" (1998,), by Don Horine, bemoans the fact that largely because of the influx of minority students admitted under the "alternative admissions program" (a program that seeks to promote a more diverse student population), the universities' academic standards have been negotiated. Every year, especially after results of standardized tests are made public, headlines copy those of the past: "Disappointment, Little Surprise at F Schools" (Miller & Flannery, 2004) and "Schools Lag in Tackling Student-Achievement Gap" (Shah, 2004). In both instances, it is minority schools that are being referenced. In the latter article, Shah reports: "According to this year's results on the Florida Comprehensive Assessment Test, black and Hispanic students again showed that they are less likely to read and solve math problems on grade level compared with their white classmates."

These findings of blacks and other minorities' substandard academic performance are common, and so the education system, local and national, has sought various ways to balance the observed inequities. For instance, in the 1960s, busing was seen as a step forward in desegregating schools. More recently, magnet programs have sought to fulfill the dual function of diversifying schools as well as promoting excellence. These attempts, however, have met with limited success. The reason for this qualified success is that the programs have been geared primarily at getting students of different races to sit together in the classroom while the curriculum and methods of instruction and assessment remain the same. Any divergence from what is deemed socially "acceptable," is frowned upon. For example, very recently, an American Indian student was denied participation in his graduation because he chose to honor his ancestry by wearing a bolo tie instead of the traditional European fare (Marimow, 2005). He was told that his "black bolo with a silver-and onyx clasp the size of a dollar was 'not acceptable.'" Even the names we give our children penalize them in the schools, and I'm sure the workplace, as long as they do no readily fit what is "expected" (Goffard, 2005).

Lamentably, too often students of a minority culture are told that who they are is unacceptable. It has been 50 years since the Supreme Court handed down its judgment in the case of *Brown v. Board of Education* in an attempt to make the playing field more equal, but the education stranglehold that existed in the old millennium still suffocates minorities in the new. As educators, we need to study innovative ways of teaching our marginalized populations, and one way of doing this is to reexamine how we address different learning styles in our teaching and in so doing make learning more palatable for all our students. One way of attempting this redefinition is to examine orature or oral language (specifically oral literature) and the integral part it plays in the development of the language and literacy skills of black students.

References

Achebe, C. (1959). *Things fall apart*. New York: Doubleday.

Achebe, C. (1979). The uses of African literature. *Okike, 15,* 8–17.

Achebe, C. (1988). *Anthills of the savannah*. New York: Doubleday.

Achebe, C. (1989). *Hopes and impediments: Selected essays*. New York: Doubleday.

Bassnett, S. (1993). *Comparative literature: A critical introduction*. Cambridge, MA: Blackwell.

Cook, D. (1977). *African literature: A critical view*. London: Longman.

Cotter, H. (1996, February 16). Keeping history fluid. *New York Times*, p. 19.

Dale, M. (2005, June 10). Schools to require African history. *Fort Lauderdale Sun-Sentinel*, p. 9A.

Finnegan, R. (1970). *Oral literature in Africa*. Oxford, UK: Oxford University Press.

Flannery, M. (1998, October 7). Most area black students stumble on state tests. *Palm Beach Post*, p. 1B.

Goffard, C. (2005, June 13). The name blame. *Palm Beach Post*, p. 1D.

Honeyghan, G. (2000, May). The rhythm of the Caribbean: Connecting oral history and literacy. *Language Arts, 77*(5), 406–413.

Horine, D. (1998, November 22). Unqualified freshmen on the rise at FAU, study finds. *Palm Beach Post*, p. 1B.

Innes, C. L. (1990). *Chinua Achebe.* New York: Cambridge University Press.

Marimow, A. E. (2005, June 11). Student denied diploma over bolo tie: 17-year-old said he wore as a way to honor his American Indian heritage. *Fort Lauderdale Sun-Sentinel*, p. 3A.

Maxwell, R., & Meiser, M. (1977). *Teaching English in middle and secondary schools* (2nd ed.). Upper Saddle River, NJ: Merrill.

Miller, K., & Flannery, E. (2004, June 10) Disappointment, little surprise at F schools. *Palm Beach Post*, p. 1B.

Miner, E. (1990). *Comparative poetics: An intercultural essay on theories of literature.* Princeton, NJ: Princeton University Press.

Moses, M. V. (1995). *The novel and the globalization of culture.* New York: Oxford University Press.

Mulligan, R. (Director). (2005). *To kill a mockingbird* [Motion picture]. United States: Universal Studios.

Obiechina, E. (1975). *Culture, tradition and society in the West African novel.* New York: Cambridge University Press.

Opekwhio, I. (1992). *African oral literature: Backgrounds, character, and continuity* Bloomington: Indiana University Press.

Pachocinski, R. (1996). *Proverbs of Africa: Human nature in the Nigerian oral tradition; An exposition and analysis of 2,600 proverbs from 64 peoples.* St. Paul, MN: Professors World Peace Academy.

Shah, N. (2004, June 10). Schools lag in tackling student-achievement gap. *Palm Beach Post*, p. 1B.

Strickland, D., & Morrow, L. (1989, December). Oral language development: Children as storytellers. *The Reading Teacher, 43*(3), 260–261.

Winkler, K. J. (1994, January 12). An African at a crossroads. *Chronicle of Higher Education, 12*, A9.

6

THE SOCIAL CONSTRUCTION OF DIVERSITY LEARNING

Reflections from a "Haole"

Scott W. Campbell

With Patricia Fonyad, Zac Gersh, Yoke-Wee Loh, and Malia J. Smith

This chapter is a reflection on three years one professor spent teaching at a remarkably diverse university on the culturally rich Hawaiian island of Oahu. Lacking a diverse background himself, the professor decided to let cultural diversity teach itself using a social contagion approach, particularly in graduate-level courses. This chapter reports on the tactics used to encourage the social construction of diversity learning and the perspectives of four former graduate students who played an integral role in the process. Opportunities and challenges associated with this pedagogical approach are included in the discussion.

The Diversity of Hawaii Pacific University and Hawaii

I would like to begin this chapter with a confession: I do not teach courses in diversity. I actually teach courses in new communication technologies, communication theory, mass media, and organizational communication. In fact, the word "diversity" does not appear in the title of any courses I have taught so far. However, for three years I was not able to escape cultural diversity as a prominent lesson in every course I taught (nor would I have wanted to, by the way). This is because I spent three years teaching at one of the most culturally diverse universities in the United States—Hawaii Pacific University (HPU).

HPU is a private teaching institution with two campuses on the Hawaiian island of Oahu. When I joined HPU in 2002, over one-fourth of its 8,500 students were international, and the remainder was evenly split between local Hawaiian residents and the students from the U.S. mainland. International students come from over 100 countries; the most represented are Japan, Taiwan, Sweden, South Korea, Germany, and Norway, in that order. The tremendous diversity among the HPU student body is no accident. Forty years ago, the university was founded with the underlying mission to promote world peace by bringing together people from around the world in scholarship. Today this principle lives on, and the university heavily recruits in countries all over the globe in order to fulfill the core objective of global citizenship. So, it is more accurate to say that I am sharing my experiences teaching *in* diversity, rather than teaching diversity as a topic per se. Nonetheless, diversity played an integral role in my pedagogical approach at HPU. It supported my efforts to ensure that students left my classes with a richer understanding and appreciation for the various cultural backgrounds at HPU and around the world.

Some may find it ironic that I taught in such a diverse environment since I grew up and spent most of my life in the Great Plains of the Midwest. Before moving to Hawaii I lived in Omaha and Lincoln, Nebraska, and in Roeland Park, Kansas, all within a three-hour drive of each other. While these cities are certainly not homogenous, they are not particularly regarded for their cultural diversity. So it's fair to say that I have had the (stereo)typical meat-and-potatoes, weekends-watching-football, midwestern upbringing. In other words, my background is not exactly culturally diverse, but that has changed since I began living in Hawaii.

Upon completion of my doctoral work at the University of Kansas, I decided to try something different—Hawaii. Different indeed! Not only is HPU extremely diverse, so is the entire island-state. One of the first things I learned when I moved to Hawaii is that there is no dominant cultural or ethnic presence on the island of Oahu. The island is truly a melting pot sprinkled with Hawaiians, Japanese, Portuguese, Filipinos, Chinese, and many other cultural and ethnic categories including my own—Haole. The term "Haole" is commonly used in Hawaii to describe white people, especially those from the U.S. mainland. The extent to which this term is meant to be an insult or merely descriptive depends on the social context in which it is used. So, I did not necessarily find it offensive to be described as Haole. In fact, I found it novel and even fascinating to be on the receiving end of such an ethnic characterization.

When I started teaching at HPU, I knew I had to harness the diversity in my classes as a rare teaching opportunity. However, as a Haole fresh off the plane with an exclusively midwestern background I was not equipped with the necessary cultural "footing" to provide my students with understanding and respect for the various backgrounds in our classes. As Aristotle would say, I lacked the *ethos* needed to teach cultural diversity to such a diverse group of students. I had to find the right approach.

The Search for a Pedagogical Approach: Determinism or Social Construction?

My search for an effective pedagogical approach led me back to the evolution of my research agenda, which explores the social implications of new communication technologies, particularly those resulting from computer-mediated and mobile communication practices. My scholarly interest in new communication technologies comes out of seven years of industry work experience. After completing my undergraduate degree, I became a communications specialist with Integrated Marketing Solutions (IMS), a consulting firm with a client list including Compaq, Hewlett-Packard, IBM, and Microsoft. The four years I spent working with these clients gave me a rich understanding of consumer electronics industries, especially those related to personal computing. These experiences coincided with the birth of the World Wide Web and the browsers that facilitated its widespread dissemination and use.

I eventually left IMS to join Sprint PCS, at the time a fledgling wireless service provider. Once again I found myself entering a technology industry at a very exciting time—the birth of wireless Personal Communication Services (PCS). Not long after I joined Sprint PCS, the company launched the first all-digital PCS network in the United States, and as a project manager I helped spread our network presence throughout the country. Along with this technological evolution came explosive growth in mobile phone subscriptions, from just 16 million globally in the early 1990s to now hundreds of millions in the United States and billions worldwide (International Tele-communication Union, 2004).

These industry experiences fueled my interest in studying the social transformations resulting from the adoption and use of new communication technologies, so much so that I decided to leave the industry for the academy. As an incoming graduate student I was eager to study the effects of computer-mediated and mobile communication devices on relationships, social networks, communities, and cultures. My initial papers were driven by such questions as: To what extent is E-mail less personal than face-to-face interaction? In what ways do the Internet and mobile phones bring people together? In what ways can these technologies make people socially isolated? These seemed like reasonable research questions at the time. What I did not realize until later in my graduate studies was that my questions had an inherent bias. I was asking questions that stressed technology's influence on society rather than pursuing a line of inquiry that explores how and why social forces shape the adoption, perceptions, and uses of communication technologies. In other words, my questions were technologically deterministic.

While there are varying degrees of technological determinism, all share the underlying assumption that new technologies are the primary cause of macro-level changes in social order as well as micro-level influences on how people view and use technological innovations (Chandler, 1996). Technological determinism can be typified by such assertions as "The automobile created suburbia," "The robots put the riveters out of work," and "The Pill produced a sexual revolution" (Marx & Smith, 1994, p. xi). Although it can be compelling, technological determinism is problematic because it implies that people are not accountable for the innovations they develop and use. Instead, this viewpoint suggests that technology evolves along a path that is followed, not created. Gurak (1995) warned that technological determinism "is frightening, for it completely ignores any human agency in the design and implementation of new technologies" (p. 4).

To make a pedagogical analogy, technological determinism can be compared to a corollary teaching style—just as social progress is considered an outcome of technological development, educational learning is considered a product of the transmission of knowledge. In both of these cases, people are viewed as passive recipients rather than active participants. In his book *Pedagogy of the Oppressed*, first published in 1970, Paulo Freire issued a warning about this pedagogical viewpoint that parallels Gurak's warning about technological determinism. In his discussion on freeing peasants from oppression through education, Freire advocated "a pedagogy which must be forged *with*, not for, the oppressed . . . in the incessant struggle to regain their humanity" (p. 48). According to Freire, education will not free the oppressed if they are not true collaborators in the process because it will perpetuate the mind-set and practice of subservient dependence.

Freire's pedagogical philosophy resonates with an alternative perspective to technological determinism—the social construction of technology. This theoretical orientation advocates that people shape technologies, not vice versa. The social construction of technology is deeply rooted in the broader schools of thought known as symbolic interactionism and constructivism. The foundation of symbolic interactionism is formulated through a set of three classic premises: (1) people know things by their meaning, (2) meanings are created through social action, and (3) meanings change through interaction (Blumer, 1969). Like symbolic interactionism, constructivism emphasizes the importance of social interaction in the creation of meaning. In fact, there are several varieties of constructivism that are specifically germane to the process of learning (see, for example, Piaget, 1970; Von Glasersfeld, 1995; Vygotsky, 1978). Although there are differences and distinctions among these varieties, common to all is the conviction that knowledge is not transmitted but rather created through social interaction.

Social constructionism is a useful framework for understanding perceptions and uses of communication and communication technologies, evidenced by research demonstrating that coworkers tend to influence each other in how they think about and use E-mail (Fulk, 1993; Fulk, Schmitz, & Ryu, 1995; Fulk, Schmitz, & Steinfeld, 1988, 1990). Building from this line of research, I have found evidence that members of close-knit social networks influence each other in how they think about and use mobile phones (Campbell & Russo, 2003). For instance, close friends and family members who vehemently complain about mobile phone use in public over time can influence one's own attitude about this social practice. In short, people are socially contagious and tend to "rub off" on one another in how they think about and use communication technologies.

When facing the challenge of teaching cultural diversity to a diverse group of students, I decided that the best strategy would be to take a page from my research and use a social constructionist approach. That is, rather than attempting to transmit knowledge about the various cultural backgrounds, I decided to design my courses in a way that would allow students to learn about cultural diversity firsthand through interactions with each other. In other words, I tried to create an environment where students would be socially contagious so that their cultural competencies would rub off on one another. This approach seemed particularly appropriate for my graduate-level seminars where enrollment would be much lower than a traditional lecture format.

Students Can Learn as Much from Each Other as from the Instructor or Reading Materials

This is something I was told by a professor who was advising me on which graduate program to attend.[1] From her perspective, the most selective programs are the best, not just because of the faculty, but because the talent among fellow graduate students is contagious through interactions in and out of class. Not only did I view this as sound advice for deciding on a graduate program, I later found it to be a useful foundation for developing courses that foster appreciation for and understanding of cultural diversity. Regardless of the course content, I wanted to make student participation a focal point because I knew students would learn more about cultural diversity from each other than they would from me, a midwestern Haole who just arrived from the mainland.

In order to accomplish this objective, I placed much of the ownership of course content and delivery on the shoulders of the students. Beyond general class discussion, this approach involved a few specific tactics. First, each student was expected to present and illustrate key concepts from the course throughout the duration of the semester. Simply reading from the course materials was unacceptable; students were challenged to find a way to bring the material to life. To meet this challenge, participants commonly used examples and anecdotes drawn from their personal experiences to effectively illustrate key course concepts. By sharing these personal, lived experiences my students created a powerful public space that supported socially constructed learning. For instance, a Japanese student in my organizational communication class provided comparisons between her workplace experiences in Japan with her workplace experiences in the United States to illustrate key

[1] My thanks to Professor Joan Aitken for giving me this helpful advice.

concepts and key terms pertaining to various managerial approaches. Her presentation provided firsthand insights into the dynamics resulting from individualistic and collectivistic tendencies in organizational life in these two countries. The student presentations and personal anecdotes frequently prompted engaging discussion and other firsthand accounts of what life is like in other countries.

Another strategy I used to foster classroom interaction was assigning case studies to which students wrote integrative responses that linked key course concepts to these real-life cases. The student-written responses served as a platform for class discussion. Often the students' cultural backgrounds played a role in how they interpreted and responded to the scenarios in the cases, which led to some enlightening moments when they shared their responses with the rest of the class. Inevitably, the in-class exchanges went beyond the written responses in ways that provided valuable glimpses into the culturally diverse lived experiences among the students in the class. One such case involved the diffusion of communication technologies in the workplace. A student from China shared stories of governmentally bounded Internet privileges, while others told of unrestricted use. This discussion evolved into examining the dissemination of mobile communication devices around the world. And some of the U.S. students were surprised to learn that their country was not the global leader in the development and use of this emerging technology.

Another strategy for facilitating the co-construction of diversity learning was to put students in small group settings to answer discussion questions, perform structured activities, and engage in problem-solving exercises. Some of the students who felt apprehensive about contributing to the entire class were better able to open up when the social dynamic was reduced to just a few individuals. In addition, this more intimate setting gave students an opportunity to get to know each other better as people with a variety of interesting backgrounds.

As intended, the collective practices of class discussion, student presentation, case study application, and group work facilitated the co-construction of knowledge of course content as well as cultural backgrounds. Through their social interactions, the students gained insights into the cultural environments peers came from, and these insights added texture to the course and provided opportunities for students to appreciate and take on the perspective of the (often very different) "other" during the process of educating the "self."

Opportunities and Challenges

The social construction of knowledge in a culturally diverse learning environment offers both educational opportunities and challenges. As noted, the opportunities include a culturally textualized (and contextualized) learning experience, enhanced perspective taking, and insights into a variety of cultures at a time when the social landscape is transforming into a more globally connected society. However, these opportunities did not come without certain challenges. One of the biggest challenges I had to face was differing levels of comfort with the high level of interaction I expected in the classroom. For instance, it did not take long for me to realize that students from Western countries tended to be more eager to share personal experiences, discuss key concepts, and challenge ideas than were students from Eastern countries. In fact, the students from Eastern countries, especially those in Asia, tended to generally be reticent during class. Upon noticing this, the initial temptation was to assume that the Asian students were simply shyer than the Western students. However, this temptation quickly vanished when I observed no substantial differences in sociability among the students while interacting with each other in the campus settings beyond the classroom.

To solve this conundrum I turned to a fellow faculty member for information and advice. He told me that the education process tends to be carried out differently in the East than it is in the West. In most Asian countries students are expected to listen as the instructor imparts knowledge, and the challenging of ideas is often considered a sign of disrespect. Of course this is an oversimplified and overgeneralized characterization of Eastern educational practices, but it was corroborated by some of my students from Japan, Taiwan, and Malaysia, as well as by scholarly research on this topic (see, for example, Liu, 2000; Miller & Aldred, 2000). This is not to suggest that reticence among Asian students should be regarded as a problem in all educational contexts. Such an assumption would be a culturally biased misperception. In many cases, Asian students who are silent during class are still actively learning and performing at very high academic levels. With this in mind, I still considered reticence a challenge to my classes because of the nature of the classes. That is, I am reporting on a pedagogical approach for graduate-level courses in communication. As one of my former students, Yoke-Wee Loh, explains below, "to learn 'communication,' it is important to communicate."

I decided to turn the challenge of reticence into a learning opportunity by bringing it up as a topic of discussion during class. Our discussion of the pedagogical practices from around the globe became a lesson in cultural diversity for everyone, myself included. Furthermore, the discussion seemed to help make the Asian students more comfortable in participating and Western students more eager to hear their contributions. In this way, we were able to turn an obstacle to the social construction of diversity learning into a valuable learning experience.

Unfortunately, not all challenges to the learning process were as easy to address. In particular, speaking English as a second language was a serious challenge for some of the international students. While most international students became proficient in English before coming to HPU, some who lacked requisite language skills struggled to constructively contribute to graduate-level discussions. These students managed to improve their fluency by attending my office hours and E-mailing their questions about the course material and our discussion of it. In addition to these outlets, students' fluency increased through informal interactions, which decreased their language barriers.

In some instances, the class was able to turn the challenge of language barriers into a learning opportunity by sharing useful words and phrases with each other. Perhaps the most valuable language lessons came from the local Hawaiian students, who usually spoke at least some of the Hawaiian language in addition to fluent English and the local pidgin dialect. Pidgin, an amalgamation of influences from several languages, is commonly sprinkled into everyday life on the island. One of my very first teaching experiences at HPU involved a lesson in pidgin. As I was handing out the course syllabus one of the Hawaiian students asked if I could provide her with "da Kine." After responding to her with a quizzical and confused facial expression, she and some of the other Hawaiian students explained the meaning of this expression. "Da Kine" generally refers to something good or desirable and can be used flexibly in a variety of contexts. In this case, the student was asking if I would hand her a class syllabus. Such lessons in the local dialect came in handy as I and other nonlocals carried out our daily lives on the island. I was quite pleased with myself when while on the beach one day I was asked if my surfboard was "good for make wave" and I knew exactly what was being asked of me. I gave the man a nod and a grin, indicating that yes, my surfboard was indeed good for catching waves.

In addition to the beneficial lessons in pidgin, the local students were also helpful in teaching some of the common Hawaiian words that appear in everyday interactions. They include "mahalo" (thank you), "ono" (tasty food), "kakua" (cooperation), "ohana" (family), "keiki" (children), "pooka" (hole), and "pau" (finished), among others. Not long after moving to Oahu, I came to realize that these words were used as often, if not more often, than their English counterparts. Frequently I would hear statements such as, "OK, folks, we need to be sure to fill in the pookas before this meeting is pau . . . mahalo for your kakua."

Reciprocal Learning: The Instructor Can Learn as Much from the Students as They Can from the Instructor

Writing this chapter has been a cathartic reflection for me because I wrote it just as I finished my last semester teaching at Hawaii Pacific University and living on Oahu. I have greatly enjoyed and benefited from my experiences over these three years. In many ways the students at HPU have taught me as much as I have taught them—in some ways they have taught me more. I attribute this to the interaction we had both in and out of the classroom. As explained above, I believe that people are socially contagious. Individuals' perceptions, attitudes, and experiences overlap and enmesh through the process of communication. For me this process has moved from the theoretical to the applied, as I reflect upon the three years I have spent teaching at a culturally diverse university situated in a culturally diverse social environment. The cultural variety that I encountered has had a profound influence on my interest in and ability to adapt to diverse populations.

I am particularly thankful to the four students who contributed narratives for this chapter. In their narratives, you will hear the themes of social construction, collaboration, and the strong influence of communication within the learning environment. Each of these individuals embodied these practices as graduate students, which made them not only excellent students, but also excellent teachers of cultural diversity. With backgrounds from Malaysia, Switzerland, Hawaii, and the U.S. mainland, the contributors collectively provide a glimpse into the culturally diverse atmosphere in and around HPU classrooms.

Student Letters

Patricia Fonyad will soon start her practical filmmaking programme at Metropolitan Film School (London).

> Dear Dr. Campbell,
>
> Growing up in Switzerland has provided me with the opportunity to know and appreciate the impressive history and cultural diversity of Europe. For example, Switzerland itself offers four idiosyncratic geographical regions and thus cultures (i.e., German, French, Italian, and Romansh). Relating to my family roots, my mother was partly Swiss and partly British, whereas my father was born and raised in Hungary. Consequently, I grew up speaking five languages, which has regularly served me to overcome barriers in communication and cultural understanding.
>
> However, my experiences relating to cultural diversity have not only been enormously beneficial to me in my personal life but also in my academic and professional life. For instance, I used to work as a legal adviser in the securities sales and trading area for a Swiss private bank for seven years. With the stock market business being a typically global industry with an international clientele, my language skills along with my understanding and respect for other cultures were always of great advantage. (It may appear rather amusing that since I have become familiar with Marxism in social science through our readings and in-class discussions, I have converted from a Swiss banking lawyer into a [neo-]Marxist thinker.)
>
> Not surprisingly, once I decided to quit my job at the bank and study communication, there was only one place I wanted to go: Hawaii, the antipode of my home country and a gathering place of different cultures. Despite or maybe because of my cultural background, I have benefited tremendously from the diverse student body at HPU—particularly in group work. Hence, it has not so much been a new experience for me to work with people from different cultural backgrounds, rather, it has served me to gain further experience on a truly global scale. For instance, for the first time I have been working with individuals from different Asian cultures, which has broadened my mind and understanding of the specific cultural characteristics

within certain countries and how to best communicate and cooperate with members of these groups.

What I have further learned is that despite the diversity across European cultures, learning and interacting in an American classroom environment often showed we Europeans that we have more in common than we may think. To illustrate, as opposed to the Americans, Europeans share similar ethical and cultural belief and value systems. Regarding organizational communication in particular, I noted the significantly different attitudes that Americans and Europeans have in terms of employment policies and thus the practical handling of diversity in the workplace.

To conclude, it has been a unique opportunity and privilege to work with people from all over the world for the common goal of constructing, increasing, and deepening knowledge and mutual understanding. Particularly, I cherish the experience that we students shared as well as the relationship between the professors and the international student body. It has at all times been characterized by high respect and genuine interest for one another. Certainly, I look forward to further developing my understanding for cultural diversity but to also make others aware of it—privately, academically, and professionally.

Zac Gersh, *doctoral student and graduate teaching assistant (Louisiana and New York)*

Dear Dr. Campbell,

I have had the good fortune and privilege to live and study in a variety of locations throughout my academic career, and Hawaii provided a most unique opportunity to learn with students and instructors from diverse backgrounds. After matriculating at Ithaca College in upstate New York, I did not quite know what to expect in the master's program at Hawaii Pacific University. Whereas before I enjoyed and prided myself on the lecture-style approach to academia in which I, the student, absorbed the course material through a linear directional flow from teacher to student, learning at HPU exposed me to the a priori with which my former thoughts on education had proceeded.

Through your teaching style, understanding the material as such was achieved through a learning process that actively sought out different interpretations from students of different backgrounds. Breaking into groups and copresenting material from the textbook allowed students to understand the meaning of the course content through the scope of a unique cultural milieu. With a wide range of backgrounds present, we as students found ourselves not only connecting with formal knowledge conveyed through communication theories, but we were also immersed in a process of learning that was uncovered through multiple layers of meaning.

The most fascinating feature about this activity was finding how people of different backgrounds approached the theories. I soon found out that the way we understood the material was often a function of race, gender, nationality, and so forth. Synthesizing the content through a process of multicultural discourse not only acclimated me to the theories as such, but provided me with a more flexible, open stance when it came time to apply the theories in conducting research. Professionally, I owe much credit in my journalist writings to my diverse experiences in the classroom; I was able to approach subjects of assignments with a healthy respect for how people of variegated political and religious beliefs form social meaning through cultural experiences.

Now, having finished a master's thesis and working on a Ph.D. at Louisiana State University, I find myself in charge of a classroom, teaching two introductory speech courses. While the majority of LSU students are white, the state is filled with examples of cultural controversy and conflict, and this extends to campus. Just this year an argument ensued on campus over the Confederate flag being waved at sporting events with the school's colors. Many students felt it was an expression of homage to their heritage, despite the real possibility that the display would offend African Americans. I felt that my duty as an instructor was not to tell them what I think is the correct stance on the issue. I applied the learning process studied in Hawaii to facilitate intercultural understanding by having the students engage each other from the different stances on the issue. The goal was to learn: What are the arguments and how are they being appropriated? Students can discover for themselves how they feel about political issues or academic theories. By drawing upon my academic experience in Hawaii, however, I see that my responsibility is to provide them with the opportunity to weigh such discourse through a learning process composed of diverse sensibilities, cultures, and approaches.

Yoke-Wee Loh, *video editor (Malaysia)*

Dear Dr. Campbell,

Living in Malaysia all my life, I remembered when I first arrived in Hawaii to pursue my master's degree in communication, everything was new to me. With students from more than a hundred countries around the world, "global citizenship" is the perfect term to describe Hawaii Pacific University. We have literally a dozen ways to say hello.

I experienced a major cultural shock while living in a foreign country. We had small classes of 20 students compared to 200 back home. The diversity of students at Hawaii Pacific University was very remarkable. However, you may still notice that students were seated in a pattern in class: international students on the right, native students on the left. So how could a professor be sure that all of his students participated in class? I was fortunate enough to be in your class during my first semester. You opened up a whole new perspective of how dynamic a class could be and made it clear that to learn "communication," it is important to communicate.

You encouraged a casual atmosphere through your mannerisms and relaxed attire. You cleverly presented yourself to us as a friend by telling personal stories about yourself ranging from major turning points to what you had for dinner. In your Introduction to Communication class, many of us did not know any communication theories. Through the course curriculum, you would incorporate experiences of different students from various cultures thus making sure that every student received credit for contributing to the class. But how would a girl who was brought up not to challenge what is in the textbook, or to think critically, speak her mind in a foreign language? Language appears to be a barrier for most of the international students. Many international students are especially conscious of how they are perceived in class. They are afraid of being alienated and, thus, tend to be very passive. Everyone in our class had an equal chance to speak. You would skillfully invite these students to speak by observing their facial expressions. Your enthusiasm in wanting to learn about other cultures made us feel proud to present our culture. This was because you acknowledged each and every opinion. You not only listened to us, but also processed our comments and responded with a different perspective.

We soon developed this mutual respect that you communicated to us for each other. After realizing that all students have the same anxiety about speaking in class, we no longer felt that we were alone. With the diversity of students, there were no longer right or wrong answers. As we interacted with each other, we opened the door to alternative possibilities in our lives. Very often, we would learn something interesting and new from each other. For example, do you know that Bulgarians nod their heads to indicate no? Instead of attending a class, I felt this experience was more like a gathering place where we learn and evolve together.

Malia J. Smith, *chief of staff for Hawaii State Senator Bob Hogue and adjunct professor (Hawaii)*

Dear Dr. Campbell,

As a native Hawaiian woman, I have had the terrific opportunity to live on the island of Oahu-Hawaii. Aside from Hawaii's beauty and pristine weather, its cultural diversity is profound. The culmination of the eclectic cultures found in Hawaii has defined it as the melting pot of the Pacific. The amalgamation of the many cultures including Hawaiian, Chinese, Japanese, Portuguese, Filipino, Vietnamese, Samoan, Tongan (to name a few) shares a part in Hawaii's diverse nature.

Although I've lived and worked with people of many cultures and ethnicities in Hawaii, I only realized the depth of global diversity through the learning processes found in my graduate courses at Hawaii Pacific University. It was captivating to ephemerally experience the course material through the perception of a Pakistani, Scandinavian, or Israeli student. Through lively discussions, interactive group sessions, and seminar presentations, various cultural perspectives were presented, dissected, and considered. Sitting in these classes I found my axioms and canonical standards were challenged.

I specifically remember participating in a group discussion with two men from Brazil, as we contemplated the relativity of time and space. I surprisingly discovered that based on their culture, it is accepting of individuals to show up late for scheduled meetings (as long as they show up within 30 minutes of the scheduled time). This revelation explained their casual attitude in showing up for class at least 15 to 20 minutes after the designated meeting time. Thus, what I defined as late, they defined as being on time. Fascinating.

The intimacy of the group settings shared among the diverse members of the class stimulated a deeper level of learning for me. Based on cultural differences I was able to gain insight on variations of theoretical perspectives. These encounters improved my critical thinking skills and opened my mind to new ideas. Although I thought I was culturally sophisticated—living in such a widely diverse environment such as Hawaii—the required class discussions allowed me to intimately hear, see, and feel other people's realities.

Currently I am the full-time chief of staff for Hawaii State Senator Bob Hogue (R-24th district), and I am also an adjunct professor at Hawaii Pacific University teaching public speaking and communication introductory courses. At the Hawaii State Legislature we encounter an array of individuals with diverse backgrounds. As chief of staff I manage an office and remain in direct contact with constituents, businesspeople, and various organizations. I handle complaints, concerns, and legislative proposals, which require excellent communication and personal skills. Through my experiences in graduate school and the lessons I've learned in diversity I have been able to apply this knowledge to influence the way I manage and lead my staff and/ or deal with public interests. I understand the importance of relating to individuals not only on a professional level but also on a personal level, which includes their background and vast cultural differences.

As an adjunct professor of an internationally recognized institution consisting of students from over 100 different countries, I embrace the differences among my students, as I know firsthand the importance and value of cultural diversity in the learning process. Thus, I emulate your teaching styles by incorporating group discussions, seminar presentations, and interactive work. Through each other my students will be able to explore the course material, share different culturally inclined perspectives, and empower themselves by taking that knowledge and applying it in future endeavors.

Reaction to Student Narratives

As I read through the narratives from my former students, I notice several themes that emerge throughout their reflections. Perhaps the most prominent theme is unanimous appreciation for HPU's aim of promoting global citizenship—certainly a worthy aim, as exemplified by Patricia's cross-cultural experience working for a Swiss bank. HPU does not take the objective of global citizenship lightly. In fact, it resides at the very core of the university's being. According to the university mission statement,

Hawai'i Pacific University is an international learning community set in the rich cultural context of Hawai'i. Students from around the world join

us for an American education built on a liberal arts foundation. Our innovative undergraduate and graduate programs anticipate the changing needs
of the community and prepare our graduates to live, work, and learn as
active members of a global society.

Many universities tout their dedication to promoting diversity, but few
are able to deliver to the extent that HPU does, thanks to its unique student
population. Clearly, the ability to learn and grow in a microcosm of our
increasingly "global society" was an experience that these four students have
not taken for granted.

Beyond their general appreciation for the cultural diversity at HPU, the
contributors provide helpful insights into how and why such a diverse educational environment can enhance the learning experience. Specifically, students navigate their educational experiences through various filters. As Zac
explains, differences in race, gender, nationality, and so on contribute to differences in the interpretation of curriculum. Therefore, immersion in a culturally diverse classroom means that students are also "immersed in a process
of learning that [is] uncovered through multiple layers of meaning." Malia's
discussion of being able to "hear, see, and feel other people's realities" also
speaks to having access to the multiple layers of meaning that can contribute
to a more robust educational experience.

I was pleased to observe that each contributor advocates the merit of
student interaction and participation as a vehicle for diversity learning. In
several places the contributors refer to group interaction, student presentation, and class discussion as processes for gaining understanding and respect
for other cultures, and they illuminate how these practices work through
helpful anecdotes. Malia's revelation about the polychronic culture in Brazil,
Yoke-Wee's lesson in nonverbal behavior in Bulgaria, Patricia's insight into
organizational practices in Europe, and Zac's appreciation for culturally divergent meanings for symbols such as the Confederate flag are all examples
of how understanding and appreciation for diversity can be engendered in
the classroom, even when the instructor has little firsthand experience to
offer.

Furthermore, I was particularly pleased to see that the former students
who are now teachers themselves are using a similar pedagogical approach.
As Malia explains, "Through each other my students will be able to explore
the course material, share different culturally inclined perspectives, and em-

power themselves by taking that knowledge and applying it in future endeavors." Zac echoes this sentiment when he notes, "Students can discover for themselves how they feel about political issues or academic theories . . . my responsibility is to provide them with the opportunity to weigh such discourse through a learning process composed of diverse sensibilities, cultures, and approaches." These comments underscore the viewpoint that learning, especially diversity learning, can be accomplished as a transaction rather than a transmission.

One of the interesting outcomes of this approach is that lines demarcating teacher and student become blurred, just as the lines separating sender and receiver are obscured when communication is viewed as a transaction rather than transmission. Yet, it is important for the instructor to play an active role as facilitator, especially in a classroom where English is not everyone's first language. Patricia and Yoke-Wee both speak English as a second language, and both highlight the importance of language in learning about other cultures. I find it interesting that Patricia discusses language as an asset, while Yoke-Wee points out challenges associated with it. Patricia explains, "I grew up speaking five languages, which has regularly served me to overcome barriers in communication and cultural understanding." Yoke-Wee notes, "Language appears to be a barrier for most of the international students. Many international students are especially conscious of how they are perceived in class." These remarks illustrate the power of language in diversity learning and how it plays the dual role of (a) opportunity and (b) challenge for instructors to (a) harness and (b) overcome.

The intersection between opportunity and challenge is where the lines separating teacher and student become more defined in the social construction of diversity learning. In particular, it is important for instructors to recognize the anxiety that may be associated with speaking a foreign language in class. One tip is to acknowledge the anxiety and remind the students that they are not alone—that other students feel the same way. Many students, regardless of their cultural background, feel nervous about speaking during class. As a graduate assistant teaching public-speaking courses I learned that students tend to be much more focused on their own impression management than the impressions of others. Emphasizing this point in class can help alleviate the fear of participation. As Yoke-Wee explained, "After realizing that all students have the same anxiety about speaking in class, we no longer felt that we were alone."

Yoke-Wee, Patricia, Malia, and Zac are very different from one another, but each now have something important in common—an appreciation for diversity and the ability to thrive in a culturally diverse environment. I am grateful to them for conveying their insights in their letters and helping to educate me about cultural diversity as I attempted to do the same for them. Like them, I was a good student of diversity. I'm still a Haole from the Midwest, but I'm much more able to take the perspective of those who are not, and I look forward to spreading the Aloha in my new life as I make the transition from Hawaii back to the Midwest, where I am now teaching at the University of Michigan in Ann Arbor.

And with that, I am "pau."

References

Blumer, H. (1969). *Symbolic interactionism: Perspective and method*. Englewood Cliffs, NJ: Prentice-Hall.

Campbell, S. W., & Russo, T. C. (2003). The social construction of mobile telephony: An application of the social influence model to perceptions and uses of mobile phones within personal communication networks. *Communication Monographs, 70*(4), 317–334.

Chandler, D. (1996). Shaping and being shaped. *CMC Magazine, 3*(2). Retrieved February 5, 2002, from http://www.december.com/cmc/mag/1996/feb/chandler.html

Freire, P. (1970). *Pedagogy of the oppressed* (Myra Bergman Ramos, Trans.). New York: Herder & Herder.

Fulk, J. (1993). Social construction of communication technology. *Academy of Management Journal, 36*(5), 921–950.

Fulk, J., Schmitz, J., & Ryu, D. (1995). Cognitive elements in the social construction of technology. *Management Communication Quarterly, 8*(3), 259–288.

Fulk, J., Schmitz, J., & Steinfeld, C. W. (1988). *Social information and technology use in organizations*. Paper presented at the annual Academy of Management convention, Anaheim, CA.

Fulk, J., Schmitz, J., & Steinfeld, C. W. (1990). A social influence model of technology use. In J. Fulk & C. Steinfeld (Eds.), *Organizations and communication technology* (pp. 117–139). Newbury Park, CA: Sage.

Gurak, L. J. (1995). Cybercasting about cyberspace. *CMC Magazine, 2*(1). Retrieved February 5, 2002, from http://www.ibiblio.org/cmc/mag/1995/jan/gurak.html

International Telecommunication Union. (2004, May). ICT Free Statistics. Retrieved July 25, 2006, from http://www.itu.int/itu-d/ict/statistics/

Liu, J. (2000). Understanding Asian students' oral participation modes in American classrooms. *Journal of Asian Pacific Communication, 10*(1), 155–189.

Marx, L., & Smith, M. R. (Eds.) (1994). *Does technology drive history?: The dilemma of technological determinism.* Cambridge, MA: MIT Press.

Miller, L., & Aldred, D. (2000). Student teachers' perceptions about communicative language teaching methods. *RELC Journal, 3*(1), 1–19.

Piaget, J. (1970). *The science of education and the psychology of the child.* New York: Grossman.

Von Glasersfeld, E. (1995). *Radical constructivism: A way of knowing and learning.* London: Falmer Press.

Vygotsky, L. S. (1978). *Mind and society: The development of higher mental processes.* Cambridge, MA: Harvard University Press.

7

INTERCULTURAL COMPETENCE

From the Classroom to the
"Real World" and Back Again

Randy K. Dillon

With Mindy Shelton, Christopher Dixon, Kurtis Lane, and Marlo Hamilton

This chapter explores how the concept and practice of intercultural competence has become a central point of the author's
pedagogy when teaching intercultural communication and multiculturalism. Letters from four former students provide commentary on key lessons learned from his introductory intercultural
communication course and how these lessons have affected their
professional and/or personal lives. The chapter concludes with
the teacher's observations on the intercultural competence that
these students display, as well as how these students have made
him reflect upon his own continued development of intercultural
competence and its influence upon his pedagogy.

Communication scholars Guo-Ming Chen and William Starosta
(2003) write that "the need for intercultural knowledge and skills
that lead to intercultural communication competence becomes critical for leading a productive and successful life in the 21st century" (p. 344).
Instruction and discussions of culture and diversity are essential for today's
college student who must be prepared for effective participation in what
Boulding (1988) refers to as a "global civic culture." In my 11 years teaching
intercultural communication and diversity courses I have emphasized the
cultivation of one's intercultural competence (Lustig & Koester, 2003). Intercultural competence involves a combination of knowledge, skills, and atti-

tude. Knowledge is the cognitive ability to be both aware of one's own communication as well as others' communication and learn ways to build better intercultural relations. The skills component depends on how the individual can apply or carry out what he or she knows. Attitude consists of one's motivation to gain more knowledge about intercultural communication and taking opportunities of applying skills one has learned (Lustig & Koester, 2003). It is through the lens of intercultural competence that my teaching of culture, communication, and diversity is guided.

I believe that some of the best teaching and learning occurs when students return with their own accounts of what they have gained from a course. Teachers can use such accounts to help these students better process their experiences and the learning that came from them. Their stories may also be used in future classes as "teaching narratives," designed to enhance comprehension and learning. To paraphrase Freire (1970), this type of instruction requires a passionate faith that students will make and remake, create and re-create what they have learned in the classroom and apply it to their own life experiences, or what they more commonly refer to as the "real world."

Through achieving intercultural competence, students gain knowledge, apply the skills needed, and are motivated to learn more if they can personalize themselves. Furthermore, intercultural communication education requires pedagogical practices that build upon conventional concepts of teaching, yet diverge in other directions such as looking at issues and outcomes that extend beyond the classroom. These assumptions about intercultural competence and how to best teach it have led me to the following question: What have been the experiences and outcomes of my students as they relate to intercultural competence?

This chapter integrates my passions of intercultural communication teaching and scholarship with the opportunity to reconnect with former students. I explain how diversity has framed my life, followed by a discussion of my teaching philosophy and the student and institutional responses to a diversity curriculum at my home institution, Missouri State University. I then briefly summarize what I found interesting about the personal perspectives and learnings shared by four former students through their letters. Central to this analysis is an exploration of the impact and the challenges that these students faced as they applied (or didn't apply) the diversity and intercultural competence lessons learned in the classroom to their own lives.

This essay draws upon the Scholarship of Teaching and Learning (SOTL), which presupposes that highly skilled teachers engage in a systematic inquiry about the process of teaching and learning outcomes (Jardine, Clifford, & Friesen, 2003). Drawing upon the SOTL perspective I will explore how these letters and interviews have encouraged me to reflect upon the philosophy and pedagogy I have used to inform my teaching of intercultural communication. The SOTL approach will also provide an assessment frame that can determine what issues of diversity and intercultural competence shared by my former students from the "real world" can be folded back into the classroom.

Developing Intercultural Competence: Early Lessons and Classroom Experiences

Personal narratives consist of "stories lived and told" (Clandinin & Connelly, 2000, p. 9), and bring together one's experience and identity (Hantzis, 1995). One of the building blocks of diversity is to understand oneself better (Kohls, 2001). Sharing one's own story is important for self-understanding, and according to Bateson (1997) "includes a dimension of justification, not only 'what I did' and 'what happened' but how and why I chose to understand it, and a readying of the self for the task that lies ahead" (p. viii).

My early experiences with diversity were lacking. I grew up in a rural area south of Kansas City, Missouri. Despite becoming "brown as a berry" in the summer, and an ancestry that included Ponca Indian and "dark Irish," I learned that I was white. The rest of the folks in my hometown of East Lynne were white. The small school that I attended until eighth grade consisted of all white students. Difference between people in my hometown pivoted on what church one went to, Baptist or Methodist, and each had different worldviews. As a Methodist I was first baptized by being sprinkled with water, whereas the Baptists across town got "dunked under" in a local pond. Baptists took a dim view of dancing, whereas the Methodists in my hometown danced.

While growing up I discovered that most multicultural diversity thrived someplace else other than East Lynne. For me, people different from a rural boy like me lived in Kansas City, or "the City" as folks called it. In fact, I had second cousins who lived in Kansas City who seemed to lead a different existence than I did. I also knew that there were blacks in Kansas City because I heard about them on the television news or heard my family talk about them. My father had a couple of black friends who worked with him at the Leeds Fisher Body Plant that was located in Kansas City. They often would hunt quail or go fishing with my dad on my grandparents' farm nearby. When I think about it, this was quite daring in the late 60s and early 70s, but my parents and grandparents never made much of it. The only stipulation for hunting or fishing on the family farm was that you had to know someone in the family.

It was not until I was 22 that I experienced a major personal and academic recognition of diversity. In my undergraduate school there was no focus on diversity, although there were students from different backgrounds and countries who attended. My graduate school experience was vastly different at the University of Southwestern Louisiana (now called University of Louisiana-Lafayette). In Lafayette I was exposed to much broader and more expansive diversities: regional differences, nationalities, ethnicities, and racial diversity as well as my introduction to the role and influence of culture in my communication courses. I began to realize that my close friends up to that point in my life had been people who looked like me, talked like me, and we shared similar backgrounds. That was all about to change.

Graduate school spurred me to learn more about the world, to live in another country in a culture where I was challenged, different, the foreigner. I wanted that experience. A few months after finishing my master's degree I moved to Osaka, Japan, where I worked as an English teacher in a culture that spoke a language I did not know, wrote in a script that was nothing I had ever learned, and possessed a worldview that intrigued and sometimes frustrated me. Living and working overseas made me more curious about how communication and culture intersect and I became amazed at my new gained competence (and confidence) of navigating foreign cultures. Yet, I realized that I had much more to learn about intercultural communication and multiculturalism. I spent the next five years working, living, and traveling in Asia and Europe before entering a doctoral program where I sought a research focus in diversity and intercultural communication.

Knapp and Woolverton (1995) conclude that "Educators hold dual class identities, one deriving from their 'class of origin' and the other from their current occupational position as teacher, administrator, counselor, or other role" (p. 555). Palmer (1998) claims "we teach who we are" (p. 2). I believe that my experiences growing up, as well as the diversity experiences from living abroad, influence my teaching philosophy and the ways I approach intercultural communication. Intercultural competence and its combination of knowledge, skills, and attitude have become a way for me to comprehend what I have learned so I can share this knowledge and skills with my students. It also encourages me to be motivated to learn more about diversity and intercultural communication so that my students have richer learning opportunities.

After earning my doctorate degree at the University of Florida I took a tenure-track position at Southwest Missouri State University, which has recently changed its name to Missouri State University.[1] The job was appealing because many Missouri State University students were similar to me when I began college. Many are from rural communities and towns and are first-generation college students. I knew that my students' lives would be affected by intercultural diversity whether they knew it or not and that they needed to learn more about becoming competent at intercultural communication.

The Missouri State University campus is located in Springfield, Missouri. According to the 2000 U.S. Census, Springfield has a population of 151,580 with over 91% white, slightly over 3% black or African American, and just over 2% Hispanic. Native Americans and Asian Americans make up about 1% each of Springfield's population. Although the city and the surrounding Ozarks are undergoing diversity changes, primarily as a result of Hispanics moving to the area, it remains one of the "whitest" cities of its size in the United States. Fall 2004 student enrollment numbers from the University's Office of Institutional Research reported an overall student headcount at 19,114, including 1,124 minority students and 467 "non-resident aliens" (p. 12) or international students (www.smsu.edu/oir/fact-book/studentinfo.pdf).

Multiculturalism efforts are important at Missouri State University, such as the highly visible International Student Services and the campus Multicultural Resource Center, which helps coordinate several diversity-type events throughout the academic year. An increasing number of Missouri State University students are also participating in Study Away Programs and taking courses that emphasize a global community perspective. "Diversity" and "multiculturalism" have become buzzwords at Missouri State just as they

---

[1] On August 28, 2005, Missouri State University changed its name from Southwest Missouri State University. Student letters may contain the term Southwest Missouri State University (SMSU), the name of the university when they were attending.

have at other university campuses across the nation. For instance, expanded enrollments in my intercultural communication course offer one example of the university's increasing interest in diversity and multiculturalism. During my first semester (fall 1994) I taught an intercultural communication course with four students enrolled. Currently it is one of the most popular courses offered within the communications curriculum with two sections during a semester and one summer section. I cannot claim sole credit for such interest. Rather, I believe students want to learn more about our world, and this intercultural communication course is viewed as one way to begin doing so.

Teachers use patterns and certain routines that work. In my classes I believe that learning is strengthened by the use of examples and focused activities where students can put into practice what they read. Boyer (1990) emphasizes that teachers need to go beyond transmitting knowledge to transforming and extending it. Hopefully, I instill in my students a yearning to go beyond what is being learned and discussed in their communication courses by encouraging them to read books, view films, and attend outside lectures. I help them realize that as productive, educated citizens they must learn in different and multiple ways, and "embrace continuous learning" (Gallos, Ramsey, & Associates, 1997, p. 212). I strive to model continuous learning, for when I learn alongside my students I see myself as a successful teacher.

Since teaching consists of a journey of discovery, the theories I follow and the methods I carry out teaching intercultural communication continue to evolve and change. Increasingly, I encourage my students that becoming interculturally competent in a global society will require them to go beyond acquiring easily accessible cultural facts. Although learning about a culture's cuisine, holidays, and ceremonial dress is interesting, and often fun, there is more to a culture that requires deeper inquiry. This inquiry involves analyzing culture on various levels including its traditions, beliefs, norms, practices, and attitudes. I urge students to look at not only how a culture is different from their own, but also why it is different. This emphasis on cultural difference may run counter to the pedagogical philosophy that cultures have many things in common and that similarities, not differences, should be celebrated. Cultural differences and the reasons behind them can sometimes be alien to what my students have been taught and experienced. At the same time I do not advocate that students give up or lose respect for their own culture's preferences. I believe that such critical analysis is essential for students to become more competent in their intercultural interactions. Otherwise, "if we don't try . . . to understand critically what is different, we run the risk of making rigid value judgments which are always negative towards the culture which is unfamiliar to us" (Freire & Faundez, 1989, p. 17).

With each new semester I hope that the intercultural communication class stimulates a culture of education that is empowering to all students (Banks, 2000). I believe that participatory dialogues can increase students' competence. Freire (1970) said, "Without dialogue there is no communication, and without communication, there can be no true education" (p. 81). In order to increase classroom dialogue I have used case studies that consist of dividing up the class into different groups that meet to discuss issues and work out various cultural dilemmas. After a certain amount of time each group must circulate to the other groups a summary of what they discussed and decided. (Over the past several semesters I have had classes post these summaries on an online electronic bulletin board that is set up for the class). Once each group has reviewed the other group's summaries, the class comes together for a participatory dialogue where explanations are made of why the group reached or did not reach its thinking on a topic, questions can be asked, and additional possibilities are explored.

Participatory dialogues have been used in other ways in my intercultural communication courses. I have always required a final project assignment from my students that asks them to explore the communication phenomena of another culture. For example, a student might compare the use of conflict styles between Culture A and Culture B, or the communication issues that surround conducting a meeting in one culture as opposed to the way a meeting is conducted in one's own culture. All students were asked to write a final research paper, as well as orally present their research to the class. For years, I felt like the results were a crapshoot. Some students demonstrated that they had done a sufficient amount of research and thinking about their chosen cultural topic, while others did a poor job because of misunderstanding the importance of thoroughly investigating a topic and presenting to the class. Many papers and, subsequently, the presentations exhibited a thrown-together, last-minute effort to get something turned in on time, resulting in frustration and disappointment not only on the part of the student, but also for fellow classmates, and of course, the teacher.

A few years ago I employed a more proactive stance in order to achieve more favorable results in the final projects. I required students to identify early in the semester what their topic would be for the final project. I have discovered that when students publicly announce to their fellow classmates what their topic is there is more follow-through toward the final completion of the assignment. Also, when students know the topics of fellow classmates they can discuss them with each other and point out resources that can help with research. As Freire (1970/1995) said, "Authentic education is not carried out by 'A' *for* 'B,' or by 'A' *about* 'B,' but rather by 'A' *with* 'B,' mediated by the world—a world which impresses and challenges both parties, giving rise to views or opinions about it" (p. 82). In addition, I offer "mini assignments" at different points in the semester that make students think about whether a topic currently being studied in class can be applied toward their topic. Students are also asked to read and discuss with one another each other's work. These dialogues occurring throughout the semester have resulted in students engaging in more critical thinking and learning about not only their topic but other classmates' topics as well. The final papers and presentations have improved.

Despite the continuing evolution of my pedagogy and methods of teaching intercultural communication one thing has remained constant in the 11 years I have taught at Missouri State University. I wonder about the impact my teaching and my courses have had on my former students. I tell students in my intercultural communication courses that they have only scratched the surface when it comes to learning about communication across cultural groups. It is my hope that they will apply more of what they have learned about intercultural communication once they leave my classes than they do in the actual class. This hope for my students leads to the following questions: What is it that they are experiencing? What are they are learning from their experiences? In what ways can their stories inform me as well as my current and future students? When I do receive this feedback it causes traditional roles to become blurred, and my former students become my teachers. This continuous loop of learning coincides well with my approach of using intercultural competence in my diversity and intercultural communication courses. Students realize that intercultural competence consists of a lifelong adventure of gaining knowledge and applying the skills. Moreover, one's attitude to be motivated to learn is essential in becoming more competent at intercultural communication.

This project of having former students write letters to me concerning what they have experienced/learned is an extension, and evidence, of continued learning in intercultural competence. I asked four students—two females and two males—who were in my intercultural classes at different times during the past 11 years to share their experiences. They each grew up within 150 miles of Missouri State University where the campus draws a large percentage of its student population. I chose these particular students because of the variety of life experiences they represent since taking my course and graduating from Missouri State University. I did not specifically ask these students to write about intercultural competence for fear that they would be restricted in trying to make their experiences fit in neatly with the components and terminology of knowledge, skills, and attitude. I incorporate those competencies in the analysis that follows their letters.

Student Letters

Mindy Shelton, export logistics operator (Texas)

Dear Dr. Dillon,

I come from a very conservative, close-knit family. My family is white and I was raised in a typical Southern Baptist home. If anything could give a glimpse of the kind of knowledge about intercultural communication my family imparted to me, it would be my dad's quote to his teenage daughters while we were in high school. During an angry fight with our father, he responded to us saying, "I have three rules in this house: no smoking, no drinking, and no dating black guys." I kept my thoughts to myself, but it was, "OK, so sex and drugs are OK?"

After college, I found a job as a customer service rep, but I wasn't happy. I wanted more out of life. Therefore, I decided to follow one of my dreams—to learn Spanish! I moved into my sister's apartment in Houston. Her boyfriend, a bilingual first grade teacher at her school, was originally from Mexico. I tried to spend as much time as possible with both of them while seeking temporary work in order to pay the bills and eventually go to Mexico for language school. My sister's boyfriend would speak to me in Spanish while we were cooking.

I was able to get hired at a Dutch company as an export logistics operator. On a daily basis I would communicate with agents in Latin American countries and customers who wished to ship chemicals to Latin America. One example of understanding intercultural communication challenges is the ex-

perience I had with our import supervisor in Rotterdam. After several months of talking via the telephone with him, I felt we had developed a nice working friendship and mutual respect. In an E-mail to him one day I bluntly stated that I had found a problem in one of our orders I had investigated on his side, and that it needed to be corrected right away. I personally felt I was direct, but in no way trying to place blame or point fingers. The E-mail was not interpreted the way I had intended. Similar situations have occurred with other colleagues of mine in Rotterdam. I often wonder why this miscommunication occurs. I partly think it has to do with the way U.S. Americans are portrayed overseas. I don't think that my Dutch colleagues expected such direct behavior from their female U.S. American counterpart.

I eventually found an incredible deal to study Spanish in Guanajuato, Mexico. For six weeks I lived in Guanajuato with an older woman in her two-story home. She only spoke Spanish. She was so helpful and always willing to do anything for anyone, but half the time I didn't know what she was asking me. Although my Spanish was improving I found it hard to communicate about simple day-to-day activities. I always forgot the word for spoon, and trying to communicate about how to do the laundry was difficult. I spent a lot of time in the outdoor cafés talking to the local wait staff and university students.

Once I had finished the language school I was hired again at the Dutch firm where I was previously employed. A Dutch man transferred to our office from the Rotterdam office. We slowly became friends and soon were officially dating. His view of the United States was typical of the way I think that many Europeans in general feel—that the United States is an arrogant country that only thinks of itself and nothing else outside its borders. We had many discussions about politics, religion, and social reform. I found that he and I think very much alike on many issues. However, when it came to relational issues, we had different ideas about such things as relationships with past partners and mutual friends. I think our communication styles were so different that we just couldn't ever get on the same plane. I don't think this was because we were born in two different countries as much as that we were two totally and completely different people.

When I think of intercultural communication I tend to think of communicating with people from other countries or other races. However, we all have our own culture based on the type of family we were raised in, the friends we hang around with, and the community in which we live. This sometimes is the hardest barrier to cross . . . the barrier that stands between you and the person next door. I think the greatest thing I learned from your Intercultural Communication class was awareness. I've always been interested in what's going on outside my own walls, but I don't believe enough people have this interest. I hope more and more students will learn to appreciate our world as a whole from taking your course.

Christopher Dixon, *enrollment manager (Missouri)*

Dear Dr. Dillon,

My name is Christopher Dixon and I am a white male who grew up in a small town in northern Missouri. From the time I could walk until the time I landed at Southwest Missouri State University in 1996, I lived in my hometown of slightly less than 10,000 people. I knew everyone in my high school, and my graduating class had around 155 people in it. For the most part, my daily contact with people from different cultures, backgrounds, and belief systems was limited.

Early on at SMSU, I met Dr. Randy Dillon who mentioned that I might want to take a course titled Intercultural Communication because it might help me have a better understanding of the world around me. It was during this class that I realized that even people who were from very similar backgrounds and seemed to be exactly the same on the surface could have views on life that varied significantly from mine! We discussed how colloquialisms, sayings, and even some words can mean different things in different parts of the country. We learned that people communicate differently depending on their socioeconomic status and depending on their position within a certain organization or entity.

Throughout the semester, our Intercultural Communication class learned that we should not fear or shy away from those who believe and/or communicate differently than we do, nor do we have to be ashamed of our own cultural experiences. Rather, we learned to be aware and sensitive to backgrounds that varied from our own. During that semester and long after the class was over, I slowly began to recognize people around me who were not only raised in a different environment, but also recognized that they held viewpoints that were quite separate from mine. They held on to their beliefs—sometimes quite passionately—and yet I could still find common ground with them. If nothing else, the class began opening my eyes to the similarities we all share as humans.

After graduating college, I accepted a position in college recruiting/admissions with a local private college. Within a short time frame I went from dealing with college students and professors to meeting people from virtually every walk of life! I met people who were on one end of the political spectrum or the other: rich or poor, old or young, straitlaced or wild, locals or immigrants. While I cannot say that I have met every type of person there is to meet, I can certainly say that I have been fortunate enough to meet people with all types of life experiences. Currently, I work in admissions in Springfield, Missouri, for a school that trains massage therapists. When people come in to meet with me they share many of their life experiences and how those life experiences have helped frame their identity.

Possibly the biggest difference that my examination and study of intercultural communication made for me was in my ability to listen to others for who they are. The class was an introduction to the idea that we can all meet others where they are. When someone comes into my office and shares his or her life experience with me, those experiences may be drastically different than my own. I may or may not agree with that person or be able to understand where that individual is coming from. But regardless of where people have been or what they believe, I can listen and learn something from them. I recently completed a book of truths and in it I wrote something to the effect of, "I have never met two people who are exactly the same. Each of us has our own unique personality that is different from everyone else on earth." Pulling from the ideas I was first introduced to several years ago in Intercultural Communication, I could probably finish the truth with something we all need to understand and live by: Not only is each of us created uniquely, our uniqueness is something to be proud of!

Kurtis Lane, *second lieutenant, U.S. Marine Corps (Virginia)*

Dear Dr. Dillon,

Understanding and applying knowledge gained in my Intercultural Communication class has greatly led to a more enriched understanding of the diversities within our society and in others. My limited understanding of cross-cultural barriers came through my experiences in the military and my time spent in Japan. In January of 1994 I was given the opportunity to spend six months in Okinawa, Japan, and to visit the mainland. I was in awe of its extreme diversity as compared to that of the United States. I sought to better understand my surroundings, knowing that I would have to return to Japan later on in my military career. After serving eight years in the military I left active duty and became a reservist in order to pursue a degree that would later lead to a future as an officer.

Dr. Dillon, your Intercultural Communication class seemed very interesting to me. I wanted a chance to learn more about dealing with the various cultures. For example, I learned in class that the military had a culture of its own and that I was a part of it. I was able to share some of that culture with my fellow classmates in a presentation given at the conclusion of the semester. The chance to learn through other students' presentations proved to be invaluable to my career and helped to enhance the whole learning process. The communication process is to be respected from both sides for mutual learning to take place. Understanding one's own culture first and how it relates to others will greatly contribute to a clearer and better understanding of the diverse cultures within this world. Respect becomes a double-edged sword that can cut both ways. I later understood that what may be acceptable in American culture can be completely rejected in Japanese culture. The same holds true for other cultures, and knowing the barriers and limits can greatly improve one's understanding through the learning process.

In the service we tend to be proud and feel a bit of ethnocentrism when it comes to viewing ourselves in the world and how we stack up to people of other countries. I feel it is important to remember that cultures are defined by their differences and that conformity can strip another culture of its true identity. In helping other countries with internal and external problems, I believe that should not involve cultural conformity. Instead it's important to preserve what makes a culture unique. My Intercultural Communication class has helped me to realize from a scholar's view the importance of autonomy and diversity. We as Americans can learn a lot from the various cultures of this world and take the good things we perceive back with us, but we should never attempt to judge another's culture.

I believe that everyone should experience a class like this; it can help enrich a person's life. Even if someone never leaves the country or the state of Missouri, the class can help one to better understand the global issues that define our place in this world. Since graduating from college in May of 2004 and returning to active duty in the military I have had a chance to exercise the teachings from this and many other classes. Intercultural Communication has helped me to better understand my place in society and to see how others contribute to our culture and to many others. You see, cultures rub off on each other; they take from one another, that is how they grow. In the military we get a chance to experience a wide range of diversity in our travel and interaction with other cultures in the world. We contribute to them and bring back with us what we learn. This helps us to grow and better understand the world in which we live.

Marlo Hamilton, *zone account manager (Missouri)*

Dear Dr. Dillon,

I am from a very small town in northwest Arkansas. When I was growing up, there were only white children in my classes, and my exposure to people of other races was very limited. It wasn't until I went to college that I made my first black friend, not to mention my first Indian friend and Asian friend. I was excited to be around different types of people and make new friends when I got to college.

In my junior year of college I took my first intercultural communication class with you. One of the first discussions we had was about the different metaphors for diversity. The class discussion was lively, as even a small, diverse crowd had strong opinions on what metaphor best described society overall. Were we a melting pot of all kinds of different people, all melting into each other and soaking up other cultures' "flavors" into one big cultural soup? Or were we a garden salad—all tossed together in the big bowl of life but still maintaining our own identities? The image that stuck with me all these years was that of a tapestry—each person was a thread in the fabric, interconnected and creating the bigger picture while still being affected, complemented, overshadowed, or interweaving with threads of different color, texture, and feel.

I lived for a while in London working as an intern at the London Chamber of Commerce and Industry. While there I had several intercultural discoveries, and I would not have appreciated these quite as much if it weren't for my study of intercultural communication. Often, I recalled a lecture about culture shock and reentry culture shock because of the visual imagery that went along with it. Stages of culture shock could be understood and visualized through the letters U and W [see Martin & Nakayama,

2007]. *The gist of the* W *hypothesis was that a person is given the opportunity to travel and go to another country. Of course, at first, you are excited and can't wait to get there. That is the top of the* W. *Then you arrive, and even though it may be exciting and new at first, slowly a feeling of homesickness approaches, which is the bottom of the first half of the* W. *Then things begin to pick up, you make a few friends, learn your way around, and start to feel as though you've conquered your new territory. That is the middle of the* W, *as you are on your way back up. Your trip may come to an end and you are excited to go home and prepare to leave. Once you arrive home, however, things aren't as exciting as they were. Things feel different, or they still feel the same even though you're different, and again, you are at the bottom of the second half of the* W. *I liked this theory because it had a happy ending; you came back up again and finished the* W *because after time, you were able to readjust to your old surroundings and remember fondly your time abroad.*

I actually lived this W *hypothesis while in London, and my being aware of the stages helped somehow. It helped to know that I was in a period of readjusting and it would take time, but inevitably I would get used to my new surroundings and learn my way around. And I did. I was able to accept my adjustment period for what it was. It was not eternal misery, but a brief period of time where I had to get used to a new place and make it comfortable. When I returned home, I knew to expect a little bit of sadness. Although I had missed my family, it wasn't long before home felt ordinary and dull compared to the excitement I eventually felt for London. But, of course, the ordinary and dull subsided, because life picked right up where I left off and I was able to cope with that as well. This* W *hypothesis stuck with me and has been in the back of my mind even with the smaller steps that I have taken in life, such as when I graduated from college and moved to an entirely new town.*

Because of my intercultural class I'm able to understand different types of people, their frame of reference, and find a way to communicate with them. In situations where people make comments about religious beliefs or specific races, I am prepared to question them on their comment and way of thinking, and come across as educated, not accusing or argumentative. I think that alone is one of the most important lessons to take away from classes in intercultural communication and diversity.

Reflections on Students' Letters: Bringing It Back to the Classroom

Receiving letters from Mindy, Christopher, Kurtis, and Marlo delighted me. If anything, it provided an opportunity to reconnect with them as they continue their lifelong lessons of intercultural communication competence and diversity. I admire Mindy's motivation to learn more about diversity, languages, and interacting with people from other cultures. Through both professional and personal interactions Mindy has acquired an acute awareness of intercultural competence. I immediately noticed in Mindy's letter how specific she used the term "U.S. American" to refer to herself. One of the first lessons I give in my intercultural courses is the specificity of language, including how one talks about oneself. Intercultural competence includes realizing that the identifier "American" includes not only persons from the United States, but also people from North, Central, and South America. Just the elegant care Mindy takes in identifying herself as a U.S. American demonstrates she is sensitive to how identity terms are used, a lesson in intercultural competence that probably served her well when she was living in Mexico.

Mindy talks firsthand about the stereotypes people from other national cultures have of U.S. Americans. For example, she mentions that "Dutch colleagues [were surprised by] direct behavior from their female U.S. American counterpart." Mindy realizes that generalizations will always be there and one must work to learn why there are such stereotypes and how to counter them. By being the target of stereotypes herself I am confident that Mindy has developed the skills to maneuver around stereotypes when communicating with people from different cultures.

Mindy's letter begins and ends with topics that illustrate her continued growth in learning more about diversity and multiculturalism. The early advice given to her about "no dating black guys" exemplifies what several of my students arriving in my intercultural communication classes think of diversity—as a black and white issue. Diversity can be a black/white issue, but diversity is much more; it is multicolor, multiracial, multinational, multiethnic, multiregional, and so on. Recognizing this helps one navigate the challenges of intercultural competence, and Mindy has learned this. Near the end of her letter she states that "we all have our own culture based on the type of family we were raised in, the friends we hang around with, and the community in which we live." Intercultural communication researchers Myron Lustig and Jolene Koester (2003) state that, "Knowledge about your own culture will help you to understand another culture" (p. 69). Mindy's awareness of who she is and her own culture is a foundation of her intercultural competence. Culture begins where the student is, and as Mindy so aptly stated, the most difficult barrier is "the barrier that stands between you and the person next door."

Mindy's references to barriers among people, even the person next door, has spurred me to consider barriers that I may be neglecting in my classes. Questions such as "What are the barriers that separate people?" and "What are the barriers that keep people at a disadvantage?" need further exploration. One barrier to take a look at is inequalities involving social economic class and the increasing digital divide. When Mindy mentions communicating internationally via E-mail it makes me think about those individuals who do not have access to E-mail and the world of the Internet.

Whereas Mindy focused on diversity, she has encountered it through people who are from different countries. Christopher focuses on the diversity he has encountered in the local community, more specifically in his work with clients in Springfield, Missouri. As a former college recruiter and in his current occupation as a recruiter for a professional massage training school, Christopher continues to work on learning how to interact with different kinds of people. Tatum (1997) clarifies such an ability:

> It should be clear that diversity is not the end in itself. It is not *just* about being friends. It *is* about being allies and becoming effective agents of change. To work effectively as an agent of change in a pluralistic society, it is necessary to be able to connect with people different from oneself. (p. 212)

Christopher is not afraid of communicating with people who are different from him. He emphasizes, "we should not fear or shy away from those who believe and/or communicate differently than we do, nor do we have to be ashamed of our own cultural experiences." This statement sums up an important lesson of intercultural competence that I hope to get across to my students.

Another important point from Christopher's letter about diversity and multiculturalism comes when he remarks, "If nothing else, the class began opening my eyes to the similarities we all share as humans." Christopher understands that intercultural competence involves cultural differences but also how people and cultures are similar. He possesses what Gallos et al., (1997) refer to as "a cardinal requirement for diversity education—holding on to differences and similarities at the same time. . . . It requires freely and passionately embracing paradox" (p. 218). Intercultural competence in my courses involves recognizing the common humanity we share. Humankind faces basic questions of the world around us and the needs that must be met. However, differences result in how these questions and needs are addressed depending on a range of values within a culture (Kluckhohn & Strodtbeck, 1961). Differences among people can be informative, but so can their similarities.

Christopher writes, "Possibly the biggest difference that my examination and study of intercultural communication made for me was in my ability to listen to others for who they are. The class was an introduction to the idea that we can all meet others where they are." Christopher's success in his workplace hinges on listening to what his clients have to say, including helping them formulate the questions they may have. Part of this listening is allowing others to feel comfortable in asking questions. Christopher's letter more than anything makes me pause to think about the importance of listening and allowing students to explore through asking questions.

In the book, *Learning to Question*, Paulo Freire, in a letter exchange with Antonio Faundez, writes:

> For an educator with this attitude there are no stupid questions or final answers. Educators who do not castrate the curiosity of their students who themselves become part of the inner movement of the act of discovery, never show disrespect for any question whatsoever. Because, even when the question may seem to them to be ingenuous or wrongly formulated, it is not always so for the person asking it. In such cases, the role of educators, far from ridiculing the student, is to help the student to rephrase the question so that he or she can thereby learn to ask better questions. (Freire & Faundez, 1989, p. 37)

Although I have known for a long time that learning through questions is an important tool for increasing intercultural competence, this "pedagogy of questioning" that Freire and Faundez refer to (p. 140) will be given more attention in my future classes. "[W]hen students are free to ask questions on a subject, it can often give their teachers a new angle, enabling them later to engage in more critical reflection" (Freire & Faundez, 1989, p. 33).

Appreciating humanity and the mutual lessons that cultures can share with one another is a central theme in the third letter from my former student Kurtis. Kurtis is different from the other three students. Before taking my course he had eight years of military service that gave him the opportunity to live and work in foreign cultures such as Japan. Even so, Kurtis says that by taking a course in intercultural communication after being overseas, it gave him a stronger self-awareness and an awareness that the military "had a culture of its own, and that I was part of it."

What I find the most provocative about Kurtis's letter is that he tackles head-on the issue of ethnocentrism. He writes, "In the service we tend to be proud and feel a bit of ethnocentrism when it comes to viewing ourselves in the world and how we stack up to people of other countries." Yet, this military officer who is proud of his service and his country is wary of being ethnocentric and writes that the United States "can learn a lot from the various cultures of this world." Kurtis seems to be able to balance the juxtaposition of military leadership and learning from others. He has chosen a military career armed with the formal knowledge of intercultural communication and its importance in today's global society. This makes me not only optimistic about his future, but also for the United States and its military (if it has officers like Kurtis). Kurtis exemplifies an important part of intercultural competence: an appreciation of the cultural differences around the world and the mutual, collaborative learning that comes with such appreciation.

Kurtis is motivated to continually learn and he successfully connects those classroom lessons with his life experiences. He says, "Since graduating from college . . . and returning to active duty in the military I have had a chance to exercise the teachings from this and many other classes." This statement coincides with what McKeachie (1994) says about the connection between teaching and lifelong learning:

> Human beings receive pleasure from doing things well. To the degree that teachers can help students develop a sense of standards that will enable them to see that they are developing increasing skill, teachers can also contribute to the goal of continued learning after the class has been completed. (p. 351)

Kurtis's letter is an example of continued critical reflection on both his intercultural interaction in the military as well as what he has learned in the Intercultural Communication classroom. He has taken into account the facts from his life and classroom experiences, but more so, has gained valuable insights for future learning.

While working on this chapter I more than ever like the pedagogical role that teacher Jennifer Obidah describes. Obidah likens herself to being "a border guide who helps students to acquire necessary skills to negotiate unfamiliar territory and consider their life experiences in light of class readings and discussions" (Enns & Forrest, 2005, p. 20). Ancis and Ali (2005) agree that "exercises that encourage students to reflect on their own experiences of privilege and discrimination may help them to better understand the lived experiences of others" (p. 96). One of the things that I can do in my classroom is to encourage students to reflect more on their own life experiences through the use of mini assignments and narratives, much like Kurtis and the other three former student contributors in this chapter have done.

The fourth letter, from Marlo, reiterates what has been said before concerning the feedback loop of students teaching and teachers learning. Marlo's letter reminds me of the importance of visualization techniques that I need to keep in my current and future intercultural communication courses. For Marlo visualization is essential in understanding the world around her. She refers to visualizing the models of cultural diversity presented early in the class, and how she sees the world as a tapestry "the image that stuck with me all these years." She uses visualization again when she relates the W hypothesis in order to understand the stages of culture and reentry culture shock she experienced with her internship sojourn to London and her return to the United States.

Throughout her letter Marlo understands being the "other," whether it is being the girl from Arkansas going to a Missouri school or being a U.S. American working in London. She has a good sense of who she is and this awareness has carried her through life changes that have occurred both inside and outside her native culture. Marlo displays empathy for those who practice a different religion, think a different way, or speak in an accent that says, "You are not from around here." She has even experienced how her nonverbal expressions are interpreted differently in another culture. These are all important skills associated with intercultural competence. Marlo may portray herself as the other, but all of us can relate to the adjustments and adaptations new living arrangements and lifestyle changes entail.

"Education is not complete until students not only have acquired knowledge but can act on that knowledge in the world" (Colby, Ehrlich, Beaumont, & Stephens, 2003, p. 7). All through Marlo's letter she acts on what she has learned concerning diversity and multiculturalism. As a teacher the most intriguing part of Marlo's letter comes in the last paragraph where she comments about being around different kinds of people. "In situations where people make comments about religious beliefs or specific races, I am prepared to question them on their comments and way of thinking, and come across as educated, not accusing, or argumentative." I would like to follow up on this further with Marlo because I believe this is a needed skill of intercultural competence that my current and future students should know more about.

Marlo's letter makes me pause and evaluate how issues of privilege and oppression are presented in my diversity and intercultural communication classes. More than ever I believe that I need to implement a social justice approach in my teaching of intercultural communication especially in the areas of how privilege is conferred and from whom. Torres (2004) writes,

> The praxis of social justice involves educators who not only "teach" students to talk about and examine critically the many things that are happening today that impact their lives, but also how to act upon their knowledge using "moments of possibilities" to confront everything that legitimates inequity and perpetuates inequality. (p. 15)

One way to work toward this goal is to help my students frame class discussions and gain awareness of issues and barriers that are a result of privilege and oppression. Ways of managing conflict that arises from differentials in power is another method that my students need to be exposed to in the classroom. In other words, not just noting the differences, but dealing effectively and working through differences leads to increased intercultural competence. For example, I could offer extra credit to students to participate in one of the many conflict management workshops offered on campus and in the local community. A service-learning project could be another way for students to work with and get a firsthand experience of working with those who may be less privileged or who have a different worldview. Learning about culture can help students themselves become empowered, liberated, and active (Nieto, 1999). Ways of working through the political, economic, and social systems to confront abuses of power, injustice, prejudice, and discrimination from a social justice perspective would add to future diversity and intercultural communication courses.

The letters from Mindy, Christopher, Kurtis, and Marlo provide several things to reflect upon my own continued intercultural competence and the pedagogy of teaching diversity and intercultural communication. What have these four former students taught me so that I can bring their real-world experiences with intercultural competence back again to my classroom? I realize that I have left out things from the students' letters that other readers would find more interesting for exploration. This is OK because the intent is for readers to discover what they want to ponder and even compare and contrast their own experiences with diversity. I know that when I revisit these student letters I will also find something new. I look forward to such an engagement.

I am impressed with all four of these former students and how they handled the intercultural situations each faced since leaving my course. These letters remind me that students take concepts learned from a course and make them their own. A lesson for me to keep in mind as a teacher is that "growth is not something done to them; it is something they do" (Dewey, 1966, p. 42). I played only a part in these students' learning about intercultural competence. Knowledge, skills, and most importantly, the attitude to be motivated to continually learn about the diverse world around them cannot be done to them. It is something each person must do for effective learning to take place.

Reviewing these student letters has made me stop and reconsider those issues that I may no longer spend time on in class. For example, for the past few semesters in Intercultural Communication I have only made a passing mention of the different metaphors that characterize U.S. cultural diversity. However, Marlo in her letter states that these metaphors made a powerful visual impact on the way that she comprehends cultural diversity. This encourages me to reevaluate: Should I go back and spend more time on these metaphors of cultural diversity for my future intercultural communication courses?

These letters demonstrate to me the diversity of my own students. Take, for example, their writing styles in each of the four letters. Mindy takes you on a personal journey. Kurtis gets straight to the point. Christopher's identity is strongly influenced by his alma mater, and this is illustrated in the respect he gives to his educational experience. Marlo will take a bit to get going, but once she does—watch out. Although this is a small sample of four students, the tone of the two female students, Mindy and Marlo, was of a more personable style, whereas the two male students, Kurtis and Christopher, wrote in a formal style referring to me as Dr. Dillon and using their formal names. I know them from class as Kurt and Chris. Even though a majority of my students are white, come from within a 150-mile radius of Missouri State University, and speak English, each is similar and different from the other.

Concluding Remarks

Gallos et al. (1997) state: "Learning about diversity in all its forms is a life-long undertaking. It is not something quickly or ever finally mastered. The more we learn, the more we realize how much there is to learn" (p. 105). I find myself at the end of this chapter wanting to know and learn more from these former students. Additional questions have been raised about the topics of diversity and intercultural competence and the teaching of such topics. Isn't that what teaching and learning is all about? I know that this interplay between teaching and learning is what made me go into the study of diversity and intercultural competence.

This project has spurred me to contact Mindy, Christopher, Kurtis, and Marlo for follow-up face-to-face interviews for additional examples and addressing new questions I have. I'm curious also about what they didn't talk about in their letters. Consequently, I have contacted other former students who are not part of this chapter to write me letters recounting their professional and personal experiences with diversity and intercultural competence. I believe that these letters and interviews from former intercultural communication students will enhance instruction and learning in my future intercultural communication courses. I will invite these former students from the real-world of intercultural competence back into my classroom to share their knowledge, their skills, and their attitudes (even when it was difficult) about intercultural communication competence with my current and future students. This connection from the real world back to the classroom provides a connection with former students that goes beyond what is usually asked of alumni—donations of money. These are donations of their experiences with intercultural competence. It continues the loop of learning, of bringing intercultural competence from the classroom to the real world and back again, that is essential in our multicultural, pluralistic world.

References

Ancis, J. R., & Ali, S. R. (2005). Multicultural counseling to training approaches: Implications for pedagogy. In C. Z. Enns & A. L. Sinacore (Eds.), *Teaching and social justice: Integrating multicultural and feminist theories in the classroom* (pp. 85–97). Washington, DC: American Psychological Association.

Banks, J. A. (2000). Multicultural education: Characteristics and goals. In J. A. Banks & C. A. M. Banks (Eds.), *Multicultural education: Issues and perspectives* (4th ed., pp. 3–30). New York: Wiley.

Bateson, M. (1997). Foreword. In A. Neumann & P. Peterson (Eds.), *Learning from our lives: Women, research, and autobiography in education* (pp. vii–viii). New York: Teachers College Press.

Boulding, E. (1988). *Building a global civic culture.* New York: Teachers College Press.

Boyer, E. L. (1990). *Scholarship reconsidered: Priorities of the professoriate.* Princeton, NJ: Carnegie Foundation for the Advancement of Teaching.

Chen, G. M., & Starosta, W. J. (2003). Intercultural awareness. In L. A. Samovar & R. E. Porter (Eds.), *Intercultural communication: A reader* (10th ed., pp. 344–353). Belmont, CA: Wadsworth/Thomson Learning.

Clandinin, D., & Connelly, F. (2000). *Narrative inquiry: Experience and story in qualitative research.* San Francisco: Jossey-Bass.

Colby, A., Ehrlich, T., Beaumont, E., & Stephens, J. (2003). *Educating citizens: Preparing America's undergraduates for lives of moral and civic responsibility.* San Francisco: Jossey-Bass.

Dewey, J. (1966). *Democracy and education: An introduction to the philosophy of education.* New York, NY: The Free Press.

Enns, C. Z., & Forrest, L. M. (2005). Toward defining and integrating multicultural and feminist pedagogies. In C. Z. Enns & A. L. Sinacore (Eds.), *Teaching and social justice: Integrating multicultural and feminist theories in the classroom* (pp. 3–23). Washington, DC: American Psychological Association.

Freire, P. (1970/1995). *Pedagogy of the oppressed.* New York: Herder and Herder.

Freire, P., & Faundez, A. (1989). *Learning to question: A pedagogy of liberation.* New York: Continuum.

Gallos, J. V., Ramsey, V. J., & Associates. (1997). *Teaching diversity: Listening to the soul, speaking from the heart.* San Francisco: Jossey-Bass.

Hantzis, D. M. (1995). *Performing experience(s)/shifting to self.* Paper presented at the Speech Communication Association Convention, San Antonio, TX.

Jardine, D. W., Clifford, P., & Friesen, S. (2003). *Back to the basics of teaching and learning: Thinking the world together.* Mahwah, NJ: Erlbaum.

Kluckhohn, F., & Strodtbeck, F. (1961). *Variations in value orientations.* Chicago: Row & Peterson.

Knapp, M. S., & Woolverton, S. (1995). Social class and schooling. In J. A. Banks & C. A. McGee Banks (Eds.), *Handbook of research of multicultural education* (pp. 548–569). New York: MacMillan.

Kohls, L. R. (2001). *Survival kit for overseas living* (4th ed.). Yarmouth, ME: Intercultural Press.

Lustig, M. W., & Koester, J. (2003). *Intercultural competence: Interpersonal communication across cultures.* Boston: Allyn & Bacon.

Martin, J., & Nakayama, T. (2007). *Intercultural communication in contexts* (4th ed., pp. 309–313). Boston, MA: McGraw-Hill.

McKeachie, W. J. (1994). *Teaching tips: Strategies, research and theory for college and university teachers.* Lexington, MA: D. C. Heath and Company.

Nieto, S. (1999). Multiculturalism, social justice, and critical teaching. In I. Shor & C. Pari (Eds.), *Education is politics: Critical thinking across differences, K–12: A tribute to the life and work of Paolo Freire* (pp. 1–32). Portsmouth, NH: Boynton/Cook Heinemann.

Palmer, P. J. (1998). *The courage to teach: Exploring the inner landscape of a teacher's life.* San Francisco: Jossey-Bass.

Southwest Missouri State University Office of Institutional Research. (2005). Student information. SMSU Factbook. Retrieved April 20, 2005, from www.smsu.edu/oir/factbook/studentinfo.pdf.

Tatum, D. T. (1997). *Why are all the black kids sitting together in the cafeteria?: And other conversations about race.* New York: Basic Books.

Torres, M. N. (2004). The role of participatory democracy in the critical praxis of social justice. In J. O'Connell, M. Pruyn, and R. C. Chavez (Eds.), *Social justice in these times* (pp. 15–31). Greenwich, CT: Information Age Publishing.

U.S. Census Bureau (2000). Springfield, Missouri. Retrieved May 12, 2005, from http: factfinder.census.gov.

8

NARRATIVE ANALYSIS OF A STRENGTHS-BASED APPROACH TO PREPARING STUDENTS FOR GRADUATE AND POSTGRADUATE EDUCATION

Karen Bullock

With Crystal Smith, Jessica Hernandez, Dalkis Muir,
and Aaron Scott Taylor

Students enter the learning environment with many strengths and learning needs. Social structures of class, race, gender, and ethnicity create varied experiences through unequal distribution of social opportunities. Those who are committed to improving the imbalance must take a proactive posture on educating future leaders about diversity and its relationship to social stratification and global functioning. Students may thrive or be inhibited by learning encounters, depending on the ability of the educator to assess and address diversity issues. This chapter exemplifies a strengths-based approach to teaching diversity and includes narratives as a tool for beginning a potentially life-changing process.

Class, race, gender, and ethnicity are macrostructures that shape microstructural educational worlds. These structures organize society as a whole and contribute to the diversity in social environments. They create varied experiences through unequal distribution of social opportunities. As a young African American girl growing up in rural North

Carolina, my awareness of class, race, gender, and ethnicity were convoluted. At times the lines of stratification were invisible, while at other times they were extremely apparent. In Warren County, where the land mass was vast and my personal scope of interaction was limited to about 8,000 people, retrospectively my exposure to diversity was derisory. By and large, the residents of the town of Manson, where most of my cultural insight and development took place, were poor—black and minimally educated. There were no clear social class distinctions. We all seemed to be equally poor and deprived of educational opportunities. An identifiably middle-class black was an anomaly in Manson. The whites in the town owned the means to production, and blacks were the laborers. No other ethnic groups resided in our town and, thus, our world was completely black and white.

In my black world, gender roles were often blurred. Men and women worked alongside one another, or there was no man present and women did the work inside and outside the home. Black men were in no better social position than black women. Our Southern Baptist values and traditions kept us content and to some degree complacent. Since most of the people in my intimate surroundings looked like me, sounded like me, shared my cultural values, and affirmed my existence, the homogeneity of my community shielded me from the complexity of the issues of diversity and the visceral impact it has on society at large.

Even though Manson was approximately 85% black, the race stratification in my social environment was blatant. The significance of race differences was distinguishable by the fact that whites were the minority in our little town, yet, they were the shop owners, the owners of the farms, bosses in the factories where most of the town's people worked, and were overrepresented as the educators in our schools. Unfortunately (or fortunately), as a child, I and my siblings were not cognizant of the unequal distribution of social opportunities. We lived happily in our single-parent household, desiring very little in spite of the fact that we had very little social capital. My mother, who went from being a domestic worker (nanny/housekeeper) to becoming a factory worker, impressed upon my three brothers and me that education was the only thing that would keep us out of factories. She would repeatedly say, "Education is the equalizer."

Warren County was/is one of the poorest counties in North Carolina. Our schools lacked resources. Our communities lacked jobs. Trying to attain the goal that my mother laid before me meant stepping outside my comfort zone, going beyond my very comfortable, predominantly black world of Manson. Taking the risk of being different. Taking the risk of being less prepared for rigorous, comprehensive educational experiences than my counterparts from more affluent families and communities. The road out of Manson and into the capital city of Raleigh was wrought with educational challenges and rewards. As a young African American woman entering North Carolina State University, I didn't think that I was equipped with the necessary resources to succeed in an institution of higher education. I never imagined that a poor black girl from a single-parent household, from the backwoods of rural Warren County could earn a master's degree from an Ivy League institution as I did at Columbia University, and a Ph.D. from Boston University, then, go on to become a college professor who educates graduate students across gender, social class, race, and ethnic differences. It was my own struggle to come to terms with social stratification in predominantly white institutions that spawned my commitment to teaching diversity and helping students understand that barriers to success can be overcome by multicultural experiences.

The unequal distribution of access and opportunities based on social structures in society can be obliterated with the appropriate educational tools and skills. Although there are a range of character traits including age, sexual orientation, and abilities that make us diverse, this chapter will focus primarily on class, race, gender, and ethnicity as components of diversity because they make up three major oppressive systems in the United States: classism, racism, and sexism.

The Raison d'Être of the Academy

To understand how class, race, gender, and ethnicity shape our lives, we must understand two appurtenances of these systems. These are hierarchies of stratification that distribute social rewards and opportunities differently, and are systems of power and subordination (Grusky, 2001). The pedagogy of sociology and social work lends itself well to the teaching of diversity, including social stratification. As an educator, my teaching philosophy is *the integration of diversity as a theme throughout the curriculum, using a strengths-based approach that combats social stratification that can cripple success in institutions of higher education.*

The raison d'être of the academy is to provide quality education to our students and prepare them to be contributing members of society. Educators accomplish this through knowing who our students are, not just in terms of their grade point averages, but also as whole individuals who have lives beyond the classroom and who look to us for guidance and direction in their future. As we communicate the values of an education to those we come in contact with, we should take into consideration the structures that make us diverse. These structures arrange groups and individuals in patterned ways and allocate society's resources unequally. They are systems of power and domination.

Class, race, gender, and ethnicity are made up of structured relationships in which the affluent dominate the poor, men dominate women, and white people dominate people of color (Feagin & Feagin, 2003). These hierarchies of domination and subordination intersect in complex ways and are operationalized through different races' and/or ethnicities' varying rights and privileges. Nevertheless, because diversity can contribute to an imbalance of power between individuals and groups, it is important to undertake the subject matter at the college level before individuals find themselves in positions of power over others. As we educators prepare our students to be directors and supervisors, practitioners and clinicians, we have a duty to address these hierarchies as a means for improving the social conditions of the environments in which we live and work.

Diversity curricula have been strongly supported in the institutions where I have held faculty appointments. Teaching in social work and sociology has given me great opportunities to infuse diversity content into curricula. Whether I teach a research class, a practice class, or a theory class, diversity is a constant theme throughout my teaching. A strengths-based approach to teaching diversity helps educators to view our students as "valued and respected for their ability to survive and adapt, and there is a sense of hope regarding each person's capability to continue to learn and develop over time in relationships with others" (Rapp & Poertner, 1992, p. 17). According to Saleebey (2001), this translates into students being engaged in ongoing communication with the educator. Students are recognized as having some authority in their lives and having the right to self-determine their career path. They are resourceful and capable of making decisions based on their own cultural values, attitudes, and norms. Inherent in the strengths perspective is the belief that students have the ability to resolve difficult situations, learn from experiences, and change their attitudes and behaviors. This is what we would want to foster in our protégés as they are exposed to diversity content and knowledge.

Diversity and Its Relationship to Social Stratification and Global Functioning

In order to bring change in society at large, the academy must take a proactive posture on the importance and significance of educating future leaders about diversity and its relationship to social stratification and global functioning. Having taught in undergraduate and graduate programs, in our homeland and abroad, I have had firsthand experience with how beneficial the learning can be to students in their formative years. Through the experience of international study abroad courses, students have been able to compare their culture to that of students in foreign countries and gain a minority perspective from a different vantage point. Having taught two courses in Mexico and two in the United Kingdom, I found that white students who enjoy the comforts of majority status in their homeland of the United States of America are deeply challenged by diversity as nonnatives and thus, as a minority. Figuring out how to develop respect for others' culture, norms, and beliefs while making the necessary adjustments to be deferential in our actions toward what is acceptable and appropriate social interaction is no easy feat. In other words, exposure to diversity challenges our social comfort level. We are more likely to choose to be in the company of people who validate our norms as opposed to annul them.

As the United States becomes increasingly more multicultural (U.S. Census Bureau, 2001), it will be imperative that professionals are equipped with training and education that guard against oppression and discrimination. The nonwhite population in the United States in 2002 made up 27% of the country's total population. That percentage is projected to increase by 11% in 20 years. By the year 2050, we can expect about 48% of U.S. citizenship to comprise people of color (Hobbs, & Stoops, 2002). The ethnic and racial makeup of the United States has changed more rapidly since 1965 than during any other period in history (Grieco & Cassidy, 2001), but political and professional leadership has changed very little.

World population is expected to increase by 29% over the next 25 years, with nearly all growth occurring in less-developed countries. There will be a slight shift toward becoming less male dominated (i.e., with a shift to a lower male-to-female ratio) than in 2000 (McDevitt & Rowe, 2002). Teaching diversity helps to prepare our students to function in a global society. Globalization has created opportunities for individuals to develop and maintain relationships across many cultures. Teaching students about culture and the significant influence it has on individual values, beliefs, and worldviews helps to prepare them for success. "Culture lives at the very heart of what it means to be human. . . . Objectivity is impossible since our understanding of the social work is inevitably filtered through the parochial worldviews that we inherit . . . from the culture into which we are born" (Angel & Williams, 2000, p. 27). These are just a few reasons why teaching diversity is important and timely. At issue is whether and how we engage the intelligence and talent of students in the deconstruction of social stratification and cultural diversity in our ever-increasing global society.

The business, political, and social interests of the United States will change with the population expansion of less-developed countries. Currently, the United States is the third most populous country on earth after China and India, yet it comprises less than 5% of the world's population (McDevitt & Rowe, 2002). The globalization of information and technology is creating new challenges to our conventional education content and curriculum. There is and will continue to be strong links between job performance and workplace diversity. For many companies, diversity equals productivity. For example, the Social Security Administration, which received one of the highest ratings for productivity and efficiency among federal agencies, is among the most diverse of any federal agency in terms of employment (Rodriquez, 2001). Organizational productivity resulting from diversely composed staff is the hallmark of successful world markets.

I have taught diversity content and entire courses on diversity in both undergraduate and graduate programs. To help prepare students for graduate and postgraduate education that will carry them into successful professional careers, faculty and administrators need to foster effective teacher-student relationships that reinforce resiliency, self-value (Brem, 2001), confidence, and sensitivity to the experiences of others. Students enter the learning environment with many strengths in addition to their weakness and need to acquire knowledge. Educators are in a unique position to affect students' lives on many levels. Education should go far beyond the mere imparting of knowledge. Students may thrive or be inhibited by the learning encounter, depending on the needs of the students and the ability of the educator to assess and attend to diversity issues. Our students rely on us to prepare them for their professional lives (Nieto, 2003). The strengths-based approach to mentoring in the teacher-student relationship can be effective across race, ethnic, gender, and class boundaries. Support provided in a mentoring capacity, particularly support that helps one to overcome diversity barriers, has been strongly correlated with career success (Denton, 1990).

For the past 11 years, I have taught diversity courses and content at predominately white institutions of higher education. I have had the dubious pleasure of preparing students to graduate from college and go on to accomplish their postgraduate professional goals. Drawing upon a perspective that emphasizes strengths and de-emphasizes social stratification fosters supportive relationships that are akin to mentoring relationships. As an African American female professor who has had my share of experiences associated with minority status in U.S. society, I have been able to bring to life the abstract concepts of human oppression and social stratification that helps both white and nonwhite students to think critically about their role in their professional, political, and social lives. A strengths-based approach to education offers an added advantage because it allows for the mentoring of students and not simply teaching them.

I define mentoring as an intense relationship in which a person with more experience and expertise (teacher) works closely with a less experienced person (student) to promote both professional and personal development. This is what I have done with many students whom I have taught to value and respect diversity. As an educator who mentors my students, I do a thorough assessment of their strengths and weakness. I nurture their autonomy, treat them as adults, help them maximize their skills, and create opportunities for them to grow and challenge. This pedagogical model incorporates mentoring, which fosters empowerment, to prepare students for success in a multicultural world. Integral to developing this pedagogical model is a commitment to education in collaboration with students, confronting ineffective systems, and strengthening existing social structures. The notion that education and empowerment are collaborative ventures supports the value of autonomy and nurtures the relationship between the teacher and student. This educational empowerment through diversity occurs when (1) engagement is viewed as a distinct activity that constitutes the initial step in developing a relationship, (2) the relationship between the teacher and the student is recognized as essential to the educational process, (3) communication focuses on the student's accomplishments and potential, (4) a student's ambitions and directives are addressed and not judged, and (5) mutual trust is established and acted upon by both the teacher and the student.

Mentoring to empower students is integral in the strengths-based approach to diversity education. The process of assisting students to discover and expend the resources and tools within and around them is empowerment. It has been recommended in the literature (Gutierrez & Lewis, 1999; Holmes, 1992; Rapport, 1990) that resources be tailored to individuals in such a way that those receiving the information have the opportunity to experience the personal power that leads to change in attitudes and behaviors. When diversity is taught, emphasis should be placed on the range of experiences, characteristics, and roles that contribute to one's survival skills, abilities, knowledge, resources, and desire that can be used to help individuals reach their goals. The strengths approach has a basic assumption that individuals have the capacity to grow, change, and adapt. Challenging our personal and professional frames that underlie traditional theories, models, and educational materials is the first step in denouncing the preoccupation with human deficits (Blundo, 2001). The traditional models are steeped in European American middle-class values and norms for well-being and human development (Fong, 2001).

A graduate education in social work helped me to begin to explore my pedagogical approach to diversity. I developed a skills set for working with individuals and groups as a social work practitioner that has been equally appropriate for my role as a college educator. If we are to prepare future professionals to work effectively with others, the general studies curriculum must include a diversity curriculum, as should content for advanced concentration courses. Students should learn that diversity is an important element of their basic skills level. For example, in teaching any subject matter, basic communication skills can be used to listen and respond to one person or to a classroom of many. The language used in classroom discourse should not be considered merely in terms of communication, as in everyday discourse. One needs to recognize and reflect on how communication in the teaching-learning process *is* educational discourse (Mercer, 1995). What we say to our students influences their lifelong decisions and actions. The oral and written language used in educational discourse serves a double function for minority students in particular. If the majority of students communicate using certain styles and patterns unfamiliar or uncomfortable for the minority student, the classroom discourse becomes problematic to minority students' learning. As formal institutions of socialization and enculturation, academic settings play a decisive role in transmitting culture by means of semiotic tools, particularly language. Successful participation in classroom discourse as a medium for knowledge building depends on having access to shared cultural knowledge, including rules of interpretation concerning educational talk and practice and educational ground rules (Edwards & Mercer, 1987). This is how we teach diversity.

Advocacy skills, including assertiveness and negotiation, should be a component of the teaching. The best way to teach diversity is to demonstrate its application to students. Educators who are involved in advocacy produce a range of opportunities for students to see this skill in action. Mentoring students typically involves some level of advocacy. Advocacy can serve students well in maneuvering through the college bureaucracy, but these skills can be used to improve the quality of life for one person or an entire community or to give voice to issues that less empowered people may not.

I typically begin teaching a diversity class by asking students to reframe their identities when they enter the educational setting. To go beyond merely abstract thoughts of diversity, I ask my students to set goals for themselves to see how they can be contributors or inhibitors to a fair and just society. As mentioned at the opening of this chapter, structures of diversity can contribute to equality and inequity. We discuss various components of diversity and the relevance to fair and just societies. Differences in race, gender, ethnicity, and class between the student and educator must be addressed as well. These structures and differential power of the institutional roles pose significant barriers to developing relationships that are conducive for mentoring in diversity (Bryk & Schneider, 2002; hooks, 1994). A body of research documents the contribution of a strong, trusting relationship between the educator and the student (Godshalk & Sosik, 2000; Johnson-Bailey & Cervero, 2002; Wright & Wright, 1987).

Having established the importance of a strengths-based perspective on mentoring to empower students, it is worth noting that other research has emphasized the significance of the development of social networks between students and teachers to enable students to succeed beyond undergraduate education. Social networks are key forms of institutional resources. Stanton-Salazar's (1997) research concluded that social networks provided support that was deemed necessary for social integration and success and were identified as "funds of knowledge associated with ascension within the educational system" (p. 11). For many students, the ability to cross cultural systems, overcome barriers, and develop the capacity to negate risk has much to do with developing resiliency and understanding of social systems in which they operate.

In graduate and postgraduate diversity education, I have been able to identify building blocks of a pedagogical framework that enables students to garner knowledge from the diversity curriculum and integrate it into their work with others in order to be principled and productive. These include (a) support, (b) empowerment, (c) boundaries and expectations, (d) constructive feedback, and (e) constructive use of time. Support consists of ways in which students are affirmed, accepted as different, given resources to meet their distinct educational needs, and appreciated for their contributions. Didactic instruction, including diversity knowledge, facts, and experiential learning, should occur in a supportive environment. Empowerment focuses on culturally specific values, attitudes, and beliefs that create opportunities for students to contribute to society in meaningful ways. In teaching and learning about diversity, each person must explore his or her own background and cultural frame of reference. The deconstruction of identities helps growth and learning to occur on a level that does not usually occur in an unstructured social environment.

Boundaries and expectations refer to clear and consistent limits to the support and empowerment that educators provide to those who are engaged in the diversity-learning environment. It is important to not become paternalistic and to maintain a professional relationship in the process. Role identification and setting limits on when, where, and how the teaching and mentoring will occur assists in adherences to boundaries and expectations. Expectations tend to change and are readjusted as students mature in their educational, professional, and personal lives. This process requires the application of diversity concepts and content that is taught in the curriculum. They are not unfamiliar to students when you begin to engage in the diversity-mentoring relationship. For example, there must be an exploration and identification of different cultures and patterns of relationships between the educator and the students. I have found students' perceptions of what is an appropriate role for them in response to diversity issues to be a function of the way they perceive social institutions have treated them (Bullock & Blundo, 2001). In other words, when students feel that they have had a supportive, fair, and equitable undergraduate educational experience, they are able to go into graduate and postgraduate education with a favorable outlook on how to bring about positive change in social conditions.

Constructive feedback is essential. An honest and open conversation about diversity and social justice must occur. Often there will be a difference of opinions during the exchange that allows for growth and insight on both sides. When I point out disparaging behaviors and attitudes that are racist, sexist, xenophobic, or homophobic, for example, students will sometimes resist and say, "That has nothing to do with racism at all." I listen to the student and ask, "How might we think differently about the occurrence?" I try to understand my students' perspectives, as I ask them to try to understand mine. I make every effort not to be dismissive and I ask the same of my students.

Critical feedback for learning is imperative when cultural knowledge is being imparted. Because it is usually tacit knowledge, taken for granted, it is seldom communicated explicitly. When students enter a course where diversity is taught, the linguistic, social, and cultural contexts of the students' everyday experiences represent the frame of reference through which they interpret and respond to what is said in the classroom discourse. Misunderstandings, originating from a discrepancy between what is assumed to be "common knowledge" (Edwards & Mercer, 1987) about people of different social statuses, races, genders, and ethnicities and what is being presented in the diversity classroom discourse arise. Critical feedback that frames the larger issues of oppression and discrimination helps those who have been fortunate enough to not experience those social vices to prepare to have meaningful relationships with those who have.

A constructive use of time cements the framework. Because educational contracts are time limited, whether it is a semester or a quarter, a summer block or one-day seminar, it is wise to set goals and objectives for the learning that are connected to a set of specific outcomes. Furthermore, the intensity of mentoring relationships demands that time spent be focused (Johnson-Bailey & Cervero, 2002), guided by insight drawn from the research and, more important, come from the observations and experiences of others.

No investigation to date has paid systematic attention to teaching diversity from a strengths-based perspective across class, race, gender, and ethnicity. This chapter presents a narrative analysis of theoretical traditions—not usually applied to teaching diversity—to exemplify the philosophy and pedagogy that prepared students for graduate and postgraduate education. The narratives include retrospective insight on what worked for students and what could be improved (Casey, 1995; Catalyst, 2001). Narrative analysis presupposes that reality is, in larger part, socially constructed, though each approaches differently the challenge of how this reality is constructed. According to Riessman (1993), narratives can provide us with a rich understanding of the world as our students experience it and enable us to create a learning environment that is based on mutual respect between the teacher and the learners.

The theory of learned behavior (Bandura, 1986) helps us to understand the intellectual imperative that highlights the importance of integrating multiple perspectives into the human experience through growth, challenge, and contrast. Discussion of students' differences in the classroom is no longer limited to cognitive style, cognitive development, motivation, and preferred physiological modality, but now includes socioeconomic class, race, ethnicity, gender, sexual identity, and abilities. I have applied a strengths-based model to teaching diversity for more than 10 years. Narratives are presented here for analysis of how this pedagogy for diversity can foster potentially life-changing education.

Student Letters

Crystal Smith, social work supervisor (Connecticut)

> *As an African American female, my early experiences with people of other races and ethnicities were partial. I lived in a drug-infested, crime-ridden, urban neighborhood. I was bused to predominately white schools. My interactions with other cultures during my school years were scarce because all of my friends were black. I was not comfortable interacting with white students.*
>
> *As I entered a predominately white college and chose my major, I found that other black students' experiences were similar to mine. Their contact with other cultures was also limited. I had two black professors (one being Karen Bullock) in graduate school and I was amazed by how much their credibility was challenged by the white students. One diversity experience in particular that stands out for me shows how resistant white students were to*

diversity. I remember a white student criticizing Professor Bullock and saying that she was an unnecessarily difficult professor. I did not agree. I shared with the student that my impressions of the professor was that she was passionate about the topic and she lectured in such a style that all students would be able to understand the concepts and complete the assignments. I felt that the white student may have been resistant because of her limited experiences with black educators. The student appeared to have a sense of entitlement and was offended by the professor's expectation for excellence. This experience reinforced how challenging it can be to promote diversity in our society and in the human services field specifically.

Diversity and its issues daily intersect with my work life. Currently, I am a social work administrator for child protection services. Cultural diversity is extremely important in my field of practice. However, my experiences have been that we professionals seldom emulate in our work what we have been trained in concerning cultural diversity. I believe that in order to become culturally competent one must immerse himself or herself in the culture, that is, learn about the norms, values, and beliefs. I believe that "knowledge" and "behavior" are mutually exclusive. What one knows might not transfer into behaviors. For example, in an investigation of a Latino family for child abuse, the white social workers described them as "enmeshed." As the supervisor, my assessment of this family and my knowledge about Latino culture told me that Latino families are close knit and often there is a matriarch or patriarch whom everyone respects. Instead of this being viewed as a positive and a strength, it was viewed as a negative by a less experienced practitioner.

As a young African American social work administrator who supervises a racially and gender-diverse staff, my experiences have been similar to my professor's, Dr. Bullock. My credibility and supervisory style are always challenged. I have supervised over 20 staff and found that the older white males and/or white females have the greatest difficulty with being supervised by a young black female. It seems to me that although we do diversity education, training, and promotion, it is still not clear how to put it into practice.

Jessica Hernandez, *graduate assistant (Connecticut)*

Dear Dr. Bullock,

As a Latina Honduran, learning about diversity has been tremendously helpful in understanding my experiences and the experiences of the communities where I work. I grew up in a mostly African American and Puerto Rican neighborhood that was economically segregated. Typically, my relationships were developed based on shared social class values and experiences that cut across racial boundaries. Many of my friends were black, and at that time, we all saw each other as being the same with the exception of a few different foods and holidays. I strongly identified with both cultures.

When I entered college, it was the first time that I was not surrounded by a majority of "my peers." I struggled to adapt to my new environment that had very little diversity. I tried very hard to surround myself with people who were more familiar, who "looked like me," so that I could feel comfortable. Unfortunately, this new environment did not share the same collective sense of community I had experienced growing up. African American and Latino students were less cohesive. I was reproached by some Latinos for "thinking I was black." It was a hard time for me. I didn't understand why these groups wanted to be so separate.

Dr. Bullock, by the time I enrolled in graduate school, the courses that you taught, which focused on the experiences of African Americans, were a great asset. I was working in communities that were very diverse and a large percentage of my clients were black children and families. I enjoyed being able to discuss different points of views and issues of diversity based on the experiences of African Americans in a classroom setting where I could learn from my peers. One of the most important concepts that I learned was how to identify the coping mechanisms that have been adopted by some members of the black community to deal with oppression. It has forced me to change my way of working with clients to include a more strengths-based perspective.

Taking your courses was the first time I was able to develop a mentoring relationship with a female of color. Interacting with you outside of the classroom made me feel comfortable with my own identity. I learned as much outside of the classroom from you sharing your experiences as I did inside the classroom. Your interest in learning about me and my culture made me feel validated. I gained more confidence in myself and in my ability to navigate throughout different cultures.

Bridging the gap between African American and Latino cultures is still an important theme for me. Most likely I will be working and living in these communities. Learning more about the particular experiences of these individuals has not only made me a better professional but it also affects the relationships that I maintain with the diverse group of friends and family in

*my life. I will rely upon the diversity education that empowered me through-
out graduate school in my postgraduate personal and professional life.*

Dalkis Muir, *financial law attorney (Massachusetts)*

*I am a native Panamanian woman who came to the United States at age
13. My family valued education and strong kinship networks. Although
Spanish is the primary language in Panama, my family spoke both Spanish
and a dialect of English. My family's educational values and success made
our transition to the United States and the English-speaking classroom of
the public education system much easier than, possibly, for some other
immigrants.*

*While pursuing my undergraduate degree, I took a sociology course with
Dr. Bullock that was focused on the black family. It was her approach to
teaching that connected me with the course. I learned that the most valuable
learning occurs through a supportive, mentoring-type exchange. I excelled
academically on the undergraduate level and was sure I could succeed in
graduate law school, especially after having passed the required graduate entrance exam. I decided to postpone entering graduate law school for one year
because of my mother's death. I needed the time to mourn her loss, which
occurred six months prior to receiving my bachelor's degree. I thought I could
fix the beginning and ending date of the grieving process. I was wrong! I
entered graduate law school and I began to grieve during my second year of
graduate law school. Because of the demands of graduate law school, I pushed
onward and it was not until a year and a half later that I realized I was
experiencing grief. The issues of diversity and how one manages school and
family commitment and values are critical. My cultural value and work
ethic made me want to keep going and producing. My connection to my
mother and her loss made me want to stop. I was conflicted. There is life
outside the classroom and students are asked to leave it at the door when we
come into the classroom. Most professors do not take cultural diversity into
consideration.*

*Understanding these challenges and dilemmas in the cultural context
can be taught in diversity classes. The diversity education that I received as
an undergraduate continues to be an educational resource for me in my personal and professional life.*

A class that focuses on diversity and understanding existing resources, values, and cultural beliefs makes it possible for students to live while they learn. Having a teacher who understood diversity and had an appreciation for different learning styles helped me to know what I needed in order to survive graduate law school. Too many times throughout my academic career, I sat in a classroom where the professor would teach a subject devoid of diversity issues. Professors conveyed the message "I am here to tell you what I know about the subject matter and whether you understand it or not is your problem, not mine." These frustrating experiences are disempowering. I found that academic success is not an individual process, nor an individual achievement. My success is attributed to my strengths of strong interpersonal relationships, guidance, and support that occurred before, during, and after I entered graduate law school.

Aaron Scott Taylor, *law student (Illinois)*

As a white male growing up in eastern North Carolina, I had limited experiences with peoples of different cultures, races, and ethnicities. As a result, my thoughts and views were shaped with bias. Feeling like something was missing from my life I yearned to escape the cultural deprivation of my small town.

As I entered the University of North Carolina Wilmington, I toyed with the many options that a university setting offers. One thing was certain: I wanted to develop academically as well as socially. After exploring a variety of course offerings, I found my calling in sociology. This discipline gave me the opportunity for more social interaction. I became intrigued with people of other cultures through various lectures and readings. From this fascination came the desire to interact and immerse myself in other cultures.

So I decided to study abroad to expand my cultural horizons. I began in Bremen, Germany, making stops in Bristol, England, and Wollongong, Australia, before finishing my degree at Copenhagen University in Denmark. It was on the second of my four study-abroad programs that I encountered Dr. Karen Bullock. She organized a course in International Social Welfare Policy at Bristol University in England. Conversations with Dr. Bullock inspired me to continue my travels in order to gain the cultural capital I would need to be successful. She remains in my life today as both mentor and friend.

I am currently a first-year law student in Chicago. I find that the cultural capital I gained through the course with Dr. Bullock has been extremely important. I still contact her regularly for guidance and advice. The knowledge and insight that I gained from her approach to educating students has helped me to be able to think on a different level than many of my colleagues in law school. I believe the primary reason for this is because my views were developed, as every student's views should be developed, through a pedagogical approach that integrates diversity in the learning experience.

I remain amazed at the ignorance and lack of cultural diversity I find throughout higher educational systems within the United States. I am similarly amazed at the lack of knowledge many of my colleagues have on social classes, life chances, and non-U.S. cultures. I find myself in day-to-day battles with my colleagues over many U.S. international policies. My immersion in so many other cultures has allowed me to approach situations with a broader perspective than many of my colleagues.

The interaction with peoples of different cultures has broadened my understanding of the world. Moreover, my ability to communicate and analyze many situations I face today in my pursuit of a legal education is shaped by the interactions and knowledge I received in my pursuit of cultural capital. The value of these experiences is exemplified in my daily life. The assimilation of oneself into the society and culture of another is an endeavor I challenge each and every student to take.

What's in the Narrative?

The narratives should raise an important question among those who have the potential to influence education in our society. To what extent are we participating in narratives of relationships between educators and students and hence creating realities in everyday lives? Socially constructed, personal meaning gained from a diversity course is different for each student. Understanding diversity among individuals requires a culturally appropriate framework that combines strengths, resiliency, and empowerment. A diversity curriculum, while designed for all students in a given course, is transcended when an individualized assessment of a student's social class, race, gender, and ethnicity is valued in the learning process. Most people understand how

others view and treat them through the lens of class, race, gender, and ethnicity (Appleby, 2001). In the United States, we continue to struggle against
oppression and discrimination. As illuminated by the narratives, the historical context and cultural background of our students influence their critical
thinking and shape their realities.

The narratives confirm that the mentoring strategy can contribute to the
effectiveness of the teaching. Three theoretical traditions—personal meaning, social context, and race relations in the learning experience—emphasize
quite different features of everyday life. Together they provide a lens to interpret how diversity education affects those who engage in it. Individuals use
resources that cultures provide to define and make sense of new and/or difficult experiences (Sue, 1998). These narratives make clear the notion that each
of us constructs explanations using taken-for-granted definitions of what it
means to have an experience versus creating an experience.

In Jessica's narrative she describes the experience of enrolling in a predominantly white institution of higher education and having to make adjustments to being the "minority." This is a fairly common experience among
students of color across the country. They are confronted with having to
navigate multiple worlds when they enter schools outside their neighborhoods (Phelan, Davidson, & Yu, 1993). Crystal expressed this as a challenge
long before entering college. These young women of color document the
difficulties that they faced when they decided to leave their majority environment for a minority experience.

Dalkis's experience of an immigrant woman faced with the trauma of
losing her mother who was the pillar of her family structure corroborates the
accounts in the literature of the significance of family networks and strong
social ties (Francis, 2000). The personal meaning tradition gives prominence
to the fact that accounts are always versions, rather than objective and impar-
tial descriptions, of reality. A narrative has the advantage of pointing to dis-
tinctive ways of ordering experiences or of constructing reality (Giles, 2002;
Riessman, 1993). The racist and sexist histories that most women of color
have survived give pause to consider the applicability of traditional Western
pedagogical paradigms. A strengths-based pedagogy embraces the commonality in the experiences of women across race, class, and ethnicity. The three
women in these separate narratives are of different ethnicities. Jessica is Honduran, Dalkis is Panamanian, and Crystal is African American. The women
were from different social classes and from different parts of the world. Yet,

they all report having benefited from diversity education. The empowerment that comes through learning about issues of diversity and the validation of one's culture helps students to develop skills of resiliency.

Dalkis tells of a law school environment that was disempowering. It is very possible that many students feel similarly. Patricia J. Williams (1992) so eloquently wrote about her experiences as a black woman in a law school that captures the essence of Dalkis's experiences. That is, the mere presence of people of color does not automatically equate welcome, nor warmth, nor well intentions in the host environment. In our dubious roles as educators who help develop our students into wonderfully intelligent professionals, we all have inherently more power than our students in the student-teacher relationship. When we try to empower them as we teach about diversity, we should be teaching them how to overcome the barriers of social stratification. One way to do so is to change the way we view others. Xenophobia is a far too common concept in our Western education systems.

Aaron describes his growth and development after taking a diversity course that helped him to attain a level of sensitivity to unassuming the challenges of social stratification. He was able to develop strengths and resiliency that now make him a well-adjusted law student. Appleby (2001) argues that oppression is "a by-product of socially constructed notions of power, privilege, control and hierarchies of differences" (p. 37). The way such concepts are defined and by whom will determine how the power and the privilege are acted upon. An analysis of Aaron's dilemmas and challenges as a white male from a rural southeastern region of the country leads me to the conclusion that white male experiences are as similar as the experiences of women of color.

In the same course that Dalkis took with me (but in a different year), I taught a white male student who was born and raised on the northern shoreline of Massachusetts. In 1995 when he was a student in my class, he worked in a police department where the only person of color in the department was an African American woman. This course was one of several that met a race/ethnic content requirement in the curriculum. When I gave an assignment to interview a black person about his or her family life, the student, whom I will call Anthony, resisted. He thought the assignment was ridiculous. (Crystal captured a similar experience in her narrative about the course she took with me at the University of Connecticut.) Anthony, in Massachusetts, didn't know any black people on a personal level, had never taken a course with a black professor, and really did not have any genuine interest in studying issues related to diversity. He admitted to taking the course because the class time fit his work schedule and he needed to meet a race/ethnic content requirement as a sociology major. Ultimately, Anthony interviewed the black woman in his department whom he had worked with for five years but had never spoken to. Admittedly, the process of interviewing his colleague changed his life forever. It allowed him to have his first positive one-on-one experience with a black person.

This student's experience was typical of the white male students who enrolled semester after semester in my diversity courses. Toporek and Reza (2001) argue that there is a natural tendency for us all to view others through our own cultural perspective and to believe that our view is the most appropriate. This ethnocentric stance along with prejudice attitudes is what I seek to reduce through the teaching of diversity. When diversity is taught using a strengths-based approach it is possible to see a shift in students' thinking and understanding about differences. This is documented in the students' narratives. Enlightened consciousness often requires a radical restructuring of entrenched belief systems and ethnocentrism (McPhatter, 1997). This is what has occurred with Aaron especially. I have had numerous conversations with him since 2001, and I see the continued growth and development that began in an undergraduate course that infused diversity throughout the curriculum.

The diversity literature contains few examples of personal and professional challenges experienced by white males. When we shift the paradigm from alienation to all-inclusive, white males must not be left out of the model. Moreover, because we know that wealth and power tend to be concentrated among a few, and white males are most likely to be in positions of power (Mills, 1959), diversity education strategies must target them. When diversity content is taught in courses that carry elective credits only, we run the risk of preaching to the choir. The students who enroll in those types of courses have already been converted into diversity "believers" or at least they are liberal minded enough to take the risk of learning more about diversity. Infusion throughout the broad-based standard curriculum creates opportunities for diversity education to occur in all courses.

The Value Latency of the Pedagogical Approach

Analyzing my students' narratives has caused me to think even more critically about my pedagogical approach to teaching diversity content in a curriculum where one might not expect to find it. Social work education in general is a good model of integrative learning. The course that Crystal took with me is one such example. The diversity content was infused throughout a research course. Diversity themes including at-risk populations were embedded into each topic area of the course. Some students felt it was overkill. A student once asked, "How many different ways can we discuss diversity?" I still do not have a definitive answer to that question. This approach to education apparently works, albeit not without resistance. For those students who resist, positive learning may still occur. Students may need more than one semester to examine their feelings about differences. The students who provided the narratives in this chapter have been engaged in diversity education and training for as many as 10 years, and as few as 3. I continue to mentor each of these students in their postgraduate lives. We continue to talk about diversity in everyday life and our conversations are ongoing. We either directly or indirectly focus our talks on diversity and the respect for differences, whether it pertains to their own career choices and directions or the lived experiences of others.

Reflecting on the narratives raises an important area of distinction, which is the degree to which we are able to teach others to respect cultural differences. Dalkis discussed her graduate experience that was intertwined with her grief and loss. Culturally her family network supported her yet depleted her of strengths. She was able to be resilient. She entered graduate school after the loss of the most important person in her support network. She completed her J.D. degree, and then completed her L.L.M. degree. How do we teach resiliency? How do we teach others to respect cultural values and norms and not to view them from a deficit perspective? Self-confidence and respect are good starting points.

The student narratives characterize the exploration of uncomfortable areas. In order to have greater respect for differences, self-reflection must occur. The open and honest discourse that allows for self-reflection can lead to feelings of vulnerability (Sanchez-Hucles, 2000). Embedded in my teaching philosophy is the commitment to demonstrate respect and foster self-confidence.

On more than one occasion, Jessica has talked with me about the feelings that she expressed in her narrative. Each time we have been engaged in the discourse, I have been intrigued by her anxiety in the cross-racial, cross-cultural encounters because she is an extremely articulate, intelligent, bilingual (which is highly valued in the professional arena) young woman who was very engaging as a student. In the two different courses that she took with me, I observed her use of a low-conflict style of interaction with peers as well as her demonstration of cooperative and conciliatory behavior during times of provocative discourse around diversity. Her style of interacting cross-racially is consistent with findings about emotional and social distress experienced by women of color in the workplace (Norwicki, Glanville, & Demertzis, 1998).

In my role as a teacher of diversity, I mentor to empower. bell hooks (1994) teaches us that in order to transgress, we must create a learning environment that has no walls. Jessica has accompanied me to professional conferences in addition to other out-of-class learning environments. In February 2004, I invited her to attend the annual meeting of the Council on Social Work Education in New York City with me. This is an example of one of the many opportunities for teaching in a mentoring capacity. On the train down to New York from Connecticut, there was time for one-on-one motivation speeches. I read over an essay that she was preparing to submit for postgraduate studies. While at the conference, she attended my presentation on technology education. There are a multitude of ways and settings conducive for teaching and learning diversity. Jessica's narrative is a testimony to her growth and development.

In an effort to reduce ethnocentrism and prejudice, the goal is to eliminate social stratification that continues to feed oppression and discrimination. Lum (2005) argues that sometimes people experience diversity as threatening and respond with emotions of anger and resentment. Crystal's characterization of the workplace is another unfortunate but not uncommon experience of black professionals in predominately white work settings. Lee and Ramirez (2000) have alluded to the fact that Eurocentric values pervade human services practice. Variation from the Eurocentric norms has often resulted in the labeling of individuals as being deviant or pathological. Until recently, human service professionals viewed culture as ancillary to the basic helping process (Marsella & Yamada, 2000), as did other disciplines, I'm sure. Culturally diverse clients were viewed from a deficit perspective and the responsibility of the client rested on the individual to adapt to Anglo norms.

Having had numerous discussions with Crystal that transcend the diversity course that she had with me, I can illuminate her narrative in addition to analyzing it. She and I as black women in our professional roles may be dealing with what has been described in the literature as cultural nuances of ambivalence and ambiguity where black-white differences in communication and management styles invoke racial tensions. Research shows that white people view the communication style of black people as more assertive, bold, emotional, and attention seeking (Cox & Nkomo, 1993). Moreover, aggressive is a trait that white people have used to characterize blacks in institutions of higher education since the early '80s (Weitz & Gordon, 1993). From the mentoring sessions that I have had with Crystal, I can attest to the stress that she experiences as a black woman in a supervisory role. She feels the need to downplay attributes that may be perceived as overly expressive and reactionary. Teaching students about these nuances in the workplace helps to prepare them for the diverse world in which we live and work.

A narrative analysis of the strengths-based approach to teaching diversity leads me to conclude that the interaction of knowledge, skills, and values organize the framework that enables me to explore different facets of my students' lives. I have infused and continue to infuse diversity content throughout the curriculum that I teach. The diversity content includes emphasis on historically oppressed populations in the United States and power dynamics. I explore with my students the macro- and microstructures of class, race, gender, and ethnicity. Showing respect earns me respect in most cases. I teach students the importance of respecting others' values, beliefs, and traditions. I make an effort to have students deconstruct their own identity and reconstruct it with a diversity backdrop. This typically brings about an awareness of self and ethnocentrism that is invaluable to the learning experience.

For example, we discuss actions such as the culturally specific etiquette of addressing individuals by preferred names and not assuming that everyone should be on a first-name basis. Language is key to establishing rapport and developing trusting relationships. Failure to recognize culturally distinct behaviors and attitudes may lead to frustrations, misunderstandings, and defensive reactions (Dana, 1998). For some students, it may cripple their ability to succeed in an academic setting. When diversity is taught using a strengths-based perspective students report positive experiences and a higher level of learning than other approaches to teaching diversity (Bullock & Blundo, 2001).

Teaching and mentoring across race, class, gender, and ethnicity can be rewarding for both the teacher and the student. Individuals bring to the learning experience a complex set of attributes including social class, race, gender, and ethnicity, which influence their cultural identities, values, beliefs, strengths, goals, and expectations. Students benefit from hearing and seeing themselves in the curriculum. This can be quite empowering. Students come to college, to us as the deliverers of wisdom, seeking the tools for success. The responsible thing that we can do is give them the foundation for changing the cascade of the American psyche and social structure. Diversity does not preclude normalcy. When we teach any and all subject matter, there are ways to include diversity content. This is a progressive pedagogical stance.

Some educators may feel that diversity should be relegated to an elective course that averts such discourse from the pedagogy of mainstream American students. When diversity is infused throughout the learning process, we reach a broader range of students and have an impact on a larger target audience. In the more intense mentoring relationships, the greatest influence of diversity education occurs. Finally, those who apply a strengths-based approach to teaching diversity should (1) periodically review the course content for updates in the available literature, (2) develop a framework to guide the learning process, (3) establish empowerment strategies, (4) identify critical success factors and associated performance indicators, as well as (5) develop a process to monitor/evaluate effectiveness of the diversity education approach. Student narratives are a good measurement tool to begin this important and potentially life-changing process.

References

Angel, R. J., & Williams, K. (2000). Cultural models of health and illness. In I. Cuéllar & F. A. Paniagua, *Handbook of multicultural mental health* (pp. 24–44). San Diego, CA: Academic Press.

Appleby, G. A. (2001). Dynamics of oppression and discrimination. In G. A. Appleby, E. Colon, & J. Hamilton (Eds.), *Diversity, oppression, and social functioning: Person-in-environment assessment and intervention* (pp. 36–52). Needham Heights, MA: Allyn & Bacon.

Bandura, A. (1986). *Social learning theory.* Englewood Cliffs, NJ: Prentice-Hall.

Blundo, R. (2001). Learning strengths-based practice: Challenging our personal and professional frames. *Families in Society: The Journal of Contemporary Human Services, 82,* 296–304.

Brem, M. L. (2001). *The 7 greatest truths about successful women.* San Francisco: Jossey-Bass.

Bryk, A. S., & Schneider, B. (2002). *Trust in schools: A core resource for improvement.* New York: Russell Sage Foundation.

Bullock, K., & Blundo, R. (2001, October). *Who is teaching diversity? A black female and white male perspective.* Paper presented at the annual meeting of the Baccalaureate Program Directors, Denver, Colorado.

Casey, K. (1995). The new narrative research in education. In M. Apple (Ed.), *Review of research in education* (pp. 211–253). Washington, DC: American Educational Research Association.

Catalyst. (2001). *Women of color: Their voices, their journeys.* Retrieved September 9, 2002, from http://www.catalystwomen.org

Cox, T., Jr., & Nkomo, S. (1993). Race and ethnicity. In R. T. Golembiewski (Ed.), *Handbook of organizational behavior* (pp. 205–229). New York: Marcel Dekker.

Dana, R. H. (1998). Cultural identity assessment of culturally diverse groups: 1997. *Journal of Personality Assessment, 70*(1), 1–16.

Denton, T. C. (1990). Bonding and supportive relationships among black professional women: Rituals or restoration. *Journal of Multicultural Counseling and Development, 11,* 447–457.

Edwards, D., & Mercer, N. (1987). *Common knowledge: The development of understanding in the classroom.* London: Methuen.

Feagin, J. R., & Feagin, C. B. (2003). *Race and ethnic relations.* Englewood Cliffs, NJ: Prentice Hall.

Fong, R. (2001). Culturally competent social work practice: Past and present. In R. Fong & S. B. C. Furuto (Eds.), *Culturally competent practice: Skills, intervention, and evaluation* (pp. 1–9). Boston: Allyn & Bacon.

Francis, E. A. (2000). Social work practice with African-descent immigrants. In P. R. Balgopol (Ed.), *Social work practice with immigrants and refugees* (pp. 127–166). New York: Columbia University Press.

Giles, H. C. (2002). Transforming the deficit narrative: Race, class, and social capital in parent-school relations. In C. Korn & A. Bursztyn (Eds.), *Rethinking multicultural education* (pp. 127–146). Westport, CT: Bergin & Garvey.

Godshalk, V. M., Sosik, J. L. (2000). Does mentor-protégée agreement on mentor leadership behavior influence the quality of a mentoring relationship? *Group and Organization Management, 25,* 291.

Grieco, E. M., & Cassidy, R. C. (2001, March). *Overview of race and Hispanic origin* (Census Overview Brief). Washington, DC: U.S. Census Bureau. Retrieved February 28, 2005, from http://www.census.gov/prod/2001pubs/c2kbr01-11.pdf

Grusky, D. B. (2001). *Social stratification in sociological perspective: Class, race, gender* (2nd ed.). Boulder, CO: Westview Press.

Gutierrez, L. M., & Lewis, E. A. (1999). *The empowerment of women of color.* New York: Columbia University Press.

Hobbs, F., & Stoops, N. (2002, November). *Demographic trends in the 20th century.* Census 2000 special report. Washington, DC: U.S. Census Bureau. Retrieved February 28, 2005, from http://www.census.gov/prod/2002pubs/censr-4.pdf

Holmes, G. E. (1992). Social work research and the empowerment paradigm. In D. Saleeby (Ed.), *The strength perspective on social work practice.* New York: Longman.

hooks, b. (1994). *Teaching to transgress: Education as the practice of freedom.* London: Routledge.

Johnson-Bailey, J., & Cervero, R. M. (2002, Winter). Cross-cultural mentoring as a context for learning. *New Directions for Adult and Continuing Education*, (96), 15–26.

Lee, R. M., & Ramirez, M., III (2000). The history, current status, and future of multicultural psychotherapy. In I. Cuéllar & F. A. Paniagua (Eds.), *Handbook of multicultural mental health* (pp. 279–309). San Diego CA: Academic Press.

Lum, D. (2005). *Cultural competence, practice stages, and client systems: A case study approach.* Belmont, CA: Thomson/Brooks/Cole.

Marsella, A. J., & Yamada, A. M. (2000). Culture and mental health: An introduction and overview of foundation, concepts, and issues. In I. Cuéllar & F. A. Paniagua (Eds.), *Handbook of multicultural mental health* (pp. 3–22). San Diego, CA: Academic Press.

McDevitt, T. M., & Rowe, P. M. (2002, February). *The United States in international context: 2000* (Census 2000 Brief). Washington, DC: U.S. Census Bureau. Retrieved February 28, 2005, from http://www.census.gov/prod/2002pubs/c2kbr01-11.pdf

McPhatter, A. R. (1997). Cultural competence in child welfare: What is it? How do we achieve it? What happens without it? *Child Welfare, 76*(1), 255–279.

Mercer, N. (1995). *The guided construction of knowledge. Talk amongst teachers and learners.* Clevedon, UK: Multilingual Matters.

Mills, C. W. (1959). *The power elite.* New York: Oxford University Press.

Nieto, S. (2003). *Affirming diversity: The sociopolitical context of multicultural education.* Boston: Allyn & Bacon.

Norwicki, S., Jr., Glanville, D., & Demertzis, A. (1998). The ability to decode nonverbal information in African American, African, Afro-Caribbean, and European American adults. *Journal of Black Psychology, 24*(4), 347–348.

Phelan, P., Davidson, A. L., & Yu, H. C. (1993). Students' multiple worlds: Navigating the borders of family, peer, and school cultures. In P. Phelan & A. L. Davidson (Eds.), *Renegotiating cultural diversity in American schools* (pp. 52–88). New York: Teachers College Press.

Rapp, C. A., & Poertner, J. (1992). *Social administration: A client-centered approach.* New York: Longman.

Rapport, J. (1990). In praise of the paradox: A social policy of empowerment over prevention. *American Journal of Community Psychology, 9*, 1–25.

Riessman, C. K. (1993). *Narrative analysis*. Thousand Oaks, CA: Sage.

Rodriquez, C. (2001, March 12). *Diversity equals productivity* (NASA Headquarters Equal Opportunity and Diversity Management Editorial Updates). Retrieved February 28, 2005, from http://www.hq.nasa.gov/office/codec/codece/editor.htm

Saleebey, D. (2001). *Strengths perspective in social work practice*. New York: Longman.

Sanchez-Hucles, J. (2000). *The first session with African Americans: A step-by-step guide*. San Francisco: Jossey-Bass.

Stanton-Salazar, R. D. (1997). A social capital framework for understanding the socialization of racial minority children and youths. *Harvard Education Review, 67*, 1–39.

Sue, S. (1998). In search of cultural competence in psychotherapy and counseling. *American Psychologist, 53*(4), 440–448.

Toporek, R. L., & Reza, J. V. (2001). Context as a critical dimension of multicultural counseling: Articulating personal, professional, and institutional competence. *Journal of Multicultural Counseling and Development, 29*(1), 13–30.

U.S. Census Bureau. (2001). *Current Population Survey*. Retrieved April 27, 2005, from http://www.census.gov/cps/cpsmain.htm

Weitz, R., & Gordon, L. (1993). Images of black women among Anglo college students. *Sex Roles, 28*, 19–45.

Williams, P. J. (1992). *The alchemy of race and rights*. Cambridge, MA: Harvard University Press.

Wright, C. A., & Wright, S. D. (1987). The role of mentors in the career development of young professionals. *Family Relations, 1*, 5.

9

BRIDGING THE TRANSGENERATIONAL GAPS BETWEEN DIVERSITY AND JUSTICE

Personal, Professional, and Pedagogical Insights from Courses on Race, Diversity, and Crime

Billy R. Close

With Isabelle Delatour, Albert Kopak, Francesca Danielle Lewis, Natasha Norton, and Vanessa Patino

This chapter examines the complex background and dynamic interaction of an African American professor and a sample of racially and ethnically diverse students formerly enrolled in undergraduate courses focusing on the theory and dynamics of racial discrimination, diversity, and criminal justice in America. The primary purpose and focus of the diversity education courses included in this analysis are to help "bridge the gaps between diversity and justice" by (1) helping students explore the different viewpoints and unreconciled positions about the current influence of racial and ethnic bias on the treatment of ethnic minority subgroups within America's criminal justice system; (2) providing a critical understanding and a conceptual framework for understanding the theory and dynamics of ethnic minority status, diversity, institutionalized racism, crime, and social policy in America; and (3) helping students realize the unique value of their familial and cultural traditions, life experiences, and worldviews. The past and present impact of the professor's pedagogical techniques and teaching philosophy on the students' intellectual growth and development, as well as their personal and professional lives, are examined through a series of personal letters and statements from the sample students. These letters reveal that the overall course objectives were met as evidenced by the students' reported increased understanding and appreciation of the subject matter, as well as an increased commitment to diversity education. Additionally, all of the student letters indicate an overwhelmingly positive and lasting effect of the course experience on their personal and professional growth and development.

M ost scholars agree that, historically, America's criminal justice system and other social institutions have not always operated at the individual or institutional level without racial and ethnic bias toward minorities (Mann & Zatz, 2002; Russell, 1998; Close, 1997; Georges-Abeyie, 1990). However, there is still considerable debate about the continued nature, presence, scope, and influence of institutionalized racial and ethnic discrimination in the contemporary criminal justice system. Not surprisingly, opposing viewpoints on definitional and methodological issues continue to characterize these long-standing debates concerning the relationship between racial discrimination and the phenomenon of disproportionate criminality among blacks and other ethnic minorities (Close, 1997; Close & Mason, 2006). Nowhere else is this debate more appropriately waged and potentially profitable than the culturally diverse university classroom. This chapter examines the complex background and dynamic interaction of an African American professor of criminology and criminal justice and students formerly enrolled in undergraduate race, crime, and justice courses related to diversity education.

The primary purpose and focus of the courses included in this analysis are to help bridge the gaps between diversity and justice by (1) exploring the different viewpoints and unreconciled positions about the current influence of racial and ethnic bias on the treatment of ethnic minority subgroups within America's criminal justice system, (2) critically examining the transgenerational relationship between stereotypical images of color and the harsh realities of crime and punishment, and (3) helping students realize the unique value of their familial and cultural traditions, life experiences, and worldviews. The recent courses taught related to diversity education include

Theory and Dynamics of Racism and Oppression; Minorities, Crime, and Social Policy; Diversity and Justice; Individual and Society; Race, Ethnicity, Crime, and Social Justice; and Seminar on Racial Profiling. As background for the analysis, the chapter also includes an examination of my personal background, unique diversity experiences, and pedagogical techniques as well. The chapter concludes with a series of personal letters and statements from formerly enrolled students, followed by my brief comments and reflections.

Difference Matters: Lessons from the Cradle

Like most southern-born African American males, my life experiences have been framed by the complex issues of diversity, institutionalized racism, and social injustice in a myriad of unique, challenging, and enduring ways before, during, and after my birth. I entered the world during the New Year's Day celebration of 1965, the 9th of 11 children born to the Reverend Frank Close Sr. and his wife, Cloia Daisy (Griffin) Close. Immediately, I was forced to suffer the ill effects of racism and poverty, while simultaneously fighting off the long arms of death that pervaded my mother's womb and snatched the life of my twin sister just as we prepared to make our "regal" entrance into the world. The previous day, instead of rushing to the nearest and technologically advanced hospital in Tallahassee, Florida, when labor pains began, the probing elbows of transgenerational poverty and racism forced my parents to drive some 60 miles away to a cheaper hospital in the small town of Donalsonville, Georgia. While there is no official record of my twin sister's death and no indication on my birth certificate that I was born a twin, the extraordinary circumstances of my birth have left me with an insatiable desire to understand a series of fundamental questions about my presence and purpose in life: (1) Why was I allowed to survive? (2) What is my purpose in life? (3) Why were blacks treated so badly? As a child, I frequently sought the answers to these questions from my parents. My parents' explanations were always the same—black lives simply weren't valued back then, blacks were treated differently, and blacks knew not to seek the right answers from the wrong people.

I was never fully satisfied with the answers my parents provided to many of my questions, but I always respected the circumstances of their lives as disadvantaged, poor black farmers trying to raise a large family in the segregated South. Despite the passage of the Civil Rights Act of 1964, the practical effect of the Jim Crow laws still deeply penetrated every aspect of my parents' and other black families' lives during this period.

Many years later, I have discovered that the answers to many of my questions were actually imbedded in the often sad but nurturing stories they shared with my siblings and me. In fact, many of these discussions at the knees of my parents and grandparents were teaching moments—invaluable links to the future, filled with wisdom, strength, protection, inspiration, and important diversity lessons. Indeed, these discussions allowed my parents to carefully imbed within each of my siblings and me sacred stories that would act as a compass for our lives and a cultural time capsule for the next generation and beyond.

Diversity lessons have contributed immensely to both my pedagogy and my primary scholarly goals as a college professor. Each and every time I share these diversity lessons with my students they remind me of my commitment to (1) use every teaching moment to inspire youth to seek higher education as a means to enhance their personal and communal growth and development, and (2) to use every teaching moment to instill within students an intense desire, commitment, and the requisite skills to confront and survive racial and ethnic injustice. The following are samples of these diversity lessons.

Kneeling Between the Rows

The most poignant and inspirational childhood diversity lesson that I can recall is that of my mother, Cloia Daisy Griffin, growing up on the farm of Rufus Jones near Bainbridge, Georgia, in the late 1940s. Born March 27, 1934, the 6th of 11 children, to sharecroppers Cleveland and Hattie Lou Griffin, my mother spent many of her early childhood days working in the cotton, corn, tobacco, and peanut fields. Life was tough and educational opportunities were few to the children of black sharecroppers. According to the farm owner's rules, having a place to stay and food to eat required that each able bodied Negro "resident" contribute to the maximum productivity of the seasonal crops. For my mother this meant rising before the sun as an adolescent to pull weeds from around the plants, feeding the chickens, raking the yards, or any number of other tedious chores. As a teenager, the work expectations increased and included raking the fences (pulling weeds, vines, and small saplings from between the wire fencing) and plowing the fields behind huge, onerous mules underneath the scorching Georgia sun.

As a teenager, on any given morning while plowing or raking the fences, my mother would listen carefully for the sound of rickety horse-drawn wagons, rumbling school buses, or giggling children passing by on their way to school. If she could detect the noise before the children saw her and hurled objects at her from the bus windows or wagons, she would lie down and hide between the rows to avoid being hit or ridiculed. My mother would tell me that the racist and derogatory remarks were much more painful than the objects thrown. However, most painful was the reality that because she was born to poor, black sharecroppers at a time when her black skin meant that educational opportunities were simply not made available, she could never climb on the bus or wagon, or even walk to the rural school.

The images of my mother kneeling between the rows of corn, cotton, and tobacco, or her lying on the dew-soaked earth with tears streaming down her cheeks is a constant reminder and a lesson to me of the value of education. The images also forever remind me of the tremendous hard work and sacrifices that she and countless others have made so that future generations of black children will not have to kneel between the rows.

Fighting and Dying for Justice

A second memorable childhood diversity lesson was the painful story of my paternal uncle—Henry Lloyd Close. Named after my grandfather, Uncle Henry was second eldest of 13 children. The year was 1947 in the small southern town of Bainbridge. One morning while working as a heavy equipment operator for a local logging company, Uncle Henry was ordered by the company foreman to step down from the Caterpillar he was operating and place some boards across a muddy area so that the foreman and some of his guests could walk across. Uncle Henry refused, arguing that his job was to operate the heavy machinery, not place boards across wet, muddy areas. Enraged by the refusal to obey, the foreman climbed onto the Caterpillar and struck Uncle Henry across the face. Big mistake! Uncle Henry leaped from the Caterpillar and proceeded to defend himself against the foreman and several of his guests who joined in to collectively assault him. Remarkably, Uncle Henry was able to single-handedly defeat his aggressors and deposit each one into the very muddy area they were trying to avoid.

Upon returning home and informing my grandmother of the incident,

Uncle Henry was severely chastised for endangering the lives of the entire family and losing his job. None of the family slept well that night for fear of violent reprisal on the part of the foreman, his friends, and the entire white community. Early the next morning, my grandmother was surprised to find Uncle Henry preparing for work. Angry and terrified, she begged and pleaded with him not to go back to the logging site. Adamant that he was only defending himself, he was owed money, had not been fired, and was not afraid, Uncle Henry returned to work.

Nauseated with fear and expecting the worst, my grandmother prayed and cried as she busied herself with her daily chores. Suddenly, the rambling noise of a truck broke the afternoon silence. My grandmother's heart shuddered and ached with pain as she slowly walked toward the front door only to see Uncle Henry's limp and deformed body rolled onto the front yard. As the flatbed truck drove away, one of several white males riding on the back of the truck remarked in a sarcastic tone, "We're so sorry that Henry got run over by that Caterpillar today." My father, who was around 13 years old, stood silently weeping next to my grandmother looking on in horror as she wept over the body of his older brother. Paralyzed with fear and nearly blinded with tears, my father ran with as much speed as his trembling legs could muster to the field where his father was plowing. Upon hearing the terrible news, my grandfather simply fell to his knees and cast his weak, shaky voice toward the heavens with a fervent prayer that no harm would come to the rest of the family. He then rose to his feet, looked into his younger son's bleary red eyes, laid a hand upon his head, and continued plowing to the end of the row. I can imagine as my father walked behind him, he heard the moaning of a familiar hymn, and together they walked slowly but boldly into the well-known uncertainty of black manhood and fatherhood.

Each time I heard this diversity lesson as a young boy, I remember asking, "Why didn't Granddaddy get his gun?" "Did Granddaddy tell the sheriff? What did the sheriff do? Did the men who killed Uncle Henry go to jail? Why did Granddaddy just keep plowing—Why didn't he quit?" Each time my questions would go unanswered. When I asked the same questions as a teenager, my father once said, "Son, there was no justice for black folks then or now, and we didn't have to tell the sheriff because he already knew. We may have been killed for complaining. . . . blacks were treated very different back then." When I ask the same questions now as an adult my father simply says, "Son, when you're black and poor, there is no justice—blacks are still treated different, please don't ask why."

Beyond my father's verbal response, I see the answer simultaneously in the dimness of his and my mother's tired eyes and in the brilliant clarity in the eyes of my siblings, nieces, nephews, and two young children. I understand the degree to which each of our personal and professional lives have been profoundly influenced by the circumstances of my partially unrecorded birth, and my mother's kneeling between the rows, and my Uncle Henry's tragic unrecorded death.

In many ways these tragic diversity lessons detailed above serve as historical prisms through which I seek a greater understanding of the unique challenges blacks face in confronting and correcting the contemporary dilemmas of diversity and injustice. What follows is an examination of the impact that these diversity lessons have on my teaching philosophy and the decision to focus on issues of diversity and justice.

A Statement on Teaching Philosophy

My teaching philosophy is grounded in the belief that the intellectual engagement and nurturing of students is one of the most rewarding, noble, and sacred responsibilities of working in the academic arena. Nowhere else is the university's mission and goal of assisting students in the pursuit of knowledge and understanding about the world in which we live, better cultivated than in the student-teacher relationship. Ultimately, the long-term success of students, faculty, and the university is dependent upon the nature and quality of the interactions between student and teacher. It is with this understanding that each and every teaching moment should be treasured.

On both a personal and professional level, my teaching philosophy is fueled by an intense desire for self-knowledge interlocked with a passion to help identify and correct the institutionalized economic, social, and political ills that negatively affected the opportunities for my ancestors, my descendants, my siblings, and my students. Understanding the enormously important and transformative role education can and has played in society, particularly as a vehicle of social reform and liberation, and given the significant numbers of racial and ethnic minorities and poor people still living within the transgenerational bonds of poverty and discrimination, faltering under the chains of despair, and dying under the guise of justice and equality for all, the opportunity to teach courses on diversity and social injustice is a tremendous opportunity to improve the social fabric of humanity.

Young, Black Male and Criminal: Origins of a Black Crimmythologist

Several contemporary researchers (Georges-Abeyie, 2001; Jones, 1972; Mann, 1993; Napper, 1977; Schur, 1969) argue along the same lines as DuBois did in 1920, that "crime" and "blackness" are oftentimes perceived as synonymous. Edwin Schur (1969) notes:

> to some extent white Americans think of Negroes as soon as they start worrying about crime problems. . . . the accuracy of our information about racial differences in crime is greatly impaired by the fact that Negroes in our society traditionally and to the present day have been discriminated against at every level in our process of administering justice. Their "categoric risk" of being formally labeled criminal is extremely high. (pp. 17–19)

The stereotypical impact of the "blackness-crime" dynamic reaches well beyond whites, blacks, and their personal view of criminals. For example, Harris and McCullough (1973) argue that while "studies of black communities have been carried out by Black and white social scientists, historically, [both] Black and white researchers have viewed and analyzed Black communities from the perspective of white norms and standards, and have generally drawn predictable conclusions from their analyses" (p. 333). In many cases, this dynamic has had a detrimental effect on how African Americans view themselves and other African Americans as well. This uncomfortable reality is illustrated in the following statement by Napper (1977):

> If one is told that an overwhelming proportion of people who are arrested are black and that the population of the jails and prisons of our country are predominately and increasingly drawn from the black community, one is forced to conclude that the argument suggesting that blackness and criminality can be used interchangeably has merit. So profound is the connection that it is extremely difficult to find someone—black or white—who will fail to conjure up images of a black male when asked to provide a portrait of a criminal. (p. 11)

The accuracy of Napper's statement was painfully revealed to me while I was an undergraduate criminology major enrolled in a course on courts and social policy. On this particular morning the professor entered the classroom and began his lecture by asking each of us to close our eyes and envision a stereotypical criminal. I was sitting in the front of the class and turned to see if my classmates were complying. All eyes were closed. As I turned back toward the professor I noticed that he was staring at me with a somewhat puzzled look. I smiled, but did not close my eyes. After about 10 seconds had passed the professor asked the class what they saw. To my surprise, the vast majority of the students responded almost in unison, "Young black male!" I turned again and this time when I surveyed my classmates, all eyes were opened but none of them would make eye contact with me. I turned yet again, this time searching for some familiar dark brown or black-brown eyes filled with empathy and situated within a black or brown body. There were only two sets of these kinds of eyes and in them I saw fear.

The silence in the room was deafening, or as my mother would say when I was a child, the room was so quiet you could hear a rat piss on cotton! Suddenly the professor's voice broke the silence with a question directed at me. "Billy, I noticed you didn't close your eyes nor answer the question. Why?" Not wanting to commit academic suicide, I struggled to ignore the violent thoughts and derogatory comments that were at the forefront of my mind. Instead, I drew upon the more palatable ones that years of similar situations and diversity lessons had prepared me with. I responded, "Because, I disagree with the criminal image described by my classmates." The professor became anxious and quickly responded with a rapid series of statements and statistics supporting the alleged "factuality" of black male criminality and implicitly the accuracy of my classmates' responses. The gist of his comments was, "Surely you know that statistics indicate that blacks commit a disproportionate number of FBI Crime Index offenses." I cringed and quickly reflected on another proverb of my mother's wisdom: "Son, when you have your hand in the lion's mouth—you have to ease it out slowly if you want to keep it." I continued, "But that wasn't the question. You did not ask about black crime rate as measured by the crime index. Nor did you identify a particular violation. Quite frankly, I feel as if there is a consensus among my classmates that I am a potential criminal simply because of my skin color and the preconceived notions they have about the predisposition of blacks to commit crime." The professor paused briefly, seemingly reflecting on my comments. He then gave me a stern look and commented that I was taking things way too seriously and moved on with the lecture.

As the professor rambled on for the remainder of the hour, I can still vividly remember pondering the significant and damning implications of the question that had been raised. What was the point of the question and its relevance to the lecture or the overall course objectives? The relevance of my response had been summarily dismissed. The majority of my classmates were junior and senior criminology majors, many of whom were preparing to become criminal justice practitioners (police and correctional officers, lawyers, judges, etc.), policy makers, or go on to graduate school. If they already had the image of Russell's (1998) "criminalblackman" imbedded in their minds, how would this affect their treatment of blacks? At that very moment, I decided that part of my professional goals would include teaching courses on the mythology of race and crime.

A number of years later while writing my dissertation, I coined the term "black crimmythology" to describe the numerous faulty myths and pseudo-scientific facts generated by racist and/or misguided scholars and laypersons to explain black criminality. Implicit in the notion of "black crimmythology" is a claim about the alleged inferiority and/or criminal propensity of black males, which can best be understood by analyzing what the racist scientist Van Evrie (1853) would argue as "a *naturally* occurring array of observable and measurable social, biological, and spiritual *defects* found in them." These allegedly innate defects are purported to express themselves in the subsequent criminal behavior of blacks and can best be understood as expressions of the unchangeable, heritable (hence transgenerational), and thus permanent condition of inferiority. Accordingly, propagators of black crimmythology routinely assert (implicitly or explicitly) that these defects (1) causally operate to make black males more likely to engage in "criminal" or "deviant" behavior, and (2) are themselves caused by acts of God, nature, or the inability of blacks to adapt (evolve) in an ever-changing society. In short, to borrow from (and adapt) the ignominious title of Van Evrie's work (1853), *Blacks and Black Criminality: The First, an Inferior Race—The Latter, Its Normal Condition*, becomes the operating principle for crimmythologists examining the theory and dynamics of back criminality.

The Decision to Research and Teach in the Areas of Race, Diversity, and Crime

A Personal and Professional Response to Life's Diversity Lessons

There can be little doubt that blacks commit a disproportionate number of FBI Crime Index offenses, and are in turn, disproportionately victimized by crimes involving physical contact. (Georges-Abeyic, 1984, p. 12)

Although criminal justice scholars and policy makers continue to debate the meaning of the disproportionately high African-American arrest rate—with some arguing that it reflects a higher offending rate and others that it signals selective enforcement of the law—there is no denying the fact that African-Americans are arrested more often than one would expect, particularly for crimes of violence such as murder, rape, and robbery. The explanation for this overrepresentation is complex, incorporating social, economic, and political factors (Walker, Spohn, & DeLone, 1995, p. 229).

> Murder may swagger, theft may rule and prostitution may flourish and the nation gives but spasmodic, intermittent and lukewarm attention. But let the murderer be black or the thief brown or the violator of womanhood have a drop of Negro blood, and the righteousness of the indignation sweeps the world. Nor would this fact make the indignation less justifiable did not we all know that it was blackness that was condemned and not crime. (As quoted by Weinberg, 1992, p. 186)

The preceding citations illustrate the subject matter of my current research interests and course instruction: probing into an unsettled debate about the content and character and the principles and policies of the American criminal justice system—in particular identifying the specific causal variable(s) that controls the response of this basic institution to one of America's largest ethnic minority populations, African Americans.

The first two citations describe the state of racial affairs at the end of the 20th century, the other at its beginning. The first two also represent the point of departure for most discussions of the African American situation in the United States of America—both then and now: a peculiar disproportionality between the ratio of African Americans in the general population and a particular economic, social, or political index. It does not matter whether we analyze criminality, family structure, health, or athletes in professional sports; one inevitably encounters various "startling statistics" that embody this disproportionality. "Startling statistics," or the "SS phenomenon," is a concept used to characterize a striking disproportionality between the ratio of African Americans in the general population with regard to a given social index. Identifying the accurate causality for this stark disparity lies at the heart of nearly every policy discussion about African Americans (Jones, 1990).

The third citation, taken from the eminent social historian and acclaimed African American sociologist William Edward Burghardt DuBois, links the startling statistics phenomenon to the focus of my research: the matter of disproportionate "black criminality" and its causality. DuBois specifies a particular cause—the "color line," or institutionalized racial oppression, as did Frederick Douglass. Implicit in the Douglass/DuBois analysis is a call for an audit of America's institutions, such as the criminal justice system, to determine their economic, social, and political tilt and decide if they reflect the constitutional imperative of nondiscrimination and coequality or the historical practice of racial discrimination and inequality. Over 100 years later the accuracy and adequacy of the DuBois/Douglass hypothesis is still being debated, and its "commanding question" of "how far differences of race are made the basis for denying to over half the world the right of sharing to their utmost ability the opportunities and privileges of modern civilization" (DuBois, 1969, p. 13) is still unsettled.

Teaching diversity education courses on the theory and dynamics of racism, diversity, and social justice at a predominantly white university is not an easy task for a young black male. In fact, without effective pedagogical techniques for conflict reduction, credibility establishment, subject matter and material engagement, and alienation and denial recognition strategies, the experience can be emotionally overwhelming—for both student and professor. My decision to focus my research and teaching on courses related to diversity education and oppression was motivated by a number of unique factors. As discussed earlier, the experiential circumstances of being born black and male in America exposes one to certain petite apartheid indignities (Georges-Abeyie, 2001).

On a practical level, while Africans Americans continue to be disproportionately represented in all phases of the criminal justice system, studies have consistently failed to develop a broad-based analytical and theoretical framework for explaining the phenomena of racial discrimination and disproportionality (Feagin & Feagin, 1978; Mann, 1993; Russell, 1992; Staples, 1975). In light of the growing discontent surrounding the burgeoning black male and ethnic minority correctional populations and the growing complaints of racial profiling, the development of sound pedagogical theory and methods to explain these phenomena is critical, not only for the discipline of criminology and criminal justice, but also for the security of a nation currently undergoing substantial demographic transformation.

On a theoretical level, traditional and contemporary criminological theory has had little success in explaining the historical or contemporary impact of race or institutionalized racism on African American criminality in particular, and minority criminality in general. Russell (1992) notes that empirical findings in this area have consistently shown the race variable to be a significant predictor of criminal conduct. However, despite the widespread presumption that race plays a role in the determination of criminality, existing research has not demonstrated how and why this happens (Klepper, Nagin, & Tierney, 1983; Mann, 1993). The discipline of criminology (as well as other related social sciences) has also failed to systematically cultivate, or recognize, a subfield or a theoretical framework that sufficiently addresses problems of *how and why* the race variable is such a significant predictor. In fact, Sagarin (1980) notes that there has been a long-standing taboo against raising this issue in criminology and criminal justice. The disciplinary stance in criminology and criminal justice is best illustrated in the following statement offered by Radzinowicz and King (1977):

> To enter into open discussion of links between race and crime is to enter a minefield. Politically the issue is dynamite. Claims that certain ethnic groups are inferior have served throughout history to justify all kinds of persecution, oppression, exploitation. So powerful is the reaction now, from the oppressed and their champions, that it is hard to investigate or discuss such issues without arousing strong feelings. (p. 23)

Wilson and Herrnstein (1985) add, "In the United States, the higher average crime rates of blacks have been used to support claims that blacks were morally inferior. . . . many persons, white and black, remembering the sad history of racism in this country, prefer not to discuss race differences in crime rates at all, for fear of either giving offense to a group that has been persecuted enough or giving encouragement to those who would continue the persecution" (p. 461). Meanwhile, the nation's jail, prison, and juvenile detention center populations are becoming blacker, and the American citizenry remains, as Wade Nobles (1986) argues, "conceptually incarcerated" by unfounded fears of savage criminals stalking the streets in search of helpless victims.

Given this context, university professors and students alike simply cannot afford to ignore the challenges and benefits of teaching about the issues of difference and racial oppression, nor continue to perpetuate the conclusions reached some four decades ago by Carmichael and Hamilton (1967):

"The whole question of race is one that America would prefer not to face honestly and squarely. To some, it is embarrassing; to others, it is confusing. . . . Anything less than clarity, honesty, and forcefulness perpetuates the centuries of sliding over, dressing up, and soothing down the true feelings, hopes and demands of an oppressed black people" (pp. viii–ix).

Throughout my research and teaching career, I have endeavored to provide students with an increased understanding and appreciation of the basic concepts that minimal competence and survival in this area requires. As discussed earlier, I believe this is best accomplished by (1) helping students explore the different viewpoints and unreconciled positions about the current influence of racial and ethnic bias on the treatment of ethnic minority subgroups within America's criminal justice system; (2) providing a critical understanding and conceptual framework for understanding the theory and dynamics of ethnic minority status, diversity, institutionalized racism, crime, and social policy in America; and (3) helping students realize the unique value of their familial and cultural traditions, life experiences, and worldviews. The following personal letters and statements are from a small sample of former students enrolled in my courses and exposed to diversity lessons over the last 10 years. These letters from young adult professionals and potential participants in the diverse future leadership of America provide a unique assessment of whether the overall course objectives were met. Following each letter I provide brief comments and reflections.

Student Letters

Isabelle Delatour, working, studying, and living abroad (London)

> *Dear Dr. Close,*
>
> *Being Haitian American and growing up in Miami, I believed you could visit another country just by driving a few miles. I always felt lucky to have grown up in this type of environment. Although perhaps the world saw me as a black female, I understand that my cultural background is more a part of who I am than my race. At some point, though, I realized that cultural diversity is often subordinated by race, otherwise why should I have to identify myself by checking only one little box: white, black, Hispanic, Pacific Islander, and other? It was quite clear that if race was important enough to be statistically recorded it must have important uses. How were these*

"statistics" used to help me, hurt me, or categorize me? I was interested in how a class titled Minorities, Crime, and Social Policy could help explain why everyone was so concerned with race and how it came to be so powerful in shaping policies that effect us every day.

For the past four years I have been living abroad (London/Minas Gerais, Brazil), and am finding that my definition of diversity has really had to expand. In this time I have had to face my own ignorance about the world and its people. Drawing upon life experiences and understanding diversity from the classroom have helped me appreciate the uniqueness of all the people I encounter.

I find that in the same way race often takes priority over cultural diversity, the use of overgeneralizations has the same diluting effect. For example, the common reference to Africa as a country or a homogenous land with the same culture, robs each country, tribe, and region of its unique qualities. Understanding diversity is a constant learning process because you find yourself unlearning so many things that you always accepted as fact. As I learned in Minorities, Crime, and Social Policy these damaging narrow-minded perspectives were in fact created and taught to us and therefore can be unlearned.

My Commentary—Quite evident in Delatour's letter is a growing appreciation for the value, uniqueness, and complexity of her own individual and cultural identity, as well as that of others. One of the primary learning objectives of my courses is to expose students to the inherent danger of relying on "ethnic monoliths." Her willingness to immerse herself in diverse cultures by exploring the world, and simultaneously move beyond the sometimes limiting opportunities for Haitian Americans in America, will provide her with an array of diversity lessons and a lifetime of personal and professional growth opportunities.

Al Kopak, *graduate student (Florida)*

Growing up on a farm in a small town did not allow me to interact with many people who were different from myself. This sheltered environment fostered unsure thoughts about the differences surrounding various racial and ethnic groups.

My high school had only a handful of minority students with even fewer teachers from backgrounds different from my own. The white, Anglo-Saxon Protestant culture overruled the geographic area in which I spent my formative years. These teachings were bred into the public school system (of which I was a part), the local government, and all the other social institutions in between. Being surrounded by these principles left me to believe that this was how American society operated. I was soon to find out that I was sorely mistaken.

When I arrived at Florida State University I discovered that many of the students were quite different. Not only did they possess physical differences, but their behavior was also something I was not accustomed to either. I was not so naive that I did not understand why we were different from one another, but I was curious about the implications that these differences had in our daily lives as we interacted with the world around us. Lo and behold, a course about the diversity of individuals in American society was being taught and my interest was instantly peaked.

During one of the first class sessions, I was bemused by a new concept introduced by the professor: dichotomous logic. For the first time in my life I understood both the subjective process and the implication of labeling people "different," which often results in us concluding that they are "right or wrong," "good or bad," "black or white." I quickly reached the conclusion that this method of thinking could be flawed in a variety of ways.

The fact that one person is different from another does not require that one is better or worse. The various physical characteristics of a person is one of the possible determinants of labeling (simply because they are clearly visible), but it is the subjective "power to define" and the resultant response to the "label" that ultimately determines the meaning we assign to differences between people.

I eventually came to the realization that diversity is something to be used and celebrated to enhance the value of cultural differences that exist in our society. However, in order to appreciate these differences, they must be valued, protected, defended, and celebrated. Not soon after I was exposed to the teachings of Professor Close, I was placed in a situation where I had the opportunity to apply what I learned.

I am currently working as a probation officer. Too often I see Hispanics, blacks, and poor whites overrepresented among the groups of people that I work with on a daily basis. Needless to say, Dr. Close's teachings have helped me develop an understanding that allows me treat to everyone equally, re-gardless of the color of their skin, their cultural beliefs, or their financial assets.

My Commentary—Mr. Kopak's comments illustrate quite vividly that positive changes in levels of sensitivity and understanding can occur in the course of confrontational discussions about diversity and justice. Oftentimes, white males have been taught to see themselves as the normative standard by which others are measured. Mr. Kopak has learned that in order to discriminate between two or more things, they first must be identified as different, then they must be hierarchically arranged. The resulting "difference" is not an inherent characteristic of the object being labeled. The objects do not define themselves. Rather difference, real or imagined is a relative, socially constructed concept.

In-depth discussions with students in my courses about the history of violence, difference, power, and white skin privilege in America forces them to legitimate their objective positions and their privileges. The objective is to instill within them an understanding and appreciation of the course concepts that they will consider beyond the semester and apply to their professional and personal lives.

Francesca Danielle Lewis, *graduate Harvard Law School J.D., class of 2006 (Alabama)*

> *Dr. Close,*
>
> *Thank you for including my experiences in your chapter on diversity and justice. After much consideration, I believe the best way to capture and reflect on the influence of your courses on my personal and professional life is to focus on the diversity and justice issues that I have confronted before and after meeting you.*
>
> *Throughout my life, the driving forces of diversity and injustice have had a tremendous impact on my life. Growing up in a black family in the small town of Opelika, Alabama, I was constantly encouraged to pursue education. I also had numerous direct observations of less fortunate people with even fewer opportunities and no support. These childhood experiences helped me develop a strong sense of my own obligation to give back, to be an advocate for others, and to defend what is right.*

My grandmother, Bertha Woolfolk Willis, was an important influence in my development of these attitudes. She was born in 1924 in Cincinnati, Ohio, and spent most of her childhood in rural Alabama. At a time when women and ethnic minorities were deprived of many rights and Americans suffered from the Depression and war, Grandma Bertha realized the dream of her ancestors. She attended college and received a master's degree in education. This was quite outstanding for a woman of her time. She went on to teach for 33 years. Nearly every day she runs into a past student who still admires her commitment to education.

In the summer of 2001 as I planned to travel to Prague, Czech Republic, Grandma Bertha was one of my main supporters. She saved up the little she had to help me make the trip. In studying the Czech criminal justice system, I wrote a research paper comparing and contrasting the presence of the Czech Republic's minority population (mostly Roma) in its criminal justice system to the presence of African Americans in America's justice system. I also studied Nazi war crimes against humanity through literature and visits to Terezine and Auschwitz. I returned with a greater appreciation for the magnitude of human suffering even beyond the boundaries of my own culture. Upon return, Grandma Bertha anxiously waited for me to recount every experience. How she marveled at the countries and landmarks I described. Although she was pleased that I had an exciting summer trip, she rejoiced in how her granddaughter had seen a different side of the world, an opportunity she never had.

That same summer, I also undertook my own "civil rights protest"; though not comparable to the civil rights activism of Grandma's past, I witnessed an injustice and sought to address it. After a friend was removed from a party because his cornrows violated the dress code of the establishment where the party was held, I wrote a letter to the editor of our local newspaper in which I expressed my disapproval of the dress code. The code associated cornrows, tattoos, skullcaps, gold chains, and jerseys with the profile of a "troublemaker." I outlined the injustice at play when a culturally unique hairstyle with roots that can be traced to thousands of years is included in the description of a likely criminal offender. The letter was transformed into a front-page report. The news of the dress code spread across the state and was covered in USA Today as well. City officials called the dress code unjust and intolerable. As a result of my letter, the city council called restaurant and bar owners together to develop a communitywide dress code. Grandma

Bertha cut out each article and celebrated my triumph with me. I came to realize that even though I missed out on the protests and boycotts of the '60s, there is still work to be done.

While completing my third year of law school at Harvard, I comprehended more clearly than ever, the lessons she bestowed upon me about my duty and my dreams for the future. I also constantly draw upon the many lessons I learned in your courses—Minorities, Crime, and Social Policy, and Directed Individual Study on Racial Profiling—and the countless numbers of hours spent in your office seeking advice and encouragement. Because of the many sacrifices made by my grandmother and parents, and because of the mentorship and insights I gleaned from your lectures and discussions, I am resolute in my commitment to giving back to the struggle for social justice. I believe I can best fulfill this commitment as an attorney. I will endeavor to use my legal skills as a ministry to others in an effort to make real the promises of democracy best articulated by the words of Frederick Douglass many years ago—that is to make sure that "American Justice, American Liberty, American Civilization, American Law, and American Christianity could be made to include and protect alike and forever all American Citizens in the rights which have been guaranteed to them by the organic and fundamental laws of the land" [speech on the twenty-fourth anniversary of emancipation, Washington, D.C., April, 1886] *without regard to race, ethnicity, or socioeconomic background.*

Thank you for the caring, thank you for the inspiration, and above all thank you for sharing with me the courage to pursue justice.

My Commentary—Lewis's letter epitomizes the significance and value of diversity lessons discussed throughout this chapter. Her acknowledgment of her parents' and grandmother's sacrifices and her willingness to both confront and correct the perceived injustice suffered by her and her guest, speaks to the embedded transgenerational aspirations of a historically oppressed people to be treated equally. Her courageous actions also speak to the values of faith, educational freedom, and knowledge that I try to instill in each of my students. Comments such as those made by Lewis and other students about the value and significance of my course and my mentorship provide invaluable sustenance to young black professors teaching in the academy. More important, her phenomenal academic and personal successes reinforce my belief that the intellectual engagement and nurturing of students is one of the most rewarding, noble, and sacred responsibilities of working in the academic arena.

Natasha Norton, M.S. in Journalism and Communications (California)

Growing up, I was frequently one of a few black kids in my elementary schools and always appeared on the "special" radar because I took honor's classes. I spent my middle-school years in an all-black intermediate school that lived up to its bad reputation. I remember being teased about the way I dressed, how long my hair was, and, of course, the way I talked—"You talk like a white person." However, thanks to my family upbringing, I felt that there should always be a comfortable place for me in school and that if necessary I would create it.

I have always liked to challenge myself intellectually, and one thing I quickly realized upon entering college is that all of my previous formal education had rendered me relatively ignorant about many aspects of African American history—I came to the realization that I had been mis-educated. While I was generally aware that opportunities for black people were not equal in America, I wanted to know why. I also wanted to be able to articulate the reasons with people of any race.

My most memorable experience in class was when Dr. Close explained the difference between individual racism and institutional racism. In the process, he let the entire class know that everyone harbored prejudices, including himself, but that he and the rest of the minority students could not engage in institutional racism. He explained that institutional racism required control of major institutions in America and blacks simply do not control major institutions under which whites must live.

As I was preparing to leave Florida State University, one of my favorite professors told me that he did not think I was ready for grad school. I was surprised because I had taken both of his honors classes and received an A in one course and a B in the other. To this day, I still question why he refused to write me a letter of recommendation but didn't hesitate to endorse other students.

Despite the professor's refusal to support my application, I am currently enrolled and performing well in graduate school at the University of California at Berkeley. In fact, the university practically begged me to come and offered me a fellowship! I graduated in the spring of 2006 with a master's degree in communication and journalism.

My Commentary—Norton's letter forces me to reflect on the fact that the presence of minority faculty members are a tremendous asset for facilitating diversity education and enhancing minority student matriculation at predominantly white colleges and universities. Oftentimes, minority faculty members can provide invaluable life support to minority students who may be suffocating for lack of attention and/or understanding from majority faculty members. While many students (both minority and majority) may exhibit academic deficiencies and other situational challenges, the mission of each university should endeavor to assist students in the maximal discovery and development of their potential. A racially and ethnically diverse faculty is a valuable asset in assisting both the student and university to reach their full potential.

Vanessa Patino, *master's in public administration, currently doctoral student in public administration (New York)*

I am a first-generation American. My father emigrated from South America in his 20s and my mother was born and raised in Puerto Rico. I am a Latina, by way of New York, who grew up in Miami. Although I feel I did not learn much in high school, I was lucky enough to go to a very diverse school, mostly Hispanic and African American students, where I learned about how to get along with other people—probably one of the most valuable lessons in life. Growing up, I was constantly exploring my identity and trying to balance the expectations at school versus the expectations at home. I knew many kids who got caught up the juvenile justice system and I was very interested in the whole process. I knew that I wanted to study criminal justice. Because I was a female, I was not supposed to move away from home to go to college. Luckily, I won the battle by convincing my parents that I would get a better education and experience being in the state capital.

In the beginning, I felt very out of place at Florida State University. It seemed everyone in my classes was white with blond hair. My dark, curly hair stood out. At that time, I believe less than 5% of the student population was Hispanic. In my criminology courses, very few professors discussed the intersection of race and ethnicity and crime. However, my first experience at discussing minorities and crime in an elective course fascinated and depressed me. It was the kind of course that challenged your belief system and made you ask lots of questions of yourself and those around you. It was the harsh truth that many people don't like to talk about. We discussed institutional racism and its by-products. A lesson that has stayed with me to this day is the concept of "social constructs," those things, words, ideas that we give meaning to—which by themselves have no meaning at all. For example, let's consider the definition of majority and minority. Why is it that people of color are the minorities, when in fact, they make up the majority of the world's population? Only if we contextualize the term within the paradigms of power and privilege do these concepts apply to people of color. Many of us accept such terminology and its implications as absolute facts.

We live in a society where there are many disparate policies, laws, and practices that remain unchanged. We explored many of these in class, including labeling and criminalization of youth. During this time, the Juvenile Role Model Development Program and curriculum was created at FSU—and the criminology department must have realized that in order for students to be able to pursue work with youth in juvenile justice settings, they were going to need courses in diversity. Dr. Close was a strong advocate of his students doing community service work with disadvantaged youth, which I found to be very rewarding and worthwhile in retrospect. I took several other courses with Dr. Close, all of which centered around the idea that we all come to a place with our very own experiences that frame our thinking and help us interpret our own realities.

It has been 10 years since my first class with Dr. Close but the discourse is far from being old. The lessons and the issues of diversity intersect with my professional and personal life on a daily basis. I work at a progressive, national nonprofit criminal justice research group. I have been working on projects that address the issues of minority youth and girls in juvenile justice. In many ways, I feel it is my responsibility to work in this field, with the slight chance that I may be able to affect public policy through informed research. I have had several experiences where I look around the room at the people making policy decisions about youth, and it is rare for minority youth to be represented. It is getting better, but there is more work to be done. It seems the courses about diversity and race and justice have awakened my senses and I am more aware of the issues and the needs. There just doesn't

seem to be any justice in the fact that less than 4% of Latinos have a gradu-
ate degree. We cannot address issues in juvenile justice, women and justice,
restorative justice, or even crime prevention without first examining the dif-
ferent cultures and our own biases. Terms like gender-responsive and cultur-
ally competent take on a new meaning. I want to keep learning and growing
more attuned. I have taken a more proactive approach to get involved in
projects that address these issues and always include data that disaggregates
by race/ethnicity and gender. Cultural competency is an important issue that
needs to be addressed and dissected for all people (practitioners, educators,
policy makers, etc.) who will be providing direct services or outreaching in
communities.

Issues of diversity are in my personal life, they are at my dinner table
when entertaining friends, and in the cultural activities I seek, in the foods
I appreciate, in the places I travel. The issues of diversity and justice are in
the news every day. Having the knowledge base enables me to question every-
thing and accept little as fact, while at the same time appreciating and being
open to many different viewpoints.

My Commentary—Patino's insatiable appetite for learning is exemplified in
her letter. The many diversity lessons she consumed during her formative
years at Florida State have obviously provided her with a healthy understanding of the nutritious and intellectual flavor that one can enjoy while learning
and growing. The cross-fertilization of perspectives that are provided in
courses designed to maximize each student's familial and cultural traditions,
life experiences, and worldviews, pay huge dividends. Confident and adequately prepared, Patino is eager to apply her experiential understanding to
the inequities faced by minorities in the criminal and juvenile justice
systems.

Summary and Conclusion

The purpose of this chapter was to examine the complex background and
dynamic interaction of an African American professor and a sample of racially and ethnically diverse students formerly enrolled in a series of diversity
education courses. While a simplistic understanding of diversity education
reveals that it is merely a label for describing difference, the myriad ways in

which being described, treated, and having to respond to being "different" have provided some unique personal and professional insights for understanding both the importance and complexity of this issue for the sample of former students enrolled in my courses. This is not only evident in the personal letters and statements provided by former students, it is also evidenced by the fact that each of the students continues to draw upon the diversity lesson to bridge the gap between diversity and justice.

America's transgenerational legacy of racial/ethnic discrimination and oppression, coupled with the inevitability of increasingly rapid demographic changes in the racial and ethnic composition of our population, will force all of us to constantly grapple with the issues of social justice. The former slave and activist Frederick Douglass argued many years ago that "where justice is denied, where poverty is enforced, where ignorance prevails, and where any one class is made to feel that society is an organized conspiracy to oppress . . . and degrade [it], neither persons or property will ever be safe." (source)

In the final analysis, this author believes that social justice requires a balance between people (racial and ethnic groups) and things (economic, educational, social, and political opportunities). Diversity education courses that effectively equip students with the personal and professional skills and the commitment to bridge the transgenerational gaps between diversity and social justice will help create this balance.

References

Carmichael, S., & Hamilton, C. (1967). *Black power: Politics of liberation in America.* New York: Vintage.

Close, B. (1997). *Toward a resolution of the non-discrimination/discrimination thesis debate in criminology and criminal justice: Revisiting black criminality and institutional racism.* Doctoral dissertation, Florida State University, Tallahassee.

Close, B., & Mason, P. L. (2006). *Efficient enforcement or biased policing in traffic stop searches: Evidence from Florida, 2000–2002.* Unpublished journal article.

DuBois, W. E. B. (1969). *Souls of black folk.* New York: New American Library.

Feagin, J. R., & Feagin, C. (1978). *Discrimination American style: Institutional racism and sexism.* Englewood Cliffs, NJ: Prentice-Hall.

Georges-Abeyie, D. (Ed.). (1984). *The criminal justice system and blacks.* New York: Clark Boardman.

Georges-Abeyie, D. (1990). The myth of a racist criminal justice system? In B. D. MacLean & D. Milovanovic (Eds.), *Racism, empiricism, and criminal justice* (pp. 11–14). Vancouver, Canada: The Collective Press.

Georges-Abeyie, D. (2001). Petite apartheid in criminal justice: The more "things" change, the more "things" remain the same. In D. Milovanovic & K. Russell (Eds.), *Petite apartheid in the U.S. criminal justice system: The dark figure of racism* (pp. ix–xiv). Durham, NC: Carolina Academic Press.

Harris, J., & McCullough, W. (1973). Quantitative methods and black community studies. In Joyce Ladner (Ed.), *The death of white sociology* (pp. 331–342). New York: Random House.

Jones, J. M. (1972). *Prejudice and racism.* Reading, MA: Addison-Wesley.

Jones, William R. (1990, August). *Institutional racism/oppression: Towards a new paradigm for uncovering neo-racism in the legal justice system.* Paper presented at the Florida State University School of Law School Symposium, Tallahassee.

Klepper, S., Nagin, D., & Tierney, L. (1983). Discrimination in the criminal justice system: A critical appraisal of the literature. In A. Blumstein, J. Cohen, S. E. Martin, & M. H. Tonry (Eds.), *Research on sentencing: The search for reform* (Vol. 2, pp. 55–128). Washington, DC: National Academy Press.

Mann, C. R. (1993). *Unequal justice: A question of color.* Bloomington: Indiana University Press.

Mann, C. R., & Zatz, M. (2002). *Images of color, images of crime.* Los Angeles: Roxbury Publishing.

Napper, G. (1977). Perception of crime: Problems and implications. In R. L. Woodson (Ed.), *Black perspectives on crime and the criminal justice system* (pp. 5–22). Boston: G. K. Hall.

Nobles, W. (1986). *African psychology: Toward its reclamation, reascension and revitalization.* Oakland, CA: Black Family Institute.

Radzinowicz, L., & King, J. (1977). *The growth of crime: The international experience.* New York: Basic.

Russell, K. K. (1992). Development of a black criminology and the role of the black criminologist. *Justice Quarterly, 9,* 667–683.

Russell, K. K. (1998). *The color of crime: Racial hoaxes, white fear, black protectionism, police harassment, and other macroaggressions.* New York: New York University Press.

Sagarin, E. (1980). *Taboos in criminology.* Beverly Hills, CA: Sage Publications.

Schur, E. (1969). *Our criminal society: The social and legal sources of crime in America.* Englewood Cliffs, NJ: Prentice-Hall.

Staples, R. (1975). White racism, black crime and American justice: An application of the colonial model to explain crime and race. *Phylon, 36*(1), 14–22.

Van Evrie, J. H. (1853). *Negroes and Negro "slavery": The first, an inferior race: The latter, its normal condition.* Baltimore, MD: J. D. Toy.

Walker, S., Spohn, C., & DeLone, M. (1995). *Color of justice: Race, ethnicity and crime in America.* Belmont, CA: Wadsworth.

Weinberg, M. (1992). *The world of W. E. B. Du Bois: A quotation sourcebook.* Westport, CT: Greenwood Press.

Wilson, J. Q., & Herrnstein, R. J. (1985). *Crime and human nature.* New York: Simon & Schuster.

DIALOGUE, REFLECTION, AND CRITICAL ANALYSIS

Self/Other Crossing Ideological Borders

Leila E. Villaverde

With Tanya O. Brown, Kazuko Matsuda, Adrienne Sansom,
and Warren Scheideman

Dialogue, reflection, and critical analysis are staples in the pedagogical experiences you will read below. As students encounter multiple discourses they are invited to question assumptions, push the envelope, and search for bridges across differences. In studying diversity, students are asked to discern the numerous borders that exist, separating self from other, to then delve into the dis-ease often resulting from such inquiry, and the necessary exploration, awakedness, and changes in practice and ideology.

Theories

This chapter discusses and questions the personal, social, and political borders of the pedagogical space in several curriculum studies and cultural foundations classrooms. There are many folk pedagogies (embedded beliefs about education) (Brunner, as cited in Bolotin, Bravmann, Windschitl, Mikel, & Green, 2000) students employ in their understanding of curriculum, teaching, and learning. In this chapter I explore the space in which course content intersects with student knowledge to produce new insight. This intersection can be rich in analysis, dis-ease, affirmation, and inquiry all riddled with initially a denial or even an "aha" experience and subsequently a rethinking of knowledge production.

My approach to curriculum theorizing is situated within a history of discourses defining curriculum as living, as life, and a lived experience (Bolotin et al., 2000). Therefore my approach to students focuses on a process of awakedness (Greene, 1981), questioning, and genuine listening through our shared living/being. The true challenge is at the core of the in-betweeness of knowledge, identity, and context. This type of transformative pedagogy that fosters a radically different respect of the self and other requires a presence of humanity through agreement and disagreement, success and failure, validation and potential, knowing and research. The experience in the classroom is as important as what students learn in order to continue a domino effect of social and educational change. The education of my students is just as much my own education as I continuously develop/evolve a clearer awareness of what it means to learn and unlearn in and through diversity (of identity, place, power, and ideology). In this chapter, a selected number of students from across the nation will share their perspectives on the curricular, intellectual, and individual lived experiences in classrooms and the courses they have taken with me.

Before I delve into the classroom space, curricular content, and pedagogical relations I want to discuss diversity and what frames of reference it has provided me. Diversity has been a floating signifier in my everyday experiences, signifying me as invisible, hypervisible, or not quite visible enough. I have negotiated not being Latina enough to being too Latina; being suspected of not speaking English (just based on my surname); seeming too young, too hard, too enigmatic (because I do not share my personal life); being questioned about my sexuality because I include queer theory in my courses; being asked to speak on behalf of all Latinos—the list of occurrences can go on and on. Every one of these experiences shapes and frames the way I look at the world, the people I interact with, and my responsibility within the classroom. I always say that no one checks his or her identity at the door when class begins, and there are times students make one's identity disruptively central to the curricular experience. I not only teach diversity through my presence; I also insistently weave it in through theory and practice. As pervasive as diversity is in the United States, we continue to treat it as an external entity, only "affecting" some people. If we continue to otherize what is core to human life we must hold ourselves accountable for being complicitous with numerous systems of inequity that deny individuals and groups civil rights and possibilities.

The encounters described above and the countless others that I experienced have converged for me into a conceptualization of diversity pedagogy—a particular way of processing and salvaging pedagogical content. I equate this process to Kubler-Ross's (1997) five stages of grief (denial, anger, depression, bargaining, and acceptance). The variations on these stages start with their title: instead of stages of grief, I consider them *stages of critical awareness*. There are times when denial (these moments happen so many times you're beyond questioning what occurred) turns into *recognition* of how ignorance of and prejudice against difference mutates continuously in various contexts. The second stage I retain as *anger*, a general frustration with the frequency of discrimination, injustice, and disregard for human life. The third stage is depression which I change to *contemplation*. Depression tends to immobilize people, yet contemplation provides a certain space for reflection and careful thought for future action (praxis). This stage allows for much needed critical analysis of the moment where one's identity collides with another's. Bargaining is the fourth stage of the Kubler-Ross model. I prefer to reframe this stage as a *negotiation* between reality and unfulfilled wishes or hopes that establish an innovative use of our imagination. Negotiation becomes the space where we thoughtfully theorize different possibilities, simulate practices for making things different for transforming unfortunate incidents to critical spaces for pedagogy (Villaverde, 1999). The fifth and final stage is acceptance, which I have changed to *consciousness/awakedness*. Consciousness/awakedness provides a different perspective and clarity about one's place, significance, and responsibility. Each lived experience and/or classroom situation presents a certain insight we can either recognize or ignore. I simply suggest there is a lot to learn from taking the time to not react, but to act in response with discernment and foresight. These stages have helped me theorize and operationalize my critical analysis and pedagogy about diversity.

Pedagogies

I started teaching multiculturalism courses in graduate school, not by personal choice but by appointment. Often graduate teaching assistants and faculty of color are slotted to teach multiculturalism courses—a decision that is typically fueled by an assumption that they possess an inherent scholarly knowledge or interest in the topic. Ironically this condition becomes a double-edged sword, particularly evidenced in course evaluations when students state the instructor had an agenda or a chip on his or her shoulder. Some of these courses are required as part of either general university curricula or specific programs. Most students are not there by choice, which could set up preexisting resistances. The classroom becomes a potentially volatile environment when the instructor overlays student resistance with thought-provoking readings, discussions, and assignments on difficult subject matter. Moreover, meaningful interaction becomes difficult when class participants offer tentative, safe responses that are usually cloaked by political correctness and proper etiquette. With that said, I thoroughly enjoyed every course on multiculturalism or diversity I taught in several universities because in each instance I learned immensely about people and how knowledge affects them. As I stated earlier, my approach was to weave diversity into the curriculum even if the course was not a designated diversity offering, and I still follow this tactic. Teaching predominantly in schools or colleges of education warrants that issues of race, class, gender, ethnicity, culture, religion, ability, language, and/or sexual orientation are fundamental in learning, teaching, leadership, and knowledge production.

The struggles I've negotiated in teaching issues of diversity have been great teachers in and of themselves. I have learned a great deal about people, human relations, respect, patience, genuine listening, and consistency. I also believe I have grown tremendously as I am continuously challenged to ask myself whether I am practicing what I believe, discuss in class, and want students to understand. The classroom has been an invaluable teacher, which for me was a welcome surprise since theory has always provided such guidance and numerous windows of possibility. Theory is a constant that pulls and pushes my thinking, cracks open spaces where there appeared to be none, and unfolds nuances of being through new languages. I believe learning is produced from struggle, at least for me that has always been the case. School/learning never seemed interesting enough, but I performed well. It was not until college that I became increasingly consumed with knowledge, reading, thinking, and with what I could do with it. It was not just any reading, but reading on critical theory, art history, contemporary art, poetry, feminist theory, psychology, and critical pedagogy. These disciplines fed me, armed me with ways of looking at the world and negotiating it. This of course would take time and change over time. As I started teaching I was eager to engage in conversation after conversation with students, hoping they would redefine themselves as producers of knowledge. My hopes or wishes would be, and still are, challenging but utterly meaningful.

My pedagogical philosophy leaks into multiple spaces, large/small classes, independent studies, informal conversations, and mentoring. My objective is for students to learn and be exposed to and critically think/question theories/works/ideologies more so than when we first met and to interpret, analyze, and synthesize tools for living and educating (in the various contexts they find themselves, both public and private). Genuine listening is, I believe, the key to crossing multiple borders between myself and students, students and students, and students and content. Many students enter the classroom with certain hesitations, defenses, and previous conceptions of what learning experiences are like (the folk pedagogies mentioned earlier in the chapter). It is important to recognize these qualities, conceptions, and behaviors as potential barriers to learning and to create a classroom environment that engenders within each student greater confidence in who they are as learners and producers of knowledge.

Often the readings and discussions challenge students' sense of familiarity, morality, and ethics and produce tangible frustrations. Students tend to internalize the inability to understand critical texts or lash out at the incomprehensibility of these texts, rather than taking the opportunity to wrestle with new knowledge and language. When we discuss gender or religion, discussions are pretty lively, but if we discuss race, ethnicity, or sexual orientation silence reigns until I bring our attention to it and begin to ask specific questions about their raced selves within an assumed heterosexual matrix. We inspect the norms, our experiences, and extract curricular possibilities. Many do not understand the fluctuation in privilege, access, and power; therefore classroom dialogue and conversation are essential to deconstructing and applying ideas. Students and faculty too often are caught in thinking of identity politics through large, monolithic categories (black, white, female, male, young, old, able, disabled, poor, rich, bad, good). Identity is much more complex and fluid most times, yet quite concrete other times; we cannot afford to shy away from these nuances and tricky junctures.

It is important for students to feel their questions and insights are respected/supported and pushed to the next level. Leaving the course unchanged means time was wasted. Two things I always stress are deep thinking/questioning, and qualifying/situating while they risk what they know, perhaps unlearn a few things, learn others, and yet relearn a few more.

I care about student growth regardless of where students are in the ideological spectrum. I want them to understand their limits and I want to push them, really push them for the sake of educational and social change. With this I unfold and develop my philosophy of learning and teaching. I have heard numerous times that I am a challenging and hard professor. I agree, but the difficulty is supported with plenty of scaffolds for students to be successful in learning. I see their studies as one context for learning; I do not only want to prepare them to excel in this context, but to excel outside of it. Students must become multilingual, fluent in various literacies and discourses. They must understand the skills of discernment and code switching.

Diversity Revisited

I want to make a few very specific statements about diversity before we move to student letters. Diversity is everywhere; it cannot be ignored. It needs to be highlighted, recognized, understood, and advocated. It is not just the individual differences, but the rich, intellectual contribution made by applying multiple lenses to comprehending texts. If diversity is understood ontologically, the spaces in between the present categorical taxonomies become important zones for contention, for political consciousness, awareness, and action. It is these in-between spaces where humanness is rediscovered, where lasting impact can occur, and the ethic of care made conditional upon what is done and said, not expected, taken for granted, or excluded, but mutually generated. While this complexity is embarked upon it is also crucial to link discussions/conversations to larger systems/patterns of inequity so that injustice is made evident. Injustice has a long legacy worldwide; public memories need to be inserted into a variety of curricula. The consistency of injustice should be made clear in order to deal with the magnitude of power and privilege, to dismantle systems of supremacy that breed such conditions as norm, natural, and business as usual. Yet if students embarking on this feel "less than" because they don't initially understand, don't have the "right" language or ideas, we run the risk of perpetuating/enacting the very dehumanizing systems we critique and work to change. Smith (1999) contends:

> There is an inextricability of Self and Other, with the Other maintained as
> a kind of Other-for-the Self. . . . Pedagogically it can be seen how this view
> sponsors a certain requirement of friendliness with others, a new kind of

ethical foundation for social relations. If I harm you, somehow my own self requirements are diminished, or at least the context of my life is harmed. . . . The interest of the teacher is not to teach, in the usual sense of imparting well-formulated epistemologies, but to protect the conditions under which students in their own way can find their way. (pp. 462–463, 467)

The following are the letters of four remarkable people I had the privilege of sharing classroom space with. Their letters echo and affirm the results of hard work, deep thinking, and unwavering commitment. My response to their narratives conclude the chapter.

Student Letters

Tanya O. Brown, education director of a multicultural arts school (Illinois)

Being biracial means that issues of race and diversity are always present. It is not uncommon for people to wonder, usually out loud, about my racial background. I have grown accustomed to people projecting their own feelings about race and interracial relationships onto me before taking time to get to know me or my personal experience. When I was younger and lacked the vocabulary and skills to talk about issues of race meaningfully, I saw being biracial as a burden. Growing up as one of a few children of color in a predominantly white, lower-middle-class suburb, survival meant blending in and trying to play down the black side of me as much as possible. I felt it was unfair because on top of dealing with the typical adolescent's issues of identity formation that any young person must face I had an additional burden that made me feel awkward and alienated.

I believe that race is a subject that affects everyone's life. If people believe that it isn't an issue, they are hiding behind the benefit of white privilege, not looking at the world realistically, and certainly not stepping outside their comfort zone in order to effect any meaningful change in their world. I now see being biracial as a benefit and a strength for many reasons. As an educator who works primarily with students of color and with teachers from a variety of backgrounds, being biracial provides a way for me to connect with the students and the teachers and to help build bridges from their shared experience. It also helps to open the door to productive and evocative conversations about race. Many of these skills I acquired through my work with Dr. Leila Villaverde. Before I met and began working with Dr. Villaverde, I saw issues of race and diversity primarily through cultural and personal lenses. I didn't have the skills or exposure to examine these issues through an intellectual lens. When things are brought into the intellectual realm, I feel they can be confronted and dealt with more effectively. Dr. Villaverde's classes were by no means easy. She is one of the toughest and most challenging teachers that I've ever had. However, she identified this as an area of growth for me without seeing this as a limitation. Instead she constantly pushed to use hard work and intelligence as my most powerful weapons in what we both see as a very important struggle for educational and social justice for all children. Her classes exposed me to the thinkers and theories that have become the foundation of my practice as an educator. It was through her example and her instruction that I learned how to use theory as a tool to inform my thoughts and actions and to inspire me when I am weary. I think the most important thing I learned from Dr. Villaverde was to never back down from a fight. Being a critical, multicultural, social reconstructionist can sometimes be a lonely place, leaving you open to people who believe schools should serve different purposes. When you have done your research and thought your arguments thoroughly, you don't have to back down from defending what you believe.

Working with Dr. Villaverde also kept me believing that there was a larger community of educators who were willing to work hard and sacrifice in order to build courageous schools that honestly talk about race and diversity. Such schools create a curriculum and school culture that empowers students with the tools of their own culture while respecting and learning from others.

As a school administrator in a high school whose stated mission is Critical Multiculturalism and Arts Integration I can now share my skills with teachers to help them to be comfortable and confident when talking about and actively confronting race and diversity issues. I am able to make the things that I have learned the foundation of our curriculum, school culture, and professional development. This is a dream come true for me, and I was especially proud and excited to let Dr. Villaverde know that such a place existed and that I was going to be a part of it.

Kazuko Matsuda, doctoral student in special education services (North Carolina)

Dear Dr. Villaverde,

Prior to taking your Feminist Theories in Education course I had considered myself more or less immune to human diversity. Being unilaterally deaf and therefore having a "disability" seemed to have been unique enough for me to learn at an early age that human experiences were quite diverse. As many individuals with disabilities would agree, having a disability does not exclude one from facing other life challenges. Indeed, it really wasn't my deafness that made my earlier life really hard. Rather, my deafness gave me a sense of who I was and sustained me from time to time during the difficult times as a young child. So, I used to consider my deafness as my single identity, if identity is an appropriate word. Otherwise, I did not have a place where I could belong, caught up between the hearing and deaf world.

I remember that I was very disturbed during the first half of the Feminist Theories in Education course. I have to emphasize that it was a true disturbance and it mainly came from earlier feminism's assertion that women, for example, housewives, were the oppressed. It contradicted an old cultural heritage and virtue held in my country and perhaps in many Asian countries, where women/housewives had important roles to be valued and appreciated. As I was reading several assigned articles I became agitated and wanted to yell to the authors of those articles, "Please do not judge someone's life condition based on your identity struggle." Then, I became confused as to whether what I had believed as "virtue" for women was merely the gender roles that women were forced to carry on their back. I also was confused as to whether I had been simply unconscious about my oppressive status as a woman. Had I been? I remember that I expressed my frustrations in my paper, assuming that you, Dr. Villaverde, would welcome my intense reactions to that particular feminist claim and let me go through the resistance process. It was a somewhat depressing period.

I recall one evening when I cried during a class as we discussed an article that touched upon Korean comfort women. Sitting next to a Korean classmate, I, as a Japanese woman, felt as if my blood froze. I was remorseful for what I had never done personally. I felt torn between shame and anger: shame as Japanese and anger as a woman. Exhausted, I went back to my apartment and started thinking why I always had such intense feelings dur-

ing this particular course. There were things I had rarely been particular about, such as my race, ethnicity, language, religion, gender, my own life history, as well as the history of my country. How had all of these shaped my interpretations of my life experiences, and how had I negotiated in and out of these issues.

On that particular evening, gender was as important an issue to me as disability. Culture, language, and nationality were also critical elements I had to negotiate throughout the course. It then became clear that I did not have to be always a woman with a disability. In order to become aware of the diversities within me, I had to abandon—at least once—what I used to rely on. My old self was threatened. Interestingly, the disturbance I originally felt turned out to be, or was transformed into, multiple selves, and which now allows me to see the world subjectively and objectively through my multiple lenses.

I do not know if transforming to something new always has to be accompanied with a certain period of unpleasantness. Even if it does, it is rewarding. It may sound contradictory but reflecting upon my learning experiences during the course, and becoming more conscious about the multiple selves within me, has given me a stronger sense (or a healthy ego). My voice is an important testimonial of the lived experiences of individuals with disabilities. The openness to my own multiplicities hopefully reflects my openness to others' voices. Diversity means different things to different people. To me at present, diversity begins with how many lenses we find in ourselves. When our multiple lenses start evoking our critical consciousness, we may find a deeper appreciation of diversities within us and others. Thank you, Dr. Villaverde.

Adrienne Sansom, *doctoral student in cultural studies and senior lecturer in dance and drama teacher education (North Carolina and New Zealand)*

Dear Dr. Villaverde,

I am writing this letter to you to let you know something of what your teaching has meant to me over the past two years. As a white (Pakeha) female growing up in New Zealand I have a particular perspective on diversity, issues of marginality, and culture that has obviously been a result of living in my country. I grew up in an ethnically diverse inner city neighborhood in a working-class family. This was my first recollection of encountering *difference. When I eventually chose my line of work in early childhood education, and more recently, dance education, I became aware that I worked in areas that were also seen as different, or, at least, of lesser importance, and, therefore, considered marginal. These formative experiences effectively shaped my views of difference and dominance.*

When I began my doctoral studies in education I discovered a program where we explored issues of marginality and difference to debunk preexisting ideologies that oppress. I was challenged by your courses to entertain sometimes very different perspectives of what it meant to be in education. It was these viewpoints of dominance as well as the notion of dismantling whiteness that became decentering devices in your classes. I was stirred to examine my own viewpoints and unravel how I perceived my positionality in relation to others. This involved being forever vigilant and suspicious of essentializing about any group of people or value/belief system while striving for democracy in education through the process of becoming engaged in open dialogue, critical reflection, and consciousness-raising.

I really felt comfortable in your classes, even though I remember times when I was challenged beyond all belief. Sometimes the conceptual language was somewhat difficult for me to comprehend, but I always felt inclined, and, indeed, invited to dig a little deeper so as to decipher the interesting and extremely thought-provoking language and the underlying concept. This was playing with the idea of "thinking the unthinkable," as well as "making the familiar seem strange," which were two of the many worthwhile quotes I remember from your courses.

Your teachings have had a long-lasting effect in how I now begin to view difference. One such way is in how I have become acutely aware of my new stance. I have had to alter my views from seeing the world from a predominantly culturally hegemonic standpoint (being raised in a time when minority cultures were ostracized) to embracing the "other." I have become more and more conscious of the dangers of appropriation of the other and know, how easily, the dominant continue their dominance through this method of acquiring the other. This pertains, in particular, to my own home country where indigenous rights are strongly espoused in both politics and education, but also places the other in a position of vulnerability through exploitation by the dominant.

My role as an educator is about taking risks and digging beneath the veneer of complacency, or even more, the insidiousness of guilt, so as to un-

earth the unknown. This relates, in particular, to how I encounter the other and cross those borders of ideological differences. Through these avenues I have been able to find a voice to express those things I believe in as agents of transformation. I will continue to push my own boundaries, inspired by what I have learned and will thirst for new knowledge because I have become even more aware of what I still do not know.

Warren Scheideman, *faculty in English and American literary history (Illinois)*

Dear Dr. V.:

In June of 2004 I graduated from DePaul University's School of Education with my Ed.D. in curriculum studies. I am in my early sixties with approximately 25 years at DePaul's School for New Learning, its progressive college of adult education. My journey to graduation took shape and definition when I entered your Assessing School Curriculum course, followed by your Special Topics: History of Curriculum. My course work was almost complete, but I did not have a focus or professional direction that felt right. I felt empty and was silent. I was having sustained doubts about curriculum, my teaching, values and directions, students, colleagues, and the world I knew—questions about the environmental context of our lives, and the curricular journey.

Critical Incident: When you introduced assessment, you announced a challenge that I immediately took very seriously. You said: "I want you all to push the envelope! I want you to question your assumptions, and push the envelope. You keep questioning your assumptions. I will be supportive. You work, develop, push the envelope, and I will be supportive!" Without ever having been a person of faith, and often lacking in engagement, I instantaneously believed you with serious engagement in learning. Experience of the syllabus, texts, and your exemplary supportive (nurturing, caring, but rigorous) class preparation signaled that you are fully supportive to risky thinking, to pushing the envelope, to questioning assumptions.

Change in Theory and Practice: You were not just talking. My own take on the state of our planet, including urban education, was that deep questioning, deep thought, and deep transformational changes are the only answers, if it isn't too late. I wanted to be with my whole heart and mind a better teacher and advisor. So I simply started to push myself, push the envelope; to push even harder on assignments and readings. For instance, in one *project I created a syllabus and cultural change background for teaching in Hong Kong.*

Dissertation as Benchmark of Transformation: *As I discovered curriculum history, my dissertation topic began to come into focus. I began to relate inner feelings and outer awareness, and my dissertation acquired the working title of* Bobbitt's Window. *It is about thinking through change, acquiring new awareness, seeing and hearing life differently, with multiculturally responsive awareness. And I was less silent! I was discovering new places for learning.*

Developing My Tool Kit: *Not too long after graduation I decided to inventory my newly acquired and expanded academic qualities. These I had gained from your courses and mentoring as chair of my doctoral committee, and I used them to create a "curricular tool kit." It is a literal construction that I made out of cardboard from shirt packaging and divided into drawers and sections. There is a section for tools: James Popham's hammer, his Mongolian abacus, the reality check, John Dewey's moral telescope, Bobbitt's Window, your Rolodex, the process of pushing the envelope. There is a list of my new computer skills. I was barely able to use a computer at the start of the dissertation. There is a drawer for popular culture, including photography and video and sections for critical theorists like Gadamer, Giroux, Habermas, Reinharz, Spivak.*

Your models of coaching, mentoring, facilitating, shifting pedagogical gears are perfect praxis *of theory. You empower your students for the diversity of life. The finest accolade of my life is when at the Final Defense, you said: "I am Dr. V. and now you are Dr. S." You share the rich gift of application of rich theory to meaningful practice. I hear and see more of life. Thank you.*

Reflections

As I read the above words from students I am humbled by the intensity and power of the lessons each took away. One can't always plan for these; one can hope and wrestle to include critical readings, assignments, and discussions, but the real work comes in the classroom and individual interactions (in or out of the class) when these elements come alive in the dynamic space of being and borders. To straddle and grapple with multiple ideologies and retain a respect for self and other through a sometimes unraveling process requires courage and strength to take the risk for pedagogical, public, and personal transformation.

In her letter, Tanya discusses the importance of gaining and developing intellectual lenses, using theory as a tool, and transforming her practice. Students often comment how difficult this exercise is and are usually resistant to individual discovery or experimentation. She recalls being challenged and using this to build bridges for change. Tanya's preparation to deal with any fight provides confidence in what she stands for. The fight is not necessarily a physical interchange, but rather the struggle and courage to go against the grain and the dominant perception of how intelligence is defined, who has it, who will succeed doing what, and so forth. In advocating for students who usually are disadvantaged by a system intending to assimilate them, Tanya successfully negotiates mounting opposition. Understanding the politics of diversity, power, history, culture, and pedagogy allows Tanya to make necessary/crucial professional and personal decisions. She has brilliantly taken these lessons to heart assisting in the construction of a multicultural arts school.

Kazuko's letter poignantly highlights the process by which she realizes the personal is political. She carefully recounts the ways through which she gained awareness of otherness, history, difference, and acceptance. To witness Kazuko's unfolding awareness as she discovered where a variety of discourses intersect through critical analysis was incredibly rewarding. Each discovery propelled poignant insight for a renewed understanding of her practice with young women who are in the juvenile system and are labeled with a learning disability. The more she studied, the greater became her understanding and search for new opportunities for the students she works with. Kazuko negotiated the struggle and discomfort of gaining insight and increased a deeper sense of self and other. She is a great example of using the self as the critical springboard for analysis before relating to the other.

Adrienne reflects on the various ways in which she understands difference and the analysis necessary to see the complexity of identity and power. She remembers being invited to dig deeper and "think the unthinkable," becoming decentered and remaining vigilant of essentialization. Adrienne is the eternal gifted student of life, of knowledge. She has taken what she has learned, carefully and introspectively theorized/applied it to both her writing and practice, as well as ultimately her being. She was open to rethinking and unlearning, two essential steps in the process of awakedness and genuinely being attentive to the other, relating to the other. Adrienne often otherizes the self in her quest to enact change, transformation, and growth. She welcomes risks and provides unbelievably supportive environments for her students.

Warren's letter resonates with Tanya's as he notes my emphasis on getting students to push the envelope and question assumptions. For Warren there was also recognition of his silence and development of his voice, a deep change in the ways there are to learn, and an acquisition of a tool kit. As he discusses the rigor of my courses and the consistency of what was said and experienced in them, Warren finds encouragement, challenge, and freedom to truly take the ideas into new horizons. He is able to chronicle his growth and creativity, as well as his assurance in his intellectual abilities. As a result Warren contends his life is richer, as he sees and hears more of it. I would consequently assert so are the lives of his students, given Warren's sincere care for their well-being.

All the letters touch upon at least one aspect of the process in becoming aware and developing critical consciousness. This is a never-ending process and I was delighted to see past students clearly illustrate varying steps in the process, however difficult yet rewarding it was. Most pleasing to read were the ways in which the courses we shared influenced their practice and thinking, in summary, their praxis. Tanya, Kazuko, Adrienne, and Warren are all educators who now undoubtedly carry a different set of priorities in their respective contributions to others' learning. Where they are, where they have arrived intellectually and pragmatically is in part a result of a rich, shared experience and allowance on their part to be present to others and to be sometimes painfully aware of their own position and identity. I am privileged to have shared the classroom with Tanya, Kazuko, Adrienne, and Warren and am delighted it was as significant to them. A deep and insightful pedagogical experience provides a rich soil to continuously cultivate new ideas, respect, and understanding of diversity and transformative learning. This is but a glimpse of our ongoing work.

References

Bolotin, P. J., Bravmann, S. L., Windschitl, M. A., Mikel, E. R., & Green, N. S. (2000). *Cultures of curriculum*. New York: Teachers College Press.

Greene, M. (1981, fall). The humanities and emancipatory possibility. *Journal of Education, 163*(4), 287–305.

Kubler-Ross, E. (1997). *On death and dying.* New York: Simon & Schuster Adult Publishing Group.

Smith, D. G. (1999). Identity, self, and other in the conduct of pedagogical action: An East/West inquiry. In W. F. Pinar (Ed.), *Contemporary curriculum discourses: Twenty Years of JCT.* New York: P. Lang.

Villaverde, L. E. (1999). Creativity, art, and aesthetics unraveled through post-formalism: An exploration of perception, experience, and pedagogy. In S. R. Steinberg, J. L. Kincheloe, & P. H. Hinchey (Eds.), *Post-Formal Reader: Cognition and Education.* New York: Falmer Press.

11

TEACHING ABOUT DIVERSITY
IN SEX EDUCATION

Steve Chandler

With Justin Williams, Kevin Coleman, Jeanette Woldman,
and Lance Raynor

The intent of this chapter is to convey some of the many opportunities presented in sexuality education for teaching about diversity. The four letters presented here by former students display how a sexuality course may impress each student differently and provide each with numerous chances to examine his or her own behavior from many divergent points of view. The pedagogical exercises that follow the students' letters emphasize a comprehensive approach to sexuality education and represent just a few of the strategies that sex educators may employ to help students relate to the experiences of others.

As an interdisciplinary study, sexuality may be approached from many perspectives that can actively challenge students' beliefs and perceptions about a practically universal experience—sex. Whether students feel that sexual behavior is mandated by biology, they are quick to discover that it presents itself in nearly infinite variety and is readily modified by culture and time. Diversity issues arise frequently and consistently in sexuality courses and these courses provide an excellent forum for teaching and learning about diversity.

Sexuality courses are typically offered in professional preparation programs in psychology, social work, sociology, health education, and biomedical disciplines. Such courses are also among the most popular electives on campuses, and students from outside these programs of study often make up the bulk of those enrolled. It has been my experience that women enroll in sexuality courses more frequently than men and it is not unusual for my classes to have about a 3 to 1 gender split. In the college classes I teach, my students have ranged in age from 18 to 66, with the majority clustered around 19 to 23. I teach at a historically black university that remains predominantly black. Nonblack students usually make up no more than 5% or 10% of my students or 1 or 2 in a typical class of 25. The nonblack students at this university of 12,000 students tend to cluster in certain majors, and most of the courses I teach do not attract many of these students. While my classes are not particularly diverse in student composition, diversity is a central theme in the mission of the institution and I feel my sexuality courses present a deep well of opportunity for teaching a large number of students at the university about diversity.

I have been teaching undergraduate sexuality courses in health education or social work since the early 1990s. I also see a limited number of clients for individual, couple, and family therapy as a registered clinical social worker intern in Florida. Since I may employ self-disclosure at opportune times as a tool in my work, I may be less forthcoming about my personal history in this chapter than others in this volume. I also feel that self-disclosure in the classroom can sometimes bias students and thereby reduce their openness to learning. I prefer to let my students or clients perceive me as I am through their own filters, and use self-disclosure selectively if I feel it may aid our work together.

I was raised in small Texas towns during the 1950s and 1960s as my family moved every year or two to follow my stepfather's work. We eventually settled in a small town of German heritage in the beautiful Hill Country region where I attended a public high school and graduated toward the end of the Vietnam war. My mother took my two older sisters and me to church regularly until we were teens, whereupon the kids rebelled and we all stopped going. The largest ethnic minority in my youth was Hispanic and that culture blended well with the other locals so that on any given day I could hear English, Spanish, or German spoken by those around me. I had few close friends outside my ethnic group; a more pressing social concern for me and my peers was whether one was a "hippie or a redneck." I wasn't much of either and never truly felt engaged in that debate. I preferred to spend my free time in outdoor activities like frolicking in spring-fed rivers or running and biking in the hills.

My family traveled little in my youth, and my exposure to diversity remained limited even through my college years. I chose a regional college 20 miles from home mostly because it was convenient and some of my friends were planning to enroll there. It turned out to be one of the most beautiful places in the world—with a spring-fed river running right through campus! After adjusting to studying for the first time in my life, I fell in love with learning and vowed to stay in college as long as possible, eventually earning two degrees from what is now called Texas State University-San Marcos. When I moved to Tallahassee, Florida, to pursue my doctoral degree in the 1980s, I was introduced to a new region, the South, and black folks replaced the Hispanic minority group I was familiar with. Diversity concerns had a greater emphasis in Florida, but the blending of cultures seemed to be replaced by a more strained, litigious integration. I liked my classmates and enjoyed my time in Tallahassee—there were hills and rivers to play in there, too. Basically, college in Texas had taught me to believe that visible differences in people were because of their genes and environment of origin and that behavioral differences were because of culture. Beyond that, I wasn't much engaged in that debate either.

Once I became employed as a professor, work helped me expand my awareness of the importance of diversity as something that could influence how my students learned. Work also provided an income sufficient for me to travel to other states and countries where I could see more clearly that diversity issues were flavored by where one happened to be. Professional training and practice continually emphasized diversity issues as important factors in how different people got along. I began to realize that diversity conflicts and the biases some people held mattered far more to other people than they did to me. In 1990, I came to work at a historically and predominantly black university, mostly because the topics I would teach appealed to me. Although some of my classmates from my doctoral program were on the faculty there, I had never been on campus before my interview.

What follows are several letters from former students about their experiences with diversity that stem in some part from their experiences in courses under my instruction. Two of the students are male and two female, one of each looks ethnically similar to most of my students and the others do not. Three were Florida residents during college and one was an international student. All earned at least the bachelor's degree; one is now entering the workforce, one is now beginning out-of-state graduate school and one finishing it, and the last is self-employed on the French Riviera. My reactions and observations about their comments follow each student's letter, then I share some key points where I emphasized diversity in the classes they had with me. I will also elaborate on some of the pedagogical strategies I employ in my courses to better allow the reader to reflect on how these strategies may have helped shape my students' perceptions about diversity.

Student Letters

Justin Williams, student in master's program in psychology (North Carolina)

> *Growing up in the South has been a great pleasure and a learning experience. All throughout elementary school, middle school, and high school my peers were either black or white. Diversity in my small town was nonexistent, and I was in high school when I met the first Hispanic. My knowledge of different cultures and ethnicities was very limited. However, upon entering college I learned about different ethnicities among black people, met and interacted with students who were from mixed parentage, and took classes from professors who were from different cultures and countries and had different religious beliefs and moral philosophies.*
>
> *During my junior year at Florida A&M University, I had the distinct pleasure of taking a class with Dr. Steve Chandler, a professor in the social work department. The FAMU social work department emphasizes diversity and strives to equip its students with the knowledge and skills they will need to effectively have an impact on the lives of blacks, whites, Latinos, Asians, and so on. In Dr. Chandler's class, we learned about the culture and ethnic differences that may hinder or facilitate social workers from delivering care to clients. The class helped me see the differences and similarities in groups of people. Even Dr. Chandler himself helped me to discover the wonder behind different ethnic groups. In the class 100% of the students were black and 90% female, and the instructor was a white male.*
>
> *Dr. Chandler's approach and perspective on diversity was different from that of the majority of the students in the class since we were black. At times the class would be fixated on the needs and concerns of black people, and Dr.*

Chandler would prod us to think outside our own ethnic and cultural needs and think about the needs of others. Aside from ethnic and cultural diversity, Dr. Chandler encouraged us to think about the special needs of the disabled, the needs of the physically and mentally impaired. One activity that he asked the class to do was to find a way to retrieve our exams from a hook on the chalkboard without talking and with a physical limitation (for example, being blind or deaf). Everyone in the class had a good time trying to figure out how to handle our new challenge, but the reality of not having use of one of the faculties that we take advantage of every day was quite disturbing. Personally, I know that from time to time I wonder what it would be like to not be able to see a car or hear my favorite music.

From Dr. Chandler's presentation on human sexuality, I made a resolution to be more open minded regarding people's sexual preferences, and I have a desire to incorporate sex therapy into my clinical practice after I obtain my Ph.D. Having Dr. Chandler as an instructor has helped me realize there are other ethnicities and cultures besides my own, and that sexuality is relative and culturally specific. I appreciate the life and professional lessons that Dr. Chandler has imparted on me while I matriculated through Florida A&M University. Now that I have graduated, I will take these skills with me into my professional career.

Commentary

Justin's letter conveys some important concepts and reveals her commitment to learning, reflection, and personal growth. I found it interesting that she did not consider the black and white environment of her youth to be diverse until a Hispanic person was introduced during high school. This reminds me of reactions by students in my classes to the Lesbian, Gay, Bisexual, Transgender, and Questioning (LGBTQ) guest panels I sometimes bring in to represent our local community center. If a panel contains only LGB members, students listen intently and challenge them about their insights and experiences, but when a panel contains a transgendered person, particularly one who is a postoperative transsexual, the class is prone to accept the simple, familiar differences of the LGB members without much comment and focus their inquiry on the more exotic member. The lesson I take from this: The greater diversity a group contains, the more likely its members are to accept its common variations.

When Justin refers to my prodding her generally homogenous class to think beyond their own ethnicity and realize that they will be serving clients from diverse groups in their professional lives, she conveys learning that I also experienced when I first became a minority teacher. Before arriving at FAMU, I was employed at a small, private liberal arts college that placed great emphasis on teaching diversity across the curriculum. Diversity there focused more on sexual, religious, and socioeconomic groups and ethnic minorities represented such a small fraction of the student body that they had little effect on campus culture. When I joined the faculty at FAMU, I assumed the community would be well aware of diversity issues, and my students and colleagues would model equity and fairness based on their experiences as members of a minority group. But as Justin conveyed, this is not always the case. What I realized after being at FAMU for a while was that what is sometimes learned by being a member of a minority group that has experienced discrimination is not how to be equitable to others, but rather how also to discriminate and be ethnocentric. Minority students don't automatically gain diversity insights by being in the minority. They need to be taught to look outside their own group, just like those from a majority. It is often assumed that preparing black students at historically black colleges will best prepare them to work in a diverse workplace. That won't happen unless diversity lessons are taught to the students there.

Justin's letter also conveys the importance of experiential learning. The lesson she describes about assigning students to groups that are uniquely disabled is a variation of a "foil stars" exercise introduced to my class by a GLBTQ group I described earlier. The intent is to enable the students to identify with others by acquiring their traits, at least temporarily. Justin found that effort "quite disturbing" but apparently thought provoking. What she didn't fully convey was the truly humorous appearance of the class as they achieved the goal of their newly created diverse group: to find a way to work together in a coordinated fashion to retrieve their recently graded exams from a hook above the chalkboard. The blind ones were quadriplegic but could speak; the mute ones could see the exams on the hook but couldn't reach them because they had no arms; the deaf students had arms but couldn't walk. The basic lesson is that the value of diversity in a group is most apparent when they must coordinate their efforts to achieve a task that individuals cannot accomplish as well on their own.

Kevin Coleman, *master's student in business (Florida)*

My name is Kevin Coleman and I am a black male who grew up in Fort Pierce, Florida. Before I came to college at Florida A&M University, I was an all-star athlete in my hometown and was well known for my athletic abilities. This made me extremely popular with my high school classmates. I attended an integrated high school where most of my classmates were white. Many of my cultural experiences were different from those of my white classmates, however, as an athlete, I was still able to have positive interaction with all my classmates regardless of ethnicity. It was during high school that I realized that with popularity comes sexual temptation.

High school athletes have plenty of opportunities to have sex when they are young and do not know about sexually transmitted diseases. They may have unprotected sex without thinking about the consequences of their actions. As a college student, my experiences in high school made me extremely interested in a course titled Human Sexuality taught by Dr. Steve Chandler. This course helped me understand the importance of practicing safer sex and it made me more aware about how sexually transmitted infections affect college students of all ethnicities. There were shocking statistics revealed in the class that showed an alarming HIV infection rate among blacks in the United States ages 18 to 24, more than among their white counterparts. The class was also able to dispel the myth that HIV/AIDS is a disease that only affects homosexuals. Through analyzing statistics and in-depth discussion, my classmates and I learned how sexually transmitted infections affect different people in the United States and abroad.

My class included students from all parts of the United States as well as some international students. The diverse backgrounds of my classmates ensured interesting discussions and differing viewpoints on the topics of sexual promiscuity and STI (sexually transmitted infections) prevention. I also learned that the transmission of these STIs has a direct connection to the economic status of citizens.

In many poor and rural regions of the United States and in developing nations, people are not properly educated on the ways to prevent the spread of STIs. The course in human sexuality helped me realize there is a direct link between high levels of infection and a misinformed or poorly educated public. The class taught me so much about the human body and how to protect it from disease. After learning important STI facts and statistics, I wanted to share everything that I learned with my fellow college students. I knew that I could save lives and prevent the spread of disease by informing other collegians about the deadly risks that come from promiscuous behavior.

Commentary

Kevin's letter reminds us that there are times when privilege and status can confer risk or harm on a group. Athletes at all levels are bestowed prestige and social privilege by many in our culture that extends beyond what is reasonably deserved for physical ability and skill and on to moral character and fecundity. We argue that athletic participation can teach sportsmanship, but it can also confer an unwarranted sense of invincibility and privilege on some athletes that may extend to sexual behaviors. Such athletes may constitute a high-risk group for physical and sexual abuse (Chandler, Johnson, & Carroll, 1999), and as Kevin implies, their status may provide them with opportunities for sexual activities that carry risk for disease and altered sex-related psychosocial development.

I wish I could credit Kevin's heightened sense of altruism to his attending my course, but it may have only helped him focus his efforts on educating his peers about the risks they face. Like many of his classmates, Kevin held at least two part-time jobs while enrolled as a full-time student. He worked in the bookstore and was a resident assistant for several semesters. In the latter capacity, he invited me to speak to first-year students in his residence hall during his final two years. He always provided a large audience and insisted that we use graphic illustrations and conduct frank discussions with the new students. From the feedback he received, he was confident that we had positively affected the students who attended.

We always tried to compare the effectiveness of STI prevention strategies that emphasize abstinence only until marriage with the more comprehensive ABC strategy (*A*bstinence is the only way you can be certain not to get an STI, but if you choose not to be abstinent, *B*e faithful to one partner in a monogamous relationship where you both get tested for STIs. If you cannot be abstinent or monogamous, always use a *C*ondom and realize it cannot protect you from some STIs). The students are quick to recognize that the abstinence-only strategy has its foundation in a value system that many of them do not entirely accept; contrary to many of their family experiences, it emphasizes marriage as the only acceptable union for the construction of a family, and that it does not acknowledge sex as a natural act that may be enjoyed for recreation as well as procreation. The students do not feel adequately informed by abstinence lessons and are concerned that trying to adhere to such a narrow view will leave many of their peers uninformed and unprotected when abstinence is breached. Because of his high school experiences, Kevin would insist that we discuss the proper use of condoms and where they can fall short for the typical user.

Jeanette Woldman, self-employed consultant for the travel industry (Principality of Monaco)

> Dear Dr. Chandler,
>
> I was born and raised in a small country town in the Netherlands, where some people still walked in wooden shoes, including myself at times. My world was filled with the tulips in spring, the windmill in town, vast green, flat lands with black and white cows, lots of rain, cold white winters and a very tight nonreligious family. My mother was a homemaker and my father raced motorbikes. Every weekend from spring to autumn Mom and Dad went with my brother and me to our RV on the forest's edge near a lake. Families from other towns were also on the camping site. I even had a girlfriend from Groningen, a big city. She did not wear wooden shoes and she spoke a different dialect.
>
> When I was about seven years old, our parents took the car and RV and went across the border to Germany. Everything was different there, at not even a day's drive! We met kids from countries we had not heard of. Some of them ate funny food and spoke in funny tongues.
>
> We continued traveling with my family every summer. We went all over Europe. We got used to different sounds, smells, tastes, sights, and people. We ate local foods, and tried our best in other languages. We made friends in different places and corresponded for many years with other kids in other countries. I never tired of new places and new friends. As a matter of fact, it only enhanced my curiosity about the world beyond.
>
> After high school I went abroad to study at an international school in the United States with mainly European students and teachers. After completing my studies, I worked on cruise ships and traveled to all the corners of

the world. In between contracts, I continued traveling to faraway places. Over 100 countries later, speaking several languages and having experienced working with over 50 different nationalities, I decided it was time to go to university. I left a management position aboard a cruise ship and moved to Tallahassee to obtain my bachelor's and master's in architecture at Florida A&M University.

I was prepared for change when I took my first class, but I never anticipated that the first things I was about to learn would be a long shot from what I had been exposed to so far. I found out that I was "white" on school forms (I never had a color before in the rest of the world), and I realized that the world here revolved around one country called "America." International news was limited to a few lines on the sixth page of the local paper, and the TV wasn't any more enlightening. United States passports holders called themselves "African American," "Irish American," "Asian American," "Indian American," and so on, most likely because they missed the very link with other countries they knew were somewhere outside their map. Very few of the professors I received instruction from had traveled abroad or were, like myself, "legal aliens." So how in the world could my horizons be broadened at university?

Education would come from quite a different angle. Most of what I'd learned so far had been on mainly practical experiences encountered by my five senses. Thanks to a very few well-lettered and open-minded American professors, my brain became enriched with everything that came from books written by great thinkers, and which was further explained by these bright minds who encouraged me to search for more meaning. My brain was provoked, tested, and triggered with all things theoretical. Neurons traveled places where they had not been before. My overall worldly experience was broadened by these educated men and women who taught me to explore the depths of my own horizons within the world I call myself.

My American experience was an interesting one, and thanks to those few wonderful professors, a truly educational adventure. When I left the United States for good with my degrees in hand, I returned to "the other world." I left "the land of the great" to include myself once more into the wonderful blend of cultures, nationalities, traditions, and languages that the world has to offer, acquiring more knowledge ever since because of my five senses and because of what I learned in America.

Commentary

Jeanette's letter helps us see that what we typically think of as important diversity issues are essentially local issues. Her rearing in Europe and subsequent travels throughout a world where widely diverse cultures can be as close to one another as states are in the United States clearly imparted not just tolerance on her, but also a rich, rewarding fascination for travel and exploration of culture, people, and places. Contrast that with someone like me who didn't hold a passport for foreign travel until I was past age 40. She was taught a different world was close at hand and enticing, I was taught it was distant and foreign and somehow threatening. I love it that she didn't know she "had a color" until she had to complete the forms for admission to our educational system. What do we really teach one another with those forms and why do we continue to use them? Some argue they help to provide equality, others that it keeps inequality alive and well.

It often takes the perception of someone from outside the United States to effectively point out the ethnocentrism and narrowness our nationalism perpetuates. When brought to our attention by foreign visitors, our response can be defensive and unwelcoming. Aren't we the citizens of the world with the reputation of poor hosts *and* poor guests? When someone like Jeanette crosses the border from France to Italy, she changes her language and respectfully adopts the customs of the new culture as easily as you or I would change a shirt. Personally, I'm lucky to be able to order breakfast or count money in either country. I'm truly happy that Jeanette was able to learn something from her stay in the United States, even if it was only from the books we had her read.

Lance Raynor, master's student in human sexuality (California)

> *When I first entered college, it was partly based on a desire to more fully understand my sexual attraction to both men and women. However, as a queer white male going to a historically black university in the South, I realized that the discussion of sexual diversity (including queer and gender-queer sexualities) was going to be more complicated than I first imagined. Coming to the university with a head full of idealism about cultural diversity and tolerance cum knowledge, I enrolled in the psychology program, thinking the*

department would be the most open to discussing sexual diversity. However, I was not prepared for the simplistic, reductionist notions of black culture presented by professors aiming for utopian visions of black nationalism via racial separatism—a kind of cultural purification program aimed at eradicating the influences of miscegenation.

During my first semester, I took a class in abnormal psychology. After arriving at the (much awaited) section on sexuality disorders, my professor plainly stated that the abnormal presence of a few homosexuals within the African diaspora was part of the castrating influences of slavery—so that some black men possessed such hatred of their own blackness and their own manhood, that they chose to adopt the unnatural practices of Eurocentric sexual depravity. According to this professor, a truly Afrocentric brother would condemn homosexuality and miscegenation in the black community and dutifully express his heterosexual desire for black women.

Later, after long lamentations about my professors' lack of intellectual insight into both cultural and sexual diversity within the African diaspora, I enrolled in a philosophy class that challenged for me the notion of race as a natural, discrete category, suggesting instead that race was a cultural creation of racist hierarchs. Throughout the class, I wondered if gender could be thought of in similar ways, but even this professor became stubborn when I challenged the notions of biological sex as a natural, discrete category. However, upon taking Steve Chandler's human sexuality course, I found that, under closer examination, sex and gender are not the clean and discrete categories that many hope for. In this course, we discussed sex as a spectrum, and the binary of male/female was shown to be a social construction, enabled by the sexist notions of heteronormativity and the limited views of medical doctors. He discussed the existence of persons—individuals who did not fit neatly into the category of male or female. Finally, I was able to make the connection between racism, sexism, and homophobia.

Drawing on this professor's descriptions of cultural variation in the expression of sexual identity, I realized that I was interested in bringing the knowledge of ethnic and cultural studies to bear on the formation of my own gender queer political activism. After graduating, I decided to travel around India for several months, and became interested in cross-cultural influences on diasporic sexualities. Now as a graduate student at San Francisco State University, I am in the process of creating an ethnographic film that asks how does intercultural communication function in San Francisco's queer and transgender neighborhood rights activism?

Commentary

Professors are indeed fortunate to occasionally have students like this one, whose passion for knowledge and understanding refuses to be extinguished by the narrow perspectives of rigid authority figures. When these rare students can suffer through what must feel like indignities and still emerge anxious to seek answers, we should be reminded of the struggles that have taken place to foster better relationships between people in the past. I will leave it to the reader to consider whether Lance experienced racism, sexism, and systemic bigotry or that he somehow misinterpreted some of his professors' points. It should be clear to anyone reading this text that sexual minorities are entitled to equal treatment in publicly funded educational institutions and are provided the same legal protections other minorities enjoy (Satterly & Dyson, 2005). I am happy that Lance appears to have realized that when no one can answer his questions, he needs to discover answers for himself.

It is challenges by students like Lance that should make professors grow. I am reminded of another psychology student who enrolled in my class. He was thoughtful and outspoken and I would often notice him frowning at some of my comments. Toward the end of the term he came to me at the conclusion of a class and said, "You know, Doc, this is a pretty good class, but you're teaching white-people sexuality." I assumed he meant the resources I was employing in the course didn't fairly reflect a diversity of views. I had already informed the class that the textbook and much of the literature in sexuality was rather narrow, that more basic research of ethnic sexual behaviors was needed. I often encourage my students to pursue graduate study in the field and thereby add to the body of knowledge. I responded to this student's comments by adding more books by black authors to the reserved readings for the course (Boyd-Franklin, 2003; Collins, 2004; King, 2004; Rose, 2003), by creating visual aids and other materials representative of behaviors of those in other cultures (Norton, 2002; Stubbs, 1998), and by introducing words or terms from other languages and cultures into the discourse of each class (Francoeur & Noonan, 2004). Students in subsequent semesters responded well to these additions and I was pleased to assume my students' comments had helped my course grow in a positive way. Now after reading Lance's letter, I am left to wonder what my student meant by "white-people sexuality" and what he perceived black people's sexuality to be.

Diversity Lessons in Sexuality

Sexuality courses may vary from institution to institution depending upon administrative guidelines and instructors' backgrounds, but they should generally follow guidelines set forth by professional organizations such as the American Association of Sex Educators, Counselors, and Therapists (AASECT) and the Sexuality Information and Education Council of the United States (SIECUS). AASECT trains and certifies sex educators, sex counselors, and sex therapists and provides continuing education for these professionals. SIECUS is a wellspring of knowledge and information for teachers and the public about sexuality. Its Web site and publications offer free guidelines for comprehensive sex education courses that outline contents along the following general concepts: human development, relationships, personal skills, sexual behavior, sexual health, and society and culture (Sexuality Information and Education Council of the United States, 2004). I will employ the SIECUS outline in the discussion that follows to highlight a few strategies for introducing diversity topics in sexuality courses.

Human Development

Human development includes information relating to sexual anatomy and physiology, puberty, reproduction, body image, sexual orientation, and gender roles. As Lance's letter implied above, I believe the examination of male and female sexual anatomy, particularly during embryonic development, is one of the most powerful topics for examining gender diversity in sexuality. Few students seem to realize that individuals begin life on a path to be either gender and are normally segregated to male or female through the influence of genes that initiate hormonal changes only after several weeks of equivocal development. The point is well taken when they are asked to ponder the vestiges of this transformation. The midscrotal raphe that runs from the perineum to the tip of the penis provides a handy example easily confirmed by self-examination.

Confronting the reality that sexual differentiation can, and often does, go awry to result in intersexed conditions further challenges the common

notion of sex dichotomy—male or female—that Western culture tries to en-
force (Fausto-Sterling, 2000). Many fascinating resources are available for
instructors to guide debate regarding treatment strategies for intersex conditions, historically viewed as birth defects to be surgically repaired shortly
after birth, but now being framed as variations that should be treated only
after personality and sexual behaviors can be assessed (Dreger, 1998; Kessler,
2000). Students can quickly see how historical precedence in the treatment
of these conditions can couple with the guidance of powerful authority figures (doctors) to convince parents that a crisis is present at birth and must
be addressed immediately without further consultation. I ask them to ponder
the impact on our society if a spectrum of sexual ambiguity was allowed to
exist.

Our exploration of the complexities of developing sexual structures can
easily lead on to an examination of the interplay of nature and nurture on
gender expression and sexual orientation. In addition to genital structures,
neurological development is also affected hormonally in utero and structural
differences in male and female and heterosexual and homosexual brains are
being described (Bear, Conners, & Paradiso, 2001). This can engender vigorous emotional discussions about what is learned and what is innate and how
we may accept bias based on sexual orientation yet renounce bias based on
physical qualities such as skin color. Students can recognize that both are
affected by genetics, environment, and behavior.

Relationships

The concept of relationships encompasses information about families,
friendship, love, romantic relationships and dating, marriage and lifetime
commitments, and raising children. The dynamics of dating and marriage
are favorite topics for many students in college sexuality classes. The concept
of a "dating funnel" is a useful visual strategy to demonstrate the date selection process, a form of discrimination people may use during partner selection. Students are asked to list characteristics or qualities they think are
necessary in a potential partner. Many cite age, ethnicity, education, income,
religious beliefs, personality traits, and physical qualities as important criteria
for identifying someone they would consider compatible. Students call out
the characteristics they consider important and these are supplemented by
others I may list. All are diagramed flowing into the mouth of a large funnel
so the students can see they are eliminating potential partners with their per-

sonal preferences. Finally, out the bottom drops "Mr. or Ms. Right." To ensure that students know themselves as well as who they consider compatible, it is common for students to be asked to write a "personal ad" that describes the qualities they possess and what they seek in another. A discussion usually follows to reveal that many people present themselves in flattering ways in their ad, and the realization arrives that perceptions of personal qualities vary between and within people.

Many students ascribe to the notion of a romantic marriage to a single life partner with whom they raise a family of children and live "until death do us part." A show of hands as to how many in the class come from this type of family helps them realize that this is an idealized concept, very different from reality in the United States (Coontz, 2005; Wolfson, 2005). Anthropological studies demonstrate that polygamy is more common than monogamy in animal and human models and that romantic marriage is a modern concept (Cott, 2000). Students may be largely unfamiliar with polyamorous relationships, those in which partners agree that they are capable of feeling love and desire for more than one person and act on these feelings by permitting themselves to have additional partners beyond their primary partner (Easton & Liszt, 1997). It is a powerful exercise to discuss the negotiations necessary for such relationships to operate happily. A short course in the history of marriage, even when limited to the United States, can lay the groundwork for a meaningful discussion of domestic partnerships, the Defense of Marriage Act, and the other forms of unequal treatment based on marital status. How society should deal with the intersexed (particularly those who do not wish to be surgically altered) and transsexuals can further complicate this discussion and challenge students to reflect on their values.

Personal Skills

Personal skills include values, decision making, communication, assertiveness, negotiation, and looking for help. A wide array of exercises may be employed to teach and reinforce these skills, with role playing a personal favorite. It is especially effective to demonstrate by example how theory and practice relate while using partner communication as the skill of choice. I often demonstrate differences in male and female communication styles as highlighted in a series of books and audiotapes from the *Men Are from Mars, Women Are from Venus* (Gray, 1992) series. Two male/female couples from the class are asked to volunteer to assume the roles of couples in committed relationships. One couple takes opposite seats in front of the class and are asked to react to the following scenario: The woman has just come home from work and seems upset. She asks permission from her partner to talk with him about what is troubling her. She reveals that while she was at work today, a male coworker touched her hair affectionately and asked her if they could get together after work sometime. This is the second time the man has asked her out and he already knows she is in a relationship.

Given this situation, the male almost always reacts as Gray predicts. He generally listens briefly to his partner's explanation of the situation, then offers a solution, often emotionally asserting that he will go down and have a talk with the man at work and make sure he understands there will be negative consequences if he continues to pursue his partner. Next, the class listens to an audiotape as Gray explains that men often "try to fix problems" whereas when women have a problem, they usually seek empathy from their partner, not solutions. We then allow the second couple to role-play the same scenario to see if they apply Gray's advice and what type of solution they come up with. This leads the class to discuss the nature of partner communication and to question whether there are ethnic or nationalistic differences in communication that could affect this scenario. When the class has a diverse composition, many differences are likely to be described.

Sexual Behavior

The SIECUS concept of sexual behavior includes sexuality throughout life, masturbation, shared sexual behavior, sexual abstinence, human sexual response, sexual fantasy, and sexual dysfunctions. This content is usually the most exciting portion of the course for the students and it clearly challenges their tolerance for diversity.

The pioneering sex researcher Alfred Kinsey awakened people in the United States to the rich diversity of sexual behavior apparent here beginning in the late 1940s. He used interviews to gather data and was famous for getting respondents to describe their behavior despite inhibitions and cultural pressures to conform to modesty. His questioning style—now often referred to by sexologists as "Kinsey questions"—made it difficult for the respondent to deny or withhold information because in order to answer the questions, the respondent had to admit to another behavior. I like to introduce his questioning techniques when discussing research methods because it provides a good segue into an examination of ethnic differences in sexual behaviors like masturbation. In the course of didactic discussion about Kinsey's techniques and findings, I will randomly select a black male student and ask him, "When you masturbate, how long does it take before you ejaculate?" Since the literature in their book describes masturbation as a common behavior, it is informative to see the young man squirm quietly for a long minute then finally say something like, "Well, I don't masturbate." From there, we can discuss biases in the literature and how it would help remedy some of these biases if a few more black students would focus their careers on sexuality research. "Here's a question for your thesis: We've just demonstrated that black males are less likely to masturbate; what is the consequence of this behavior?"

Most sexuality courses use explicit videos to some degree to describe sexual behaviors. I recommend great care be taken in selecting such material. Videos should be marketed as educational material, not as pornography, and be narrated by recognized sexology professionals. Strive to present a broad representation of diversity within the films—not just in sexual behaviors—but also in the ethnicity, age, and physical attractiveness of the actors. Realize that in our culture some students may feel uncomfortable viewing people of other or mixed ethnicities having sex. They may not have fully considered before viewing sex among people their parents' or grandparents' age that their relatives are, or at least once were, sexually active. Heterosexual students, particularly male heterosexuals, may feel uncomfortable viewing homosexual acts, and many students, regardless of gender or sexual orientation, may feel uncomfortable viewing anal sex. All of these scenarios provide powerful opportunities for introspection and class discussion as they challenge the assumptions many of us live by. Students who have attended my courses usually become desensitized to such differences and may become more tolerant of these behaviors as they become more knowledgeable about them.

The use of sexually explicit media, particularly video, has become more controversial in recent years as conservative activists speak out in an attempt to reform what may be used in college-level sexuality courses. This debate can be instructive, leading to discussions about what constitutes decency, especially regarding community standards and pornography. A quick comparison between a sexually explicit educational video and a pornographic video played on two televisions set side by side with the sound turned down can be employed to emphasize that what constitutes education or pornography is often open to local interpretation.

It is important to inform students at the beginning of a sexuality course that explicit media will be used in the course. It is also important that students be aware in advance of what the general content of the films will be before they view them. This point is particularly valid for survivors of sexual violence and those with abortion sensitivity. Never permit students who are not enrolled in the course to just "sit in" on a film. Students who are not enrolled may want to drop in or those enrolled may want to invite a friend who is not enrolled to sit in for the day, but these students are not prepared by successive exposure to increasingly intense media to view the behaviors they may see, and it may have unintended, contrary effects on them. Likewise, I rarely show an entire film, but usually queue films to specific segments that make only the precise points I wish to convey.

Sexuality courses also examine unusual and/or dysfunctional sexual behaviors such as paraphilias and other behaviors classified in the *Diagnostic and Statistical Manual of Mental Disorders* ([*DSM-IV-TR*], American Psychiatric Association, 2000). For students who are just being introduced to clinical training through their sexuality course, what exactly constitutes pathological behavior can create vigorous debates about the cultural determinants of deviancy (Laws & O'Donohue, 1997). Examining some behaviors that were historically praised as normal but are now considered immoral and/or illegal (e.g., the ancient Greek practice of mentoring boys both sexually and professionally by prominent men in the community) can reflect the influence of changing times on culture. Other examples reflect how behaviors once classified as pathological (e.g., homosexuality in the United States prior to the 1970s) may gain acceptance as normal variations when knowledge increases and values change.

For clinically oriented classes, understanding a client's right to self-determination in sexual preference and sexual expression may be dramatically introduced by employing case studies. Texts, professional Listservs, and guest speakers are good sources of case studies, especially when the presenting problems are the subject of current professional debate (Goldstein & Brandon, 2004; Leiblum & Rosen, 2000). One example I use is that of the client who called a local sex therapist for advice because he was concerned that his partner was experiencing pain upon penetration. The therapist scheduled an appointment for the client expecting to treat dyspareunia or a similar pain disorder based on the telephone discussion. When the client arrived, he had his pet pig in tow and the therapist invited them both into the office assuming that the man had no place to keep the animal during his appointment. The pig joined the client on the couch and as the session proceeded the therapist listened as the client described his concerns about his partner's feelings during sex. After the client's description the therapist finally asked the client, "Why don't you just ask your partner if it hurts?" Upon hearing this, the client turned to the pig (his partner) then back to the therapist and exclaimed, "But she can't talk!"

The students usually understand at this point, as the therapist did, that the presenting problem was not a pain disorder but a relationship problem for a zoophile. However, they usually are in discord when asked how the therapist should treat the problem: Should she begin to counsel the client about his unusual sexual desire and affection for his pet? Or should she call a local veterinarian for advice about whether the pig could typically accommodate a penis the size of the man's without discomfort? Presented with this case, the students can join in the debate between animal rights activists and zoophiles and ultimately contemplate the client's right to self-determination. This scenario ended with the client leaving the therapist's office after only one session feeling satisfied with her advice and happier in his relationship.

Sexual Health

I have employed a vast array of strategies to get my students to attend to sexual health concerns. I usually invite a Planned Parenthood health educator to class to discuss contraception and to display models and products that students need to be aware of. As my students are predominately African American, the health educator and I confer prior to her or his first presentation about some of the unique features of this ethnic group, such as the historical transgressions this population has experienced. This gives me confidence the educator understands and can properly address any resistance the students may express toward products and services discussed. We also discuss preferences and behavior patterns displayed by this group that may require the presentation to have a slightly different emphasis than for other audiences. After the presentation, the class will discuss the historical basis of their suspicions (e.g., the "Tuskegee Experiment" and the "Mississippi appendectomy") and predict what effect this history will have on acceptance of future sexual health products and services, such as vaccines for human papilloma virus or human immunodeficiency virus.

Attitudes about abortion are surveyed within each class as a noncredit part of the unit exam on sexual health. This allows us to compare and contrast the class's views with statistics in the literature and from previous classes. It also introduces them to qualitative research techniques and allows for a segue into a discussion about infectious diseases.

As Kevin's letter reflects, the risk of sexually transmitted infections (STIs) weighs heavily on many students. The lesson always contains discussion of incidence and risk factors, and features reliable graphic images of symptoms and treatments. I also like to perform a classic epidemiology exercise to highlight the effect of abstinence, monogamy, and condom use (the ABC model) on transmission. In this exercise, 25 index cards are prepared with a typically male or female name written in the upper-right-hand corner of each card to represent the person receiving the card. In the middle of each card is written either no name (abstinence), one name (monogamy), or from two to four names (multiple partners) to indicate the sexual partners of the person. (To give this exercise a gender-bending twist, I like to mix the gender concurrence on the cards to reflect heterosexual, homosexual, and bisexual possibilities.) On the back of 5 cards I print "STI" to indicate the person is infectious. On the back of 5 other cards I print the word "Condoms" to indicate that person strictly uses condoms. The cards are distributed to persons of the appropriate gender reflected by the name in the upper-right-hand corner and as I read out those names one by one, the student who holds the corresponding card stands and first reads the names of his or her sex partners and each of these students are asked to stand. Next the cardholder turns the card over and reveals his or her disease status and condom use practices. This gives his or her partners a sense of relief or anxiety depending upon the cardholder's status. As the activity proceeds, it is apparent how easily infections may spread. We conclude by discussing the risk/benefits of each type of relationship and the protection limits of condoms.

Society and Culture

This SIECUS concept contains sexuality and society, gender roles, sexuality and the law, sexuality and religion, diversity, sexuality and the media, and sexuality and the arts. This content is pervasive in sexuality courses and integrated from beginning to end. Before beginning to discuss culture and society, I like to first remind students that biological diversity transcends humankind. Students are encouraged to acknowledge that humans are only 1 of an estimated 30 million species in the world today—and we are yet to prove nearly as successful at sexual reproduction as others that have preceded us or coexist with us still (Torrey & Yolken, 2005). It is often beneficial to challenge students' homocentrism by presenting them with a sampling of reproductive strategies of other species as distant from us on the phylogenic ladder as bacteria and as near to us as apes. There are numerous vivid, amusing examples that may be employed to pique students' interest (Judson, 2002). I like to encourage students to question, "Where do we derive the notion that humans possess or deserve stewardship of the Earth?"

Contrasting the divergent sexual behaviors of our closest phylogenic relatives begins to impress students with the variety of acceptable sexual expression displayed by similar animals and can help them draw parallels about how much human behavior may vary. For example, the violence and jealousy displayed in the patriarchal culture of the chimpanzee contrasts well with the sexually gregarious, peaceful matriarchal culture of the bonobo (de Waal & Lanting, 1997). Likewise, a sampling of evidence from paleoanthropology can raise further questions about our origins and challenge students' egocentrism about modern Homo sapiens' place among other hominids that have a far longer history of reproductive success (Sykes, 2001). I find many students hold a rather narrow view of our biological origins and inflate the significance of man's place in the system of life on Earth, especially when thinking about the role of pathogens in the loss of past forms and their threat to present ones.

Another challenge to commonly held views comes from examining the origins of civilization and its influence on sexual behavior. Prehistory presents an opportunity to challenge gender roles by reflecting on times when women were revered for their fecundity and believed to possess the power to improve the fortunes of a community simply by raising a skirt and exposing their life-giving vulva to an approaching army, demon, or drought (Blackledge, 2004). With the domestication of animals and the subsequent revelation of the male role in fertility, prehistory indicates women were then demeaned, and that living in larger communities gave rise to social mores, laws, and governments to regulate collective conduct and ensure the security of property, including wives and children. It must not be lost on students of sexuality that equity for women is a recent construct—hardly a century old in the United States—and one that is certainly not universally accepted in the modern world.

Sexuality instructors should guard against presenting a myopic view of recorded history, discussing only the roots of Western culture by tracing civilization briefly from the Fertile Crescent, to the Greeks, Romans, Europeans, and on into the late 19th-century United States when the formal study of sexuality began to emerge here. This treatment discounts the contributions of significant coexisting cultures in Africa, Asia, and the Western Hemisphere prior to European colonization. This view has been criticized not only as Eurocentric, but also sexist (Fausto-Sterling, 2000). Some students may conclude that such treatment reflects "European-American" sexuality and may feel marginalized or dismissed by this instruction.

The influence of religions on sexual expression presents another opportunity to discuss the diversity of beliefs and behaviors. Most sexuality courses compare the sexual practices advocated by major religions, usually highlighting Judaism, Hinduism, Taoism, Islam, and Christianity. This may be the first opportunity for many students who ascribe to a faith to examine the views of other religions, particularly those with divergent views. The realization that some religions view passionate sexual behavior as a spiritual ideal and a step on the path to enlightenment, while others see it as a necessary but begrudged duty, may stir self-examination. Examining the evolution of their own religion toward its modern incarnation can be a profound experience for a class where every sneeze typically elicits a small chorus of "Bless you."

Considering the influence of Christianity on Western sexual behavior, I spend significantly more time on its teachings. Many students are surprised that efforts to regulate sexual practices have played significant roles in the rise of the Catholic Church, the papacy, the Protestant movement, the Puritan migration to colonial North America, and periodic conservative movements in the United States (Nardo, 1999).

The customary practice of circumcising males in the United States is one of the first postpartum opportunities to explore cross-cultural diversity, especially when contrasted with female circumcision as historically practiced here and currently practiced in other parts of the world. A vague misconception persists that male circumcision is practiced in the United States for religious or hygienic purposes, despite few religions other than Judaism advocating it and the American Academy of Pediatrics' disavowing its routine performance for more than 30 years (Ellwood, 2005; Planned Parenthood Federation of America, 2003). When religious reasons are cited, students are surprised to learn that the practice was not common outside

Jewish tradition until a conservative Christian movement popularized the practice for both male and females in the mid-1800s, primarily as a means to reduce children's urges to masturbate. They are quick to condemn cultures that currently practice female circumcision and agree with laws that ban its practice in the United States, yet they hesitate to see how cutting away the male foreskin could be similarly unreasonable.

Sexual Diversity: Pedagogy in Action

Justin's letter conveys the effectiveness of one of my favorite class activities to allow students to experience sexual diversity. As she mentions, it can also be modified to give students a feel for living with disabilities (Kaufman, Silverberg, & Odette, 2003). Before class begins, count the number of students expected in class and arrange for enough colored self-adhesive foil stars so that you can form four groups, in this case to represent heterosexual, bisexual, homosexual, and intersex individuals. (While the color of the stars is not relevant, gold stars may have value in some contexts so you may wish to explain to the class that the colors are meaningless.) Two groups will be larger and approximately equal in size, say, red and blue stars to represent hetero- and bisexual individuals; a third group will be smaller, about 10% of the class, say, silver stars to represent homosexual individuals; and the final group will consist of only one individual, a green star, to represent the intersexual.

When class begins, advise the students that they will be involved in an experiential activity that day using the foil stars. Show them the package of stars and demonstrate how they work by peeling one off and sticking it on the back of your hand. Next have them close their eyes and sit quietly in their seats as you distribute the stars, placing one on the forehead of each student. Explain to them that they are not to open their eyes until you instruct them to and that they may not speak during the activity until you ask them to. Instruct them that they may not touch their star until the activity concludes.

Randomly distribute the stars by applying one to the forehead of each student in class. Once the stars are distributed, tell the students to open their eyes, stand up, and without talking, walk around and arrange themselves into groups by finding people like themselves. What you should see is that the students will wander about, gesture, nod, and eventually manage to find their groups. The intersex person is often rejected by the others and they may turn their backs or gesture that she or he doesn't belong. This person may hang around the margin of a rejecting group or eventually give up and stand alone.

After everyone appears to have found a group, ask members of the hetero- and bisexual groups to comment about how they knew which group they belonged to. Ask an individual member of the homosexual group how that person figured out he or she didn't belong in the larger groups, and how it felt to realize he or she was somehow different. Finally, ask the intersex individual how he or she felt upon realizing that there was no group for that person. Ask the class how it felt to accept or reject other people.

The intent of this chapter is to convey some of the opportunities presented in sexuality education for teaching about diversity. The letters written by my former students give some idea of how a sexuality course may impress each student differently, offering each chances to examine his or her own behavior from many divergent points of view. The exercises presented here represent just a few of the many that sex educators may employ when they wish to help students relate to the experiences of others. I encourage you to emphasize diversity in your discipline as it likely presents similar opportunities to those described here for sex education.

References

American Psychiatric Association (2000). *Diagnostic and statistical manual of mental disorders—IV—text revision*. Washington, DC: Author.

Bear, M., Connors, B., & Paradiso, M. (2001). *Neuroscience: Exploring the brain* (2nd ed.). Baltimore: Lippincott Williams & Wilkins.

Blackledge, C. (2004). *The story of V: A natural history of female sexuality*. New Brunswick, NJ: Rutgers University Press.

Boyd-Franklin, N. (2003). Black families in therapy (2nd ed.). New York: Guilford Press.

Chandler, S., Johnson, D., & Carroll, P. (1999). Abusive behaviors of college athletes. *College Student Journal, 33*(4), 638–645.

Collins, P. H. (2004). *Black sexual politics: African Americans, gender, and the new racism*. New York: Routledge.

Coontz, S. (2005). *Marriage, a history: From obedience to intimacy or how love conquered marriage*. New York: Viking Adult Press.

Cott, N. (2000). *Public vows: A history of marriage and the nation*. Cambridge, MA: Harvard University Press.

de Waal, F. B. M., & Lanting, F. (1997). *Bonobo: The forgotten ape*. Berkeley: University of California Press.

Dreger, A. (1998). *Hermaphrodites and the medical invention of sex*. Cambridge, MA: Harvard University Press.

Easton, D., & Liszt, C. (1997). *The ethical slut: A guide to infinite sexual possibilities*. San Francisco: Greenery Press.

Ellwood, A. (2005). Female genital cutting, "circumcision" and mutilation: Physical, psychological and cultural perspectives. *Contemporary Sexuality, 39*(1), i-viii.

Fausto-Sterling, A. (2000). *Sexing the body: Gender politics and the construction of sexuality*. New York: Basic Books.

Francoeur, R., & Noonan, R. (2004). *The Continuum complete international encyclopedia of sexuality*. New York: Continuum International.

Goldstein, A., & Brandon, M. (2004). *Reclaiming desire: Four keys to finding lost libido*. New York: Rodale.

Gray, J. (1992). *Men are from Mars, women are from Venus*. New York: HarperCollins,

Judson, O. (2002). *Dr. Tatianna's sex advice to all creatures*. New York: Metropolitan Books.

Kaufman, M., Silverberg, C., & Odette, F. (2003). *The ultimate guide to sex and disability: For all of us who live with disabilities, chronic pain, and illness*. San Francisco: Cleis Press.

Kessler, S. (2000). *Lessons from the intersexed*. New Brunswick, NJ: Rutgers University Press.

King, J. L. (2004). *On the down low: A journey into the lives of "straight" black men who sleep with men*. New York: Broadway Books.

Laws, D. R., & O'Donohue, W. (1997). *Sexual deviance: Theory, assessment, and treatment*. New York: Guilford Press.

Leiblum, S., & Rosen, R. (2000). *Principles and practice of sex therapy* (3rd ed.). New York: Guilford Press.

Nardo, D. (1999). *The rise of Christianity*. San Diego, CA: Greenhaven Press

Norton, B. (2002). *Eastern erotica: Chinese, Indian, and Japanese eroticism in art and literature*. Hod Hasharon, Israel: Astrolog Publishing.

Planned Parenthood Federation of America. (2003). Masturbation: From myth to sexual health. *Contemporary Sexuality, 37*(3), i-viii.

Rose, T. (2003). *Longing to tell: Black women talk about sexuality and intimacy*. New York: Farrar, Straus and Giroux.

Satterly, B., & Dyson, D. (2005). Educating all children equitably: A strengths-based approach to advocacy for sexual minority youth in schools. *Contemporary Sexuality, 39*(3), i-viii.

Sexuality Information and Education Council of the United States. (2004). *Guidelines for comprehensive sexuality education: K–12th grade* (3rd ed.). Washington, DC: Author.

Stubbs, K. (1998). *Secret sexual positions: Ancient techniques for modern lovers*. Tucson, AZ: Secret Garden Press.

Sykes, B. (2001). *The seven daughter's of Eve*. New York: Norton.

Torrey, E. F., & Yolken, R. H. (2005). *Beasts of the earth: Animals, humans, and diseases*. New Brunswick, NJ: Rutgers University Press.

Wolfson, E. (2005). Ending marriage discrimination: America in a civil rights movement. *SIECUS Report, 33*(1), pp. 13–18.

12

LETTER FROM THE EDITORS

Moving Toward Best Practices in Teaching Diversity

Linda L. Lampl, Deborah A. Brunson, and Brenda Jarmon

D ear Reader,
 We recognize hope when we see it—and we see it shining brightly in this collection of chapters that presents pedagogies about the teaching of differences within and between human groups—more commonly known as "diversity." And, our hope is that the work in this volume supports the effort to move diversity education in the academy from higher education's periphery to a place at the core of its agenda. Devorah Lieberman affirms this need for sustained focus upon diversity education in the opening chapter: "Bringing diversity issues into program and course curricula requires a thoughtful process that includes classroom management, student learning outcomes, and assessment." The contributions in *Letters from the Future* support the ongoing efforts to integrate diversity curricula into a wide array of disciplinary-, interdisciplinary-, and multidisciplinary-focused course content across the academic spectrum.

As coeditors, scholars, and participants in the human drama, we believe that the teaching and learning experiences about diversity chronicled here constitute powerful philosophies, pedagogies, and practices that support a social justice perspective. From this perspective, diverse populations navigate from society's margins into its fully engaged interior. These diverse voices, which strain to express their experiences, their needs, their expertise, and their values, are attended to as they become engaged participants in society. We envision the social justice perspective as foundational for society's institutions (including the academy), but this view is not yet the norm. As we worked on the final stages of this book, a stark reminder of this distinction surfaced through statements of former U.S. Secretary of Education Dr. William Bennett, who placed race on the agenda when he commented that abortion of babies expected to have black skin would resolve problems with crime in the United States—while at the same time distancing himself from the horrific thought with protestations that such action would be morally reprehensible (Raspberry, 2005). We immediately thought of contributor Earl Sheridan's reflection on W. E. B. DuBois and the limitations of education as *the* way to end racism in the U.S. In chapter 4, "Curriculum and Race," Sheridan observed:

> Racism *is* too tough an opponent. Education alone will not eradicate it. It is naive to believe that it is *only* ignorance that makes people racist. Many knowledgeable people use their knowledge to perpetuate racism. (p. 75)

Indeed, powerful people such as a former U.S. secretary of education have and will continue to use their knowledge of the political system and human communication to place ideas on the public agenda then dodge and weave to avoid responsibility. Yet Sheridan aptly pushes hope to the forefront as he points out that education is nonetheless an effective "weapon" that can be used to "defeat racism."

Emerging Practices

Our intent has been to contribute to the body of knowledge now available on the pedagogy of diversity by listening to the stories of how teachers approach the topic and by examining the shelf life of such teachings through the voices of their former students, captured through narrative letters. In keeping with that mission, we revisited the individual chapters and stories to glean what may be called the "emerging best practices" used by these accomplished educators to reach and teach their students. While we acknowledge that the experiences presented in this book offer a multitude of how-to and food-for-thought examples, we revisit seven strategies, tactics, and techniques found to be important and effective by these individual teachers and students that we believe can be put to immediate use in the classroom, and beyond.

1. Place diversity on the agenda as a teachable topic regardless of the substantive content.

The inherent strength of an interdisciplinary volume is that the reader may encounter a singular concept from multiple perspectives, and we believe that the contributors to *Letters from the Future* provide evidence to support this assumption. We see examples of pedagogy from these contributors where either singular or multiple components of diversity have been integrated into the course content. Some examples in this volume include Karen Bullock's experiences with social work students (chapter 8), education curricula with strong diversity focus (Leila E. Villaverde, chapter 10), courses in English composition (Patricia Brown McDonald, chapter 5), and Earl Sheridan's Blacks in American Politics course (chapter 4). We also hear endorsements of diversity as a teachable topic that provides important frames of reference for these teachers' work, and for the intellectual, experiential work they expect from their students.

Villaderde, who teaches education courses in curriculum and cultural foundations, situates her instruction within a diversity pedagogy, finding space for it across course content: "As I stated earlier my approach was to weave diversity into the curriculum even if the course was not a designated diversity offering, and I still follow this tactic" (p. 209). Brown McDonald addresses the need to facilitate successful, meaningful self-expression of black students through presenting non-Western literature in the English curriculum. She notes the effect that this exposure has had upon her student Aquilla Copeland as well as herself: "Like myself, Aquilla had also read the literary greats, the so-called canons of Western literature, but none had penetrated her psyche as did the Afrocentric authorship of Edwidge Danticat (Haitian), Zora Neale Hurston (African American), and Jamaica Kinkaid (Antiguan)" (p. 89). A notable departure from the courses one typically expects to incorporate diversity components is featured in this volume through the biology course taught by Muriel Lederman (chapter 3). As she observes in "Biological Diversity," a feminist perspective is a rare frame of reference for scientists, which makes its inclusion in her molecular cell biology course an innovative, progressive effort. "My pursuing these issues led me to realize that how we teach science most often reinscribes the social conditions and disciplinary conventions that make science inimical to women and other groups. I eventually developed a strategy that I think might overcome this barrier" (p. 46).

As higher education struggles to integrate the need for diversifying its curricula with the ability of its academic units to do so, administrators must encourage opportunities to expand these curricular offerings. Lieberman (chapter 1) concludes her essay by expressing the need for institutional support of diversity initiatives that include curricula change, among other areas that need growth and development: "It is critical that the upper administration finds ways to articulate publicly its own personal beliefs in these issues. These messages can be conveyed . . . through promotion and tenure practices, through research support, and through hiring and promotion practices. Faculty, staff, and students must populate the committees that recommend policy about diversity within and across the curriculum" (p. 23).

2. Go beyond teaching "about" diversity to "doing diversity"; from telling to showing students how to appreciate differences; and to understanding why the ability to function across groups is of growing importance.

The terms "modeling" and "mentoring" come to mind here or, to use the vernacular of the business world, when we think of someone who does diversity we think of someone who "walks the talk." We are talking about the teachers who lead by example.

Karen Bullock (chapter 8) draws from her own life history to illustrate the pain and issues associated with racism, bringing first-person realism to her students. Bullock makes mentoring her style, not a task assigned by job description, but instead because she understands what it will take for these individuals who aim toward social work to participate in the current hierarchies structured by class, race, gender, and ethnicity.

> . . . because diversity can contribute to an imbalance of power between individuals and groups, it is important to undertake the subject matter at the college level *before individuals find themselves in positions of power over others* [italics added]. As we educators prepare our students to be directors and supervisors, practitioners and clinicians, we have a duty to address these hierarchies as a means for improving the social conditions of the environments in which we live and work (p. 156)

Bullock and her students remind us that the hard part about diversity is not between the covers of a text or in the classroom exam; the challenge is in enactment, in engagement in everyday life, in everyday roles—in the mode of what might be called "continuous improvement" (Walton, 1986).

Yet, in keeping with the theme of diversity itself, we see that Steve Chandler (chapter 11) perceives that self-disclosure can bias students, leading him to "let my students or clients perceive me as I am through their own filters."

Lieberman draws on the literature to remind us that diversity in the academic setting should not be limited to the student body. We need to address the topic of diversity within the faculty—yet this consideration requires thoughtful approach. Chandler, however, brings forth an observation that reminds us again of Sheridan's take on DuBois—that education is not enough to end racism and, we might add, ethnocentrism. Drawing from the learnings of a student and from his own experience at a historically black college or university, Chandler notes:

> . . . I assumed the community would be well aware of diversity issues, and my students and colleagues would model equity and fairness based on their experiences as members of a minority group. . . . What I realized . . . was that what is sometimes learned by being a member of a minority group that has experienced discrimination is not how to be equitable to others, but rather how also to discriminate and be ethnocentric. (p. 227)

3. Be prepared for a paradigm shift—even if you need to shift your own gears.

In our interactions with others, each of us brings our way of seeing the world. This template provides the framework through which we contextualize situations, groups, individuals, and events. We see these "lenses" enacted through a paradigm or worldview, and paradigmatic examples are present throughout *Letters from the Future*.

James McFarland, a clinical social worker (chapter 2), reminds us that "liquidity of thought" is required to navigate effectively in a diverse world on a day-to-day basis—as teachers and as practitioners. He was not only reminded by experience with his client and the court that he needed to recognize and respect this quality to think from multiple perspectives (liquidity of thought), but that his professional role may also require him to realize where others were not doing so, and to adjust his approach to them accordingly.

Muriel Lederman's worldview (chapter 3) as shaped by science was shaken by experience and exposure, ultimately leading her to question the pedagogy of the field she calls home. Lederman combined her personal story of gender and the culture of science with revelations that emerged through contact with feminist theories. Through her "self work" in this area, she was able to also mentor other scientists and students who were attracted to a paradigmatic structure of science from a feminist perspective. And, the powerful words of James Fogelman, a former student of Earl Sheridan's (chapter

4) informs teachers of the power of paradigms, and the influence a learning environment may wield when students are faced with a paradigm shift:

> I decided to do my best to remove the cognitive filters I had put in place regarding blacks, racism, and discrimination, and actually "learn." The course did not attempt to pass judgment, but present facts. . . . Two key influential individuals who had a profound impact on my understanding were W. E. B. DuBois and the Reverend Vernon Johns. These men broke through my complacency and created an awareness in me that has not let me lower my own awareness of how discrimination and institutional racism remain underwritten evils that are still a threat to our society today. (p. 82)

4. Prepare a safe haven for students at all points on the diversity compass to explore their own stories and the stories of others.

The act of storytelling, whether written or spoken, provides the student with a vehicle to validate his or her experiences, unfiltered, labeled, or categorized by social scientists or other professionals. These stories are real; in some cases, they are intimate, divulging details that may evoke embarrassment or shame. Coincidentally, the instructor who creates the safe haven to sort out and share lived experience also provides students with an opportunity to hear stories they could not hear elsewhere. Through the work in this volume, references emerge through students' narratives that addressed having the space to speak their experiences, and feeling supported by their teacher to do so. Examples of this emergent voice follow.

- Yoke-Wee Loh, former student of Scott Campbell (chapter 6)
  With the diversity of students, there were no longer right or wrong answers. As we interacted with each other, we opened the door to alternative possibilities in our lives. Very often, we would learn something interesting and new from each other. (p. 122)

- Kazuko Matsuda, former student of Leila Villaverde (chapter 10)
  My voice is an important testimonial of the lived experiences of individuals with disabilities. The openness to my own multiplicities hopefully reflects my openness to others' voices. . . . When our multiple lenses start evoking our critical consciousness, we may find a deeper appreciation of diversities within us and others. (p. 215)

5. Expose, expose, expose. Engage, engage, engage.

By exposure, we mean that students must be systematically introduced to diversity curricula, and the nature of that contact should be both varied and sustained. Lieberman reports that the "most effective pedagogical strategies involve intense exposure to diversity issues." In her foundational chapter, she describes instructional practices that pedagogy researchers have linked to positive, effective learning outcomes. These practices are often developed with consideration of the content matter being taught (e.g., is the topic Gay and Lesbian Issues? Race? Gender?). For example, Lieberman cited research that found gay and lesbian issues are best presented through a panel discussion that includes questions and answers. Steve Chandler uses such an instructional design when he schedules a class presentation by Lesbian, Gay, Bisexual, Transgender, and Questioning panelists. Interestingly, he notes that students respond differently to these panels, based upon their composition. Lieberman also cited research that indicates that students' class ranking—sophomore as opposed to senior, for example—can determine the most appropriate instructional mode to apply as one introduces diversity content that is often new, strange, and a challenge to individuals' worldviews.

A true measure of the impact of any curricula is the student's self-motivation to extend himself or herself beyond the course requirements, and to accept a model of "continuous, lifelong learning" as he or she completes a program. We find this high motivation to embrace continuous, lifelong learning represented throughout student letters in this volume. Three examples of this realization follow.

- Aquilla Copeland, former student of Patricia Brown McDonald (chapter 5):
  Your teaching approach is analogous to the duty of a diligent gardener. With each and every encounter, you planted a seed in me that encouraged me to think individually and critically about literature. Even now that I'm attending a different college, you're ever present to aid me in cultivating my sprouting ideas. (p. 87)

- Malia J. Smith, former student of Scott Campbell (chapter 6):
  As chief of staff I manage an office and remain in direct contact with constituents, businesspeople, and various organizations. I handle

complaints, concerns, and legislative proposals, which require excellent communication and personal skills. Through my experiences in graduate school and the lessons I've learned in diversity I have been able to apply this knowledge to influence the way I manage and lead my staff and/or deal with public interests. (p. 123)

- Kurtis Lane, former student of Randy Dillon (chapter 7):
Intercultural Communication has helped me to better understand my place in society and to see how others contribute to our culture and to many others. You see, cultures rub off on each other; they take from one another, that is how they grow. In the military we get a chance to experience a wide range of diversity in our travel and interaction with other cultures in the world. We contribute to them and bring back with us what we learn. This helps us to grow and better understand the world in which we live. (p. 141)

We have added engagement or "experience" to the strategy of exposure, drawing on David Kolb's theory (1984) on experiential learning. Kolb noted that "Learning is the process whereby knowledge is created through the transformation of experience" (p. 41). Mark K. Smith (2001), in a review of Kolb's work, reports that other scholars tend to divide life experience from classroom, short-term experiences. We do not assign primacy to the various venues for learning but do suggest that teachers may want to engage students via life stories and simulation and games. Several authors provided specific references to packaged culture simulation games such as BaFáBaFá (www .simulationtrainingsystems.com). Chandler (chapter 11) used a "foil stars" exercise, apparently brought to the classroom setting by guest panelists, and Warren Scheideman, Villaverde's former student (chapter 10), created his own tool kit in order to better assess and catalog the resources he was bringing with him into academe as a Ph.D. Film and other media can be introduced, in part to generate discussion. For instance, Earl Sheridan (chapter 4) notes his use of the highly acclaimed *Eyes on the Prize* documentary series on the civil rights movement because "this gives the class the chance to see and hear some of the people who took part in the civil rights movement, the famous and the not so famous. Seeing the newsreel footage and hearing interviews with people who participated often has a visceral effect on the students. I also sprinkle in my own experiences where pertinent" (p. 76).

Clearly, the options for engagement between students, as well as between students and teachers, seem limitless.

6. "The meaning of the word is not in the word but is in the sender and the receiver" (DeVito, 1991, pp. 98–99).

One of the basic principles of human communication is that the meaning of a word—and indeed the collection of words that form a message—is not inherent in the word; the individuals who create the message and the individuals who receive and interpret the message create the meaning. The classroom educator, the individual students, and the gathering known as "the class" create meanings over and over, and each of the meanings that are attached to words, sentences, and other units in the message are grounded in culture and experience.

Diversity is about race, ethnicity, gender, sexual preference, ability, class, belief systems—the meanings of which are all engendered by culture—but be sure that diversity is more than race! Steve Chandler (chapter 11) puzzles over comments made by a former student that Chandler was "teaching white-people sexuality." Yet another student felt at times that the class would be fixated on the needs and concerns of black people, although Chandler prodded them to think outside their own ethnic and cultural needs and think about the needs of others. Aside from ethnic and cultural diversity, Chandler encouraged his students to think about the special needs of the disabled, the needs of the physically and mentally impaired. One activity that he asked the class to do was to find a way to retrieve their exams from a hook on the chalkboard without talking and with a physical limitation (for example, being blind or deaf). Everyone in the class had a good time trying to figure out how to handle their new challenge, but the reality of not having the use of one of the faculties that most humans take for granted was disturbing but a very important learning tool that we see as an emergent practice: make sure that the senders and receivers understand concepts and the experiences. Practice or experiential learning goes a long way toward enhancing cultural sensitivity and cultural competency.

7. Remind ourselves of the diversity that occurs within the individual as well as between individuals and groups.

Complexity is the basis of human experience. Although we (or others) may try to essentialize our "self" by focusing upon one aspect of identity in isolation (such as race or gender) each of us possesses multiple identities that may be dominant (agent) or nondominant (target), given the context in which we find ourselves. Beverly Daniel Tatum (2000) observed how we try to juggle and negotiate these multiple "selves" as we engage others in both our public and private spaces. "Integrating one's past, present, and future into a cohesive, unified sense of self is a complex task that begins in adolescence and continues for a lifetime. . . . The salience of particular aspects of our identity varies at different moments in our lives" (p. 10). She further observes the interplay between dominant and nondominant, or target, status: "When we think about our multiple identities, most of us will find that we are both dominant and targeted at the same time. But it is the targeted identities that hold our attention and the dominant identities that often go unexamined" (p. 11). Encountering and engaging multiple identities (within self and others) is a challenge—a daunting task, and we see the conflicts that emerge as we reach to meet the challenge—both within the self and as one extends outward to other groups. The journey, the struggle, and the reward of engaging multiple identities are powerfully expressed throughout these essays and the narratives contained in them. There are numerous examples in this volume, but three are offered here.

- Teacher Leila Villaverde (chapter 10):
  Diversity has been a floating signifier in my everyday experiences, signifying me as invisible, hypervisible, or not quite visible enough. I have negotiated not being Latina enough to being too Latina; being suspected of not speaking English (just based on my surname); seeming too young, too hard, too enigmatic (because I do not share my personal life); being questioned about my sexuality because I include queer theory in my courses; being asked to speak on behalf of all Latinos—the list of occurrences can go on and on. (p. 207)

- Lance Raynor, former student of Steve Chandler (chapter 11):
  Drawing on this professor's descriptions of cultural variation in the expression of sexual identity, I realized that I was interested in bringing the knowledge of ethnic and cultural studies to bear on the formation of my own gender-queer political activism. After graduating, I decided to travel around India for several months, and became interested in cross-cultural influences on diasporic sexualities. (p. 233)

- Isabelle Delatour, former student of Billy R. Close (chapter 9):
  Being Haitian American, and growing up in Miami, I believed you could
  visit another country just by driving a few miles. I always felt lucky to
  have grown up in this type of environment. Although perhaps the world
  saw me as a black female, I understand that my cultural background is
  more a part of who I am than my race. At some point though, I realized
  that cultural diversity is often subordinated by race. (p. 259)

In each of these passages, one can detect the struggle to find the center, to reach equilibrium, or the congruence expressed through Carl Rogers's work (1961) where the inward conception of self aligns itself with one's outward behavior. But again, that alignment can shift, morph, and turn in upon itself based upon the prevailing context of the moment or of the time of life. This need to "flex" multiple identities is captured in Delores V. Tanno's (2000) "Names, Narratives, and the Evolution of Ethnic Identity," where she reflects upon the shifting ethnic identity she has experienced through such ethnic names as Spanish, Mexican American, Latina, and Chicana. She summarizes the significance of this identity shape shifting as healthy, necessary, and empowering: "What, then, am I? The truth is that I am all of these. Each name reveals a different facet of identity that allows symbolic, historical, cultural, and political connectedness. These names are no different than other multiple labels we take on. For example, to be mother, wife, sister, and daughter, is to admit to the complexity of being female" (p. 27).

Concluding Thoughts

As we bring our letter to closure, it is our heartfelt wish that this edited volume provides the reader with examples, tactics, techniques, strategies, and an interdisciplinary volume that demonstrates the breadth and depth of movement from *teaching about diversity* to *doing diversity*. We believe that action truly does speak louder than words.

We were very deliberate about broadening the scope of diversity by assembling a multitude of diversity among our contributors (students and teachers) and interdisciplinary thoughts about diversity, culture, and academia's role in researching, examining, developing, and contributing to the diversity knowledge base. It is important to not only teach and research about diversity but it is academia's role to generate and transmit what we have learned into learning tools for the communities in which we live. Moreover, as stated earlier, our hope is that the work in this volume supports the effort to move diversity education in the academy from higher education's periphery to a place at the core of its agenda.

Our quest to engage former students to garner their input through the use of "narratives" proved to be ingenious and quite fruitful, particularly moving from what they learned in our diversity classes to how they are making a real-life application of what they have learned. This volume is no accident. It is a testament to how important it is to not only address pedagogy and learning exclusively from the perspective of the teacher but to hear from students about their learning experiences within the academic setting. The "power of narratives" as a powerful conduit for effective diversity and multicultural pedagogy allowed our contributors (students and teachers) to storytell, and what wonderful stories we have collected. Stories ripe and overflowing with practical applications of how students have applied these learning experiences to their everyday lives.

Sonia Nieto (2002) says it profoundly as she discusses language, culture, and teaching with input from participants: "If a community is created in which all voices are respected it seems to me that itself is a noble first step—a deeper sense of bonding and caring can develop despite the real differences that exist" (p. 247).

It is our earnest hope that we have instilled food for thought and provided our readers with a repertoire of resources to either begin this journey, continue this journey, or to strengthen this journey. At the very least, we believe this volume will promote more exchange of ideas and generate collaborative initiatives that bring about change and transformation.

References

DeVito, J. A. (1991). *Human communication: The basic course* (5th ed.). New York: HarperCollins.

Kolb, D. A. (1984). *Experiential learning: Experience as the source of learning and development.* Englewood Cliffs, NJ: Prentice-Hall.

Nieto, S. (2002). *Culture and teaching: Critical perspectives for a new century.* Mahwah, NJ: Erlbaum.

Raspberry, W. (2005, October 10). A better cure than abortion. *Washington Post,* pp. A19. Retrieved from http://www.washingtonpost.com/wp-dyn/content/article/2005/10/09/AR200510090 055 1.html

Rogers, C. (1961). On *becoming a person: A therapist's view of psychotherapy*. Boston: Houghton Mifflin.

Smith, M. K. (2001). David A. Kolb on experiential learning, *the encyclopedia of informal education*, http://www.infed.org/biblio/b-explrn.htm.

Tanno, D. V. (2000). Names, narratives, and the evolution of ethnic identity. In A. Gonzalez, M. Houston, & V. Chen (Eds.), *Our voices: Essays in culture, ethnicity, and communication* (3rd ed., pp. 25–29). Los Angeles: Roxbury.

Tatum, B. D. (2000). The complexity of identity: "Who Am I?" In M. Adams, W. J. Blumenfeld, R. Castañeda, H. Hackman, M. L. Peters, X. Zúñiga (Eds.), *Readings for diversity and social justice: An anthology on racism, sexism, anti-Semitism, heterosexism, classism, and ableism* (pp. 9–14). New York: Routledge.

Walton, Mary (1986). *The Deming management method*. New York: Putnam.

PART THREE

RESOURCES

D iversity plays out across the academic spectrum as a subject that can be taught, researched, and integrated. The papers and letters presented within this text represent specific perspectives on the topic, situated within particular contexts. Yet readers may want to know more about teaching diversity as a subject or want to find substantive materials to use in the classroom. For those individuals, we offer additional resources that we believe offer the potential to expand student and teacher knowledge and insight.

We approached this section from a research perspective—where might we go to find more information on the intersection of diversity and teaching and what terms might we follow to the potential resources. In this light, we built this section as a pathfinder for those who want to go beyond the stories presented in this book.

We begin with key terms that might be used to find additional resources. We also present references for key abstracts, bibliographies, collections, databases, guides and series; journals; books and reports; articles; news media; film, TV, radio, and Internet; initiatives; and organizations of interest. Web-based resources including reports and articles are embedded in the categories identified above. This is not an exhaustive listing but simply a point of entry to the topic.

Key Terms

Ableism
African American teachers
Assessment
Culture of teachers
Discrimination in education
Diversity management
Education
Environmental justice

Evaluation
Feminist teaching
Film as teaching tool
Gender
Heterosexism
Literature as teaching tool
Literature as tool
Master teachers

Mentors	Racism
Multicultural	Scholarship of Teaching and Learning
Multicultural education	Social justice
Multiculturalism	Storytelling
Narrative	Teacher-student relationships
Patterns of childhood	Teachers as learners
Pedagogical practices	Teaching

Abstracts, Bibliographies, Collections, Databases, Guides, and Series

Birmingham Civil Rights Institute
520 Sixteenth Street North
Birmingham AL 35203
Phone: 205-328-9696
Toll Free: 1-866-328-9696
Fax: 205-251-6104
http://www.bcri.org/index.html

The Archives Division of the Birmingham (Alabama) Civil Rights Institute provides online access to a wealth of materials from the 1950s and 1960s associated with events in Birmingham and other parts of the United States. The Online Resource Gallery provides access to additional materials including audio of the stories of individuals involved in civil rights activities.

http://www.bcri.org/archives/index/index.htm
http://www.bcri.org/resource_gallery/overview/index.htm#

Black Studies Center (http://bsc.chadwyck.com/marketing)

Materials in this database include *Schomburg Studies on the Black Experience*, a database detailing the African experience in America; the African American newspaper *Chicago Defender*; and *International Index to Black Periodicals Full Text*. Available from ProQuest Information and Learning at www.il.proquest.com/chadwyck/.

Diversity: A Selected and Annotated Bibliography, 8(1), 1996–2001. Published by Oryx Press, an imprint of Greenwood Publishing Group, Inc., in conjunction with James Rhem & Associates, Inc. (ISSN 1057-2880).

This bibliography focuses on materials from the cognitive and learning styles literatures on socioeconomic diversity within the classroom. See http://www.ntlf.com/html/lib/suppmat/81divbib.htm.

FedStats
http://www.fedstats.gov

FedStats is a gateway to statistical information produced, used, and distributed by the U.S. government. Resources are provided by topic and by agency; it includes a cross-index of topics by agency. This site also includes maps and links to agency data sets including the U.S. Census Bureau, Bureau of Economic Analysis, and Bureau of Justice Statistics.

Office of Human Relations Programs. *Diversity Database*. University of Maryland. http://www.inform.umd.edu/EdRes/Topic/Diversity/about1.html.

Web-based, searchable resource includes syllabi, information on diversity initiatives nationwide, and materials for specific areas of diversity including gender, age, religion, and national origin.

Gender and Student Evaluations: An Annotated Bibliography

This bibliography provides some 50 entries on the topic of gender and evaluation of students. The materials were prepared at the Center for Research on Learning and Teaching at University of Michigan. See http://www.crlt.umich.edu/multiteaching/gsebibliography.pdf

IUPUI Multicultural Classroom Resource Guide

This guide provides an annotated bibliography, readings, Web links, syllabi, and other materials such as multicultural teaching modules. The guide is produced by Indiana University/Purdue University at Indianapolis (IUPUI). See http://www.opd.iupui.edu/diversity/resource_guide.htm

SAGE Race Relations Abstracts
SAGE Publications USA
2455 Teller Road
Thousand Oaks, CA 91320

Abstracts are published quarterly in association with the Institute of Race Relations; they contain summaries of articles, book reviews, and conference papers from more than 300 publications. Titles are available at www.sra.sagepub.com.

Sen, S. (1999). Readings on Race, Gender, Class and Ethnicity: Results of a Class Survey. Council of Planning Librarians, Bibliography 353. *Journal of Planning Literature*, *13*(4), 481–499.

This bibliography draws from the planning literature in the 1990s to set out nine broad categories that include community planning, public policy, and natural resource planning. The bibliography begins with the statement "Planning educators are recognizing the needs to incorporate the issues of race, gender, class, and ethnicity into their planning curricula."

Race, Gender, and Affirmative Action: Resource Page for Teaching

This collection of resources was prepared by Elizabeth Anderson, Department of Philosophy, University of Michigan, eandersn@umich.edu. See http://www-personal .umich.edu/~eandersn/biblio.htm

Runnymeade Trust. *The Real History Directory*. See http://www.realhistories.org.uk
Runnymede Trust
Suite 106, The London Fruit & Wool Exchange
Brushfield Street
London, E1 6EP, England
Phone: 020 7377 9222
Fax: 020 7377 6622
E-mail: info@runnymedetrust.org

The Runnymede Trust was created in 1968 with a mission to fight social injustice and racial discrimination. The site includes links to a number of resources including the *Runnymede Bulletin*, a quarterly journal on race relations. The *Real History Directory* provides materials for teachers, students, and others to teach and learn about cultural diversity in the United Kingdom.

Teaching Diversity: People of Color

Rios-Bustamante, A. (Ed.), *Teaching Diversity: People of Color Series* (1993–2002); *Teaching Mexican American History* (2002); *Teaching African American History* (2001); *Teaching Asian American History* (1997). Washington, DC: American Historical Association Committee on Minority Historians, American Historical Association.

The series is intended to provide methods and strategies for teaching and researching what are known as "previously underrepresented racial and ethnic groups." The series includes titles such as *Teaching Mexican American History*, *Teaching African American History*, and *Teaching Asian American History*. Each booklet addresses gender issues within the context of the specific topic.

Journals

American Anthropologist
American Behavioral Scientist
American Journal of Education
Chronicle of Higher Education
College Teaching
Communication Research
Cornell Hotel and Restaurant Administration Quarterly
Critical Inquiry
Critique of Anthropology
Cultural Studies Critical Methodologies
Curriculum Inquiry
Educational Studies
Ethnic and Racial Studies
European Journal of Cultural Studies
Feminism and Psychology
Feminist Teacher
Group Processes & Intergroup Relations
Harvard Educational Review
Independent School
International Journal of Cultural Studies
Journal of Black Psychology
Journal of Black Studies
Journal of Communication Inquiry
Journal of Contemporary Ethnography

Journal of Educational Research
Journal of Homosexuality
Journal of Language and Social Psychology
Journal of Negro Education
Journal of Planning Literature
Journal of Teacher Education
Journal of Urban History
Journalism
Language Arts
Michigan Quarterly Review
Oxford Review of Education
Personality and Social Psychology Bulletin
Race & Class
Review of Higher Education Sex Roles
Social Education
Social Justice
Social Studies of Science
Sociological Quarterly
Theory into Practice
Urban Education
Western Journal of Black Studies
Women and Education
Women's Studies Quarterly
Work and Occupations
Youth & Society

Books and Reports

Adams, M., Castañeda, R., Hackman, H. W., Peters, M. L., & Zúñiga, X. (Eds.) (2001). *Readings for diversity and social justice: An anthology on racism, anti-Semitism, sexism, heterosexism, ableism, and classism.* London: Routledge.

Anderson, D. Z., & Zuercher, B. (2001). *Letters across the divide: Two friends explore racism, friendship, and faith.* Grand Rapids, MI: Baker Books.

Banks, J. A. C. A. M. B. (Ed.). (1995). *Handbook of research on multicultural education.* San Francisco: Jossey-Bass.

Bell, D. (1992). *Faces at the bottom of the well: The permanence of racism.* New York: Basic Books.

Berlak, A., & Moyenda, S. (2001). *Taking it personally: Racism in the classroom from kindergarten to college.* Philadelphia: Temple University Press.

Bransford, J. D., Brown, A. L., & Cocking, R. R. (Eds.). (1999). *How people learn: Brain, mind, experience, and school.* Committee on Developments in the Science of Learning. Commission on Behavioral and Social Sciences and Education. National Research Council. Washington, DC: National Academy Press.

Cose, E. (1993). *The rage of a privileged class: Why are middle-class blacks angry? Why should America care?* New York: HarperCollins.

Decker, E. (Ed.). (1998). *Situated stories: Valuing diversity in composition research.* Portsmouth, NH: Boynton/Cook.

González, A. M. H., & Chen, V. (Eds.). (2004). *Our voices: Essays in culture, ethnicity, and communication.* Los Angeles: Roxbury.

Kivel, P. (2002). *Uprooting racism: How white people can work for racial justice.* Gabriola Island, British Columbia, Canada: New Society Publishers.

Loewen, J. W. (1995). *Lies my teacher told me: Everything your American history textbook got wrong.* New York: Simon & Schuster.

Loewen, J. W. (2005). *Sundown towns: A hidden dimension of American racism.* New York: New Press.

Moyenda, S., Berlak, A. (2001). *Taking it personally: Racism in the classroom from kindergarten to college.* Philadelphia: Temple University Press.

Nieto, S. (2002). Conflict and tension, growth and change: The politics of teaching multicultural education courses. In S. Nieto (Ed.), *Language, culture, and teaching: Critical perspectives for a new century* (pp. 227–256). Mahwah NJ: Erlbaum.

Perry, P. (2002). *Shades of white: White kids and racial identities in high school.* Durham, NC: Duke University Press.

Rankin, Susan R. (2003). *Campus climate for gay, lesbian, bisexual, and transgender people: A national perspective.* New York: The National Gay and Lesbian Task Force Policy Institute. Retrieved from http://www.thetaskforce.org

Takaki, R. (1993). A *different mirror: A history of multicultural America.* Boston: Little, Brown.

Tatum, B. D. (2003). *"Why are all the black kids sitting together in the cafeteria?" and other conversations about race.* New York: Basic Books.

Wolf, C. (1980). *Patterns of childhood.* New York City: Farrar, Straus and Giroux.

Articles

Alexander, B. K. (2004). Passing, cultural performance, and individual agency: Performative reflections on black masculine identity." *Cultural Studies Critical Methodologies, 4*(3), 377–404.

Asirvatham, Margaret. (n.d.). Enriching science through diversity. Retrieved from http://www.colorado.edu/ftep/diversity/div12.html

Barnes, B., Palmary, I., & Durrheim, K. (2001). The denial of racism: The role of humor, personal experience, and self-censorship. *Journal of Language and Social Psychology, 20*(3), 321–338.

Beasley, K., Corbin, D., Feiman-Nemser, S., & Shank, C. (1996, summer). "Making it happen": Teachers mentoring one another. *Theory Into Practice, 35*(3), 158–165.

Berry, V. T., & Shelton, V. (1999). Watching music: Interpretations of visual music performance. *Journal of Communication Inquiry, 23*(2), 132–151.

Bliss, A. (n.d.). Diversity and language: ESL students in the university classroom. Retrieved from http://www.colorado.edu/ftep/diversity/div11.html

Britzman, D. P., & Pitt, A. J. (1996, spring). Pedagogy and transference: Casting the past of learning into the presence of teaching. *Theory Into Practice, 35*(2), 117–124.

Brown, E. L. (2004). What precipitates change in cultural diversity awareness during a multicultural course: The message or the method? *Journal of Teacher Education, 55*(4), 325–340.

Buttny, R. (1999). Discursive constructions of racial boundaries and self-segregation on campus. *Journal of Language and Social Psychology, 18*(3), 247–268.

Chenoweth, K. (1998). Poll confirms that Americans want diversity on campuses. *Black Issues in Higher Education, 15*(18):12–14.

Deggans, E. (2004, July 6). Racial jokes rampant on radio. *St. Petersburg Times.*

Dirks, D., & Rice, S. K. (2004). "Dining while black": Tipping as social artifact. *Cornell Hotel and Restaurant Administration Quarterly, 45*(1), 30–47.

Dixon, T. L., & Linz, D. (2000). Race and the misrepresentation of victimization on local television news. *Communication Research, 27*(5), 547–573.

DuPraw, M. E., & Axner, M. (n.d.). Working on common cross-cultural communication challenges. Retrieved from http://www.wwcd.org/action/ampu/crosscult.html

Evans, D. C., Garcia, D. J., Garcia, D. M., & Baron, R. S. (2003). In the privacy of their own homes: Using the Internet to assess racial bias. *Personality and Social Psychology Bulletin, 29*(2), 273–284.

Flick, D. (n.d.). Developing and teaching an inclusive curriculum. Retrieved from http://www.colorado.edu/ftep/diversity/div13.html

Hartman, A. (2004, spring). The rise and fall of whiteness studies. *Race Class, 46*(2), 22–38.

James, C. (2005, March 31). Critic's notebook: When it comes to casting, love conquers color. *New York Times.*

Jones, A. (1996, spring). Desire, sexual harassment, and pedagogy in the university classroom. *Theory Into Practice, 35*(2), 102–110.

Ladson-Billings, G. (1996, spring). Silences as weapons: Challenges of a black professor teaching white students. *Theory Into Practice, 35*(2), 79–86.

Ladson-Billings, G. (1996, fall). "Your blues ain't like mine": Keeping issues of race and racism on the multicultural agenda. *Theory Into Practice, 35*(4), 248–255.

Lamb, R. (1996, spring). Discords: Feminist pedagogy in music education. *Theory Into Practice,* 35(2), 125–132.

Lassiter, M. D. (2004). The suburban origins of "color-blind" conservatism: Middle-class consciousness in the Charlotte busing crisis. *Journal of Urban History, 30*(4), 549–582.

Lee, E., & Leets, L. (2002). Persuasive storytelling by hate groups online: Examining its effects on adolescents. *American Behavioral Scientist, 45*(6), 927–957.

Lewis, A. E. (2003). Everyday race-making: Navigating racial boundaries in schools. *American Behavioral Scientist, 47*(3), 283–305.

Lowe, John P. (2003). Authentic Assessment Toolbox. Retrieved from http://jonathan.mueller.faculty.noctrl.edu/toolbox/index.htm

Luke, C. (2003). Global mobilities: Crafting identities in interracial families. *International Journal of Cultural Studies, 6*(4), 379–401.

Miller, S. C., Olson, M. A., & Fazio, R. H. (2004). Perceived reactions to interracial romantic relationships: When race is used as a cue to status. *Group Processes Intergroup Relations, 7*(4), 354–369.

Nelson-Barber, S., & Harrison, M. (1996, fall). Bridging the politics of identity in a multicultural classroom. *Theory Into Practice, 35*(4), 256–264.

100 questions and answers about Arab Americans: A journalist's guide. (2001). *Detroit Free Press.* Retrieved from http://www.freep.com/jobspage/arabs/arab13.html

Patton, T. O. (2001). Ally McBeal and her homies: The reification of white stereotypes of the other. *Journal of Black Studies, 32*(2), 229–260.

Phillion, J. (1999, spring). Narrative and formalistic approaches to the study of multiculturalism. *Curriculum Inquiry, 29*(1), 129–141.

Piland, W. E., Hess, S., & Piland, A. (2000, August). Student experiences with multicultural and diversity education. *Community College Journal of Research & Practice, 24*(7), 531–547.

Saavedra, E. (1996). Teachers study groups: Contexts for transformative learning. *Theory Into Practice, 35*(4), 271–278.

Schaafsma, D. (1996, spring). Things we cannot say: "Writing for your life" and stories in English education. *Theory Into Practice, 35*(2), 110–117.

Shah, H., & Nah, S. (2004). Long ago and far away: How US newspapers construct racial oppression. *Journalism, 5*(3), 259–278.

Sizemore, D. S. (2004). Ethnic inclusion and exclusion: Managing the language of Hispanic integration in a rural community. *Journal of Contemporary Ethnography, 33*(5), 534–570.

Sleeter, C. E. (1996, fall). Multicultural education as a social movement. *Theory Into Practice, 35*(4), 239–248.

Stearns, E. (2004). Interracial friendliness and the social organization of schools. *Youth Society, 35*(4), 395–419.

Sullivan, R. E. (2003). Rap and race: It's got a nice beat, but what about the message? *Journal of Black Studies, 33*(5), 605–622.

Timmermans, S. (2003). A black technician and blue babies. *Social Studies of Science, 33*(2), 197–229.

Tips for teachers: Sensitivity to women in the contemporary classroom. (2000). Retrieved from http://bokcenter.fas.harvard.edu/docs/TFTwomen.html

Tovares, R. (2002). Mascot matters: Race, history, and the University of North Dakota's "Fighting Sioux" logo. *Journal of Communication Inquiry, 26*(1), 76–94.

Vallas, S. P. (2003). Rediscovering the color line within work organizations: The "Knitting of Racial Groups" revisited. *Work and Occupations, 30*(4), 379–400.

Weathers, M. D., Frank, E. M., & Spell, L. A. (2002). Differences in the communication of affect: Members of the same race versus members of a different race. *Journal of Black Psychology, 28*(1), 66–77.

Wiggins, Grant. (1990). The case for authentic assessment. *ERIC Digest.* Retrieved from http://ericae.net/db/edo/ED328611.htm

Williams, D. (2004). Improving race relations in higher education: The jigsaw classroom as a missing piece to the puzzle. *Urban Education, 39*(3), 316–344.

Yelvington, K. A., Goslin, N. G., & Arriaga, W. (2002). Who's history? Museum-making and struggles over ethnicity and representation in the Sunbelt. *Critique of Anthropology, 22*(3), 343–379.

Yoshinaga-Itano, C. (n.d.). Diversity, individual differences, and students with disabilities: Optimizing the learning environment. Retrieved from http://www.colorado.edu/ftep/diversity/div13.html

News Media

The news media worldwide are a rich source of information about teaching and education and of classroom content or food for thought for teachers and students alike. In addition, the media may be said to set the agenda for how the peoples of the world are portrayed.

Recent headlines in the United States include such topics as:

- Williams, R. L. (2005, August 14). Tyson denies race claim black workers say bathroom at Ashland marked "whites only." *Birmingham (Alabama) News,* p. 1D.

- Associated Press. (2005, June 29). Mexican stamp called offensive to blacks. CNN.com. Retrieved from http://www.cnn.com.

Issues of diversity are universal; hence, the following are links to access the media around the globe:

NewsLink provides a Web-based index to newspapers, radio/TV, and magazines around the world. Newspapers are grouped according to the Americas and Other Continents. Radio/TV entries are grouped according to TV stations, radio stations, and networks; listings include ethnic and alternative stations and connections to networks worldwide. See http://newslink.org/

New California Media (NCM) is an association of more than 700 ethnic media organizations. Its Web site includes links to media that are African, African American, Asian, Southeast Asian, European, Latino, and Middle Eastern, among others. Includes radio and news feeds. See http://news.ncmonline.com/home/

American Indian Radio on Satellite (AIROS) bills itself as "All Indian Radio, Every Day, Everywhere." AIROS provides Native news, music, entertainment, and issues programming distributed through Public Radio Satellite System. See http://airos.org/

Film, TV, Radio, and Internet

Africans in America

Public Broadcasting Service (PBS)
1320 Braddock Place
Alexandria, VA 22314
http://www.pbs.org/wgbh/aia/

Africans in America is a six-hour TV series that traces the African experience through four parts from 1450 through 1865. Web site includes resources for teachers and a youth guide. Resource section includes historical documents, people and events, and modern voices.

Asian-Nation: The Landscape of Asian America
http://www.asian-nation.org

Asian-Nation, also known as "Asian Americans 101," is a private Web site that claims to be a one-stop information resource. The site features an overview of the historical, demographic, political, and cultural issues that affect the Asian American community. The site was designed to educate, provide information, and connect searchers with other sources of information linked to Asian Americans.

Hampton, H. (Producer). *Eyes on the prize I: America's civil rights years, 1954–65* [Videocassette]. Alexandria, VA: PBS Video, 1986.

Eyes on the Prize is the most inclusive television documentary depicting the civil rights movement in the United States. The series focuses on the events, issues, triumphs, and tragedies of ordinary people in the United States during a time called "the Second American Revolution." This resource was intended to help teachers introduce and open discussion with their students on the issues of the civil rights movement between 1954 and 1965 in America.

Matters of Race

Public Broadcasting Service (PBS)
1320 Braddock Place
Alexandria, VA 22314
http://www.pbs.org/mattersofrace/lm_locations.shtml

Matters of Race is a series that considers race in modern-day United States. Includes visits to North Carolina, California, South Dakota, Arizona, and Hawaii. Addresses the concept of race in cross-cultural settings and looks at the future of race in the United States.

Reality Checks Software

Robert C. Maynard Institute for Journalism Education
1211 Preservation Park Way
Oakland, CA 94612
Phone: 510-891-9202
Fax: 510-891-9565
http://www.maynardije.org/about/
http://www.maynardije.org/programs/realitychecks/

Originally known as the Institute for Journalism Education, the IJE was renamed in 1996 after the death of cofounder Robert C. Maynard. While the organization's original mission was to increase opportunities for minority journalists, the institute offers numerous resources including Reality Checks Software, which is available as a diagnostic tool for news organizations to "assess the diversity of [their] sources and the completeness of [their] coverage."

Skin Deep

California Newsreel
P.O. Box 2284
South Burlington, VT 05407
Phone: 877-811-7495

Fax: 802-846-1850
E-mail: contact@newsreel.org
http://www.newsreel.org/main.asp
http://www.newsreel.org/nav/title.asp?tc = CN0085

Reid, F. (Producer/Director). (1995). *Skin deep: College students confront racism* [Documentary]. San Francisco: California Newsreel.

Skin Deep is a film created by Academy Award-nominated filmmaker Frances Reid. In the film, Reid documents the journey of a diverse group of college students from universities such as University of Massachusetts, Texas A&M, Chico State, and University of California at Berkeley. The students are followed from a challenging racial awareness workshop where they are forced to tackle each other's racial intolerances and go back to their campuses and homes in an attempt to understand why people think the way they do.

Initiatives

Understanding Race and Human Variation

American Anthropological Association (AAA)
2200 Wilson Blvd, Suite 600
Arlington, VA 22201
Phone: 703-528-1902
Fax: 703-528-3546

The AAA currently works under a three-year (2004–2007) grant from the National Science Foundation to develop educational materials on what race is and is not, the origins of the concept of race, and racism in practice in the day-to-day world. Materials consist of a traveling museum exhibit and educational materials for teachers, scientists, and the general public. The project will draw from recent scholarly research and will include activities such as conferences.

Inclusive Excellence: Diversity, Inclusion, and Institutional Renewal

Association of American Colleges and Universities (AACU)
1818 R Street NW
Washington DC 20009
Phone: 202-387-3760
Fax: 202-265-9532
http://www.aacu.org/issues/diversity/index.cfm
http://www.aacu.org/inclusive_excellence/index.cfm

Inclusive Excellence is one of a number of continuing initiatives fostered by the AACU to focus on diversity in higher education. Founded in 1971, the AACU today concentrates on "deploying diversity as an educational asset for all students, and preparing future graduates for socially responsible engagement in a diverse democracy and interdependent world." Other current initiatives include the Bildner New Jersey Campus Diversity Project, the James Irvine Foundation Evaluation Project, and the BellSouth Foundation College-Going Minorities. AACU also hosts a Web site called Diversity Web and other online resources, including the *Diversity Digest,* on diversity and education at www.diversityweb.org/index.cfm.

National Association for Ethnic Studies (NAES)

Western Washington University
516 High Street/MS 9113
Bellingham, WA 98225
Phone: 360-650-2349
Fax: 360-650-2690
http://www.ethnicstudies.org/

The NAES is a nonprofit organization that "promotes responsible scholarship and advocacy in the diverse fields of inquiry which constitute ethnic studies." Founded in 1972, the NAES is interdisciplinary; members include students, teachers, civic and governmental organizations, and others interested in the study and advocacy focused on ethnicity and ethnic topics.

National Women's History Project

National Women's History Project
3343 Industrial Drive, Suite #4
Santa Rosa, CA 95403
Phone: 707-636-2888
Fax: 707-636-2909
http://www.nwhp.org/

The National Women's History Project is a nonprofit organization with a mission to "recognize and celebrate the diverse and historic accomplishments of women by providing information and educational materials and programs." Founded in 1980, the original impetus was to put women into the history books. Accomplishments include designation as the week of March 8th as National Women's History Week. The Learning Place and Catalog include resources for teaching about the diversity of the role of women in history.

Social Justice Education

University of Massachusetts
159 Hills South
Amherst, MA 01003
Phone: 413-545-3610
http://www.umass.edu/sje/index.html

Social Justice Education at University of Massachusetts-Amherst offers an interdisciplinary master's and doctoral program to examine and apply knowledge of social diversity and social justice in the educational system across the spectrum from kindergarten through higher education.

Teaching Tolerance

Southern Poverty Leadership Law Center
400 Washington Avenue
Montgomery AL 36104
Phone: 334-956-8200
Fax: 334-956-8483
http://www.tolerance.org/teach/

Initiated in 1991, the Teaching Tolerance project provides materials for use in the K–12 environment and the college-university setting. Recent curricula include "The Power of Words," which helps students with how to deal with slurs and epithets, and "The Children's March," which recounts the role of young people in the segregation movement. Resources include Web links, a handbook, lesson plans, and materials appropriate according to age/grade level.

Teaching Tolerance is a product of the Southern Poverty Leadership Law Center based in Montgomery, Alabama. SPLLC uses education and litigation to foster tolerance and diversity.

Diversity in the United States
Civil Rights in the United States

U.S. Department of State
Bureau of International Information Programs
http://usinfo.state.gov/usa/diversity/
http://usinfo.state.gov/usa/civilrights/

Diversity in the United States and *Civil Rights in the United States* are collections of news and reports on diversity and civil rights; includes archives and links to other areas on the same topics. Also includes links to gender-related materials.

Organizations of Interest

American Anthropological Association (AAA)
2200 Wilson Blvd, Suite 600
Arlington, VA 22201
Phone: 703-528-1902
Fax: 703-528-3546
www.aaanet.org/

The AAA is the largest organization of anthropologists in the world. Founded in 1902, the AAA consists of sections and section interest groups including the Association of Black Anthropologists, Association of Latino and Latina Anthropologists, and Association of Lesbian and Gay Anthropologists; Web sites and resources are available for each of these organizations at the AAA site. In addition, the AAA sponsors programs on women's issues and minority issues.

Gay-Straight Alliance Network (GSA)
605 W. Olympic Blvd, Suite 610
Los Angeles, CA 90015
Phone: 213-534-7162
Fax: 213-553-1833
www.gsanetwork.org

The Gay-Straight Alliance Network is a youth-piloted organization that unites school-based GSAs with community resources. Through peer support, leadership promotion, and training, GSA Network supports young people in creating safe environments in schools and assists students in supporting each other and learning about homophobia, educating the school community about the issues facing homosexuals, and helping to do away with discrimination, harassment, and violence.

National Association for the Advancement of Colored People (NAACP)
4805 Mt. Hope Drive
Baltimore MD 21215
Phone: 807-NAACP-98
www.naacp.org

Since its inauguration in 1909, the NAACP has worked to guarantee the equality of all residents and to achieve equality of rights and eliminate race prejudice among the citizens of the United States. The NAACP also seeks enactment and enforcement of laws securing civil rights.

National Council of La Raza
Raul Yzaguirre Building

1126 16th Street, NW
Washington, DC 20036
Phone: 202-785-1670
www.nclr.org/

National Council of La Raza represents the Hispanic community in Washington, DC. The NCLR operates programs including ones on education, health, farmworkers, and immigration. NCLR also provides information on policies and it issues an NCLR position paper annually.

National Organization for Women (NOW)
1100 H Street NW, 3rd floor
Washington, D.C. 20005
Phone: 202-628-8669 (628-8NOW)
Fax: 202-785-8576
www.now.org

The National Organization for Women is America's largest association of feminist advocates. Since its beginning, NOW's goal has been to bring about equality for all women. With 500,000 members and 550 chapters, NOW works to stop harassment and discrimination in schools, the workforce and justice system, and in all areas of life.

National Society of Black Engineers
1454 Duke Street
Alexandria, VA 22314
Phone: 703-549-2207
http://www.nsbe.org/

The National Society of Black Engineers is the largest student-managed organization in the United States. The NSBE's mission is "to increase the number of culturally responsible Black engineers who excel academically, succeed professionally and positively impact the community." The 10,000-member organization consists of chapters organized by university/college, precollege, and alumni. The individual chapters offer resources independent of the NSBE site. For example, see the University of Wisconsin-Milwaukee NSBE Chapter at http://www.uwm.edu/StudentOrg/NSBE/table.html for information on black history and black inventors and engineers.

The National Urban League (NUL)
120 Wall Street
New York, NY 10005
Phone: 212-558-5300

Fax: 212-344-5332
www.nul.org

Established in 1910, the National Urban League is the oldest community-based movement in the United States. The NUL is dedicated to showing African Americans that they have the power to enter the economic and social majority. Its mission is to facilitate economic self-reliance, parity, power, and civil rights of African Americans through programs, advocacy, and research.

Patricia Brown McDonald is associate professor of English at Palm Beach Community College, where she teaches literature, composition, and developmental courses. She has developed an Afro-Caribbean course that is now offered at that institution and she has published in the *Florida Comparative Studies Journal*. Her scholarly and teaching focus is the exploration of marginalized voices in the literary field.

Deborah A. Brunson is director of the Upperman African American Cultural Center and associate professor of communication studies at the University of North Carolina Wilmington. She has published articles on teaching, diversity, and leadership. Her teaching interests include interracial communication, leadership, communication theory, and diversity.

Karen Bullock is an assistant professor in the School of Social Work at the University of Connecticut. She is chair of the Black Studies Substantive Area and teaches graduate courses in research methods, gerontology, and Black studies. Dr. Bullock has presented nationally and internationally and published in the areas of race and ethnic differences. Her health-focused research has appeared in the *Journal of Families in Society, Education & Ageing, Social Science and Medicine,* and *Social Work.* She is the recipient of a Soros Foundation Award and is currently a John A. Hartford Faculty Scholar in the School of Social Work at the University of Connecticut.

Scott W. Campbell is assistant professor of communication studies and Pohs Fellow of Telecommunications at the University of Michigan-Ann Arbor. His research explores the social implications of new media, with an emphasis on mobile communication practices. His recent studies have investigated cross-cultural trends, mobile phone use in social networks, and use of the technology in public settings. Campbell's research appears in *Communication Monographs, Journal of Applied Communication Research, Communication Education, New Media & Society, Communication Research Reports, Qualita-*

tive Research Reports in Communication, and other scholarly venues. In addition to pursuing his own research, Professor Campbell is co-editing a new series on mobile communication studies through Transaction Publishers. Prior to joining the University of Michigan in 2005, Professor Campbell worked in the wireless industry, earned a Ph.D. from the University of Kansas, and spent three years teaching and conducting research at Hawaii Pacific University on the island of Oahu.

Steve Chandler is a professor in the Department of Health, Physical Education, and Recreation at Florida A&M University in Tallahassee. He is a certified sexuality educator of the American Association of Sex Educators, Counselors, and Therapists (AASECT) and was editor-in-chief of its publication, *Contemporary Sexuality*, from 2002 to 2006.

Billy R. Close is the president of Paradigm Consultants & Associates, Inc., founder and president of Beyond The Athlete, Inc., and currently an assistant professor of criminology and criminal justice at Florida State University (FSU). Close earned his M.S. and Ph.D. degrees in criminology and criminal justice from FSU. He has also served as assistant and acting director of the FSU Black Studies Program, research consultant to the Racial and Ethnic Bias Study Commission for the Florida Supreme Court, and as co-principal investigator of the Florida Highway Patrol and Racial Differences in Traffic Stops and Driver Treatment study. His current research interests include theory and dynamics of racism and crime, racial profiling, sports and crime, ethnicity and methodology, Black crimmythology, conflict reduction, and multiculturalism. Close has received numerous academic, service, and athletic honors, including FSU's Martin Luther King Distinguished Service Award, 2001; the FSU University Teaching Award, 1999–2000; the McKnight Doctoral Fellowship, 1989; the Florida Education Fund's Russell V. Ewald Award for Academic Excellence and Human Service, 1991; and induction to the Inaugural Hall of Fame Class at Lincoln High School in 1999.

Randy K. Dillon is professor and director of graduate studies in the Department of Communication, Missouri State University. He teaches courses in intercultural communication, communication theory, communication methods, small-group communication, and interpersonal communication. His research interests include the use of public dialogue to help communities and organizations discuss important sensitive issues. He has published articles in *Human Systems, International Journal of Listening,* and *Communication Teacher.* Dillon received the 1998 and 2006 University Award for Teaching and the 2002 College of Arts and Letters Service Award at Missouri State University. In 2000, he was recognized with a national award for academic advising by the National Academic Advising Association.

Michelle Howard-Vital is currently serving as interim chancellor for Winston-Salem State University, one of the sixteen constituent universities of The University of North Carolina, located in Winston-Salem. Prior to this position, she served as associate vice president for academic affairs at University of North Carolina–General Administration. In the latter capacity, she reviewed academic programs for the UNC system and led teams to review all postsecondary, nonpublic institutions seeking to offer degrees in North Carolina. Dr. Howard-Vital is the author or articles, chapters, and presentations, and she is the co-author of the book *Entering School Leadership.*

Brenda "BJ" Jarmon is associate professor and chairperson of the Department of Social Work at Florida A&M University. Her research, teaching, and publication interests include issues related to cultural diversity and designing cultural sensitivity models; examining the impact of media on abstinence education; and the effects of welfare reform, foster care, and domestic violence on children and their families. She has published refereed journal articles, book chapters, newspaper articles, and written many technical reports as well as secured over two million dollars in sponsored research projects during her academic career. She has held numerous state, national, and gubernatorial appointments. Dr. Jarmon is a nationally and internationally sought-after educational consultant, staff trainer, motivational speaker, and frequent guest on television and radio talk shows. She is the author of *Lift Every Voice: African American Students Surviving in Higher Education,* the foreword in *Journey to the Ph.D.* (2003), "What It Takes to Be Successful on Standardized Tests" in *Graduate and Professional School Success* (2003), and "Unwritten Rules of the Game" in *Sisters of the Academy* (2001).

Linda L. Lampl is president/CEO and co-founder of Lampl Herbert Consultants. She works as a practicing anthropologist and organization development consultant within the firm, which is based in Tallahassee, Florida.

Lampl holds undergraduate and graduate degrees in cultural anthropology and a doctorate in communication research from Florida State University.

Muriel Lederman is retired from the biology department and Women's Studies Program at Virginia Tech in Blacksburg. She holds an A.B. degree from Barnard College and a Ph.D. from Columbia University, both in the biological sciences. Her scientific research has been in the field of molecular virology and her work in feminist sciences studies has included coediting *The Gender and Science Reader.* Her current interest is critical pedagogies for science.

Devorah A. Lieberman is provost and vice president for academic affairs at Wagner College in New York City. She assumed this position in January 2004, having been vice provost and special assistant to the president at Portland State University in Oregon. Devorah received her Ph.D. in intercultural communication (1984) from the University of Florida and concurrently received her certification in gerontology. As provost and vice president for academic affairs at Wagner College, Devorah oversees all academic, curricular, and student-related elements of the college. She sees her primary role as furthering the academic excellence that exists at Wagner. As an academic she continues to publish in the higher education literature and to present in higher education venues. Her most recent publications have focused on academic institutions as learning organizations, issues of diversity in higher education, and creating community-based learning locally, nationally, and internationally.

Earl Sheridan is professor of political science at the University of North Carolina Wilmington. He received his B.A. degree in political science from Appalachian State University and his M.A. and Ph.D. degrees from the University of Tennessee at Knoxville. His research has been in the area of ideology and race.

Leila E. Villaverde is an associate professor in the Department of Educational Leadership and Cultural Foundations, University of North Carolina-Greensboro. She is also the director of the Master's degree in Women's and Gender Studies. She teaches courses in curriculum studies, feminist theory, aesthetics and education, and cultural foundations. Villaverde authored *Sec-*

ondary Education; coedited *Dismantling White Privilege: Pedagogy, Politics, and Whiteness* and *Rethinking Intelligence: Confronting Psychological Assumptions About Teaching and Learning*. She has written numerous articles and chapters on aesthetics, creativity, curriculum, critical pedagogy, and identity politics. She is currently working on two manuscripts, *Women's and Gender Studies: A Primer* and *Curriculum and Creativity in the Extreme Classroom: Lessons on Transformation*.

INDEX